SCHOOL IMPROVEMENT *AFTER* INSPECTION?

School Improvement
after Inspection?
School and LEA Responses

edited by

Peter Earley

P·C·P

Paul Chapman
Publishing Ltd

Copyright © BEMAS (British Education Management and Administration Society) 1998
First published 1998

Paul Chapman Publishing Ltd
A SAGE Publications Company
6 Bonhill Street
London EC2A 4PU

SAGE Publications Inc
2455 Teller Road
Thousand Oaks, California 91320

SAGE Publications India Pvt Ltd
32, M-Block Market
Greater Kailash-I
New Delhi 110 048

British Library Cataloguing in Publication Data

School improvement after inspection? school and LEA responses – (BEMAS)
1. School management and organization – Great Britain
2. School improvement programs – Great Britain
I. Earley, Peter
371.2′00941

ISBN 1 85396 417 4
    1 85396 402 6 (pbk)
Library of Congress catalog card number

Typeset by PDQ Typesetting, Staffordshire
Printed and bound in Great Britain by Athenaeum Press, Gateshead

A B C D E F   3 2 1 0 9 8

Contents

Notes on Contributors

Vanessa Aris is Head of Careers in an independent school and is a member of the Independent Schools Inspectorate. She is Chair of the Governing Body of Brookfield School, Cheltenham. Her educational interests include the development of learning and teaching styles and their effect on the self-esteem of adults and children.

Doug Close is a management consultant in education and Principal of Close Associates, an independent group providing consultancy and inspection services. He was a HMI, specialising in management and in computing/IT. After an early career in computing and management in industry and commerce, he moved into higher education as a senior lecturer and then head of department in two polytechnics. He is a registered inspector of schools, having led about 30 secondary inspections to date, and an HEFCE assessor in universities. Personal consultancy projects include headteacher mentoring, quality management and improvement, management development and information systems strategy in schools, colleges and universities.

Nigel Cromey-Hawke is Head of Faculty in a north Somerset comprehensive school, conducting part-time doctoral research on an ESRC studentship into the long-term effects of school inspection. He is co-author (with Valerie Hall and David Oldroyd) of the Management Self-Development Secondary programme (1997) for the University of Bristol. He is also an associate of CLIO (Culture and Learning in Organisations) Centre for Management and Policy Studies at the university.

Jacqueline Davies is a Research Officer in the Management Development Centre at the Institute of Education, University of London and is also currently completing an MSc in Research Methods. She is working on the impact of OFSTED on secondary schools and previously worked on parental involvement in schools.

Jim Davies, Brookfield School, began his career at a London comprehensive, before moving to Gloucestershire where he taught in three different schools. He moved into 'special needs' in 1981. He has recently taken early retirement, and is currently enjoying family life.

Tony Dimmer is a Primary Consultant with Surrey Education Services Curriculum and Management Consultancy. Prior to joining Surrey in 1994, he spent twelve years as a primary headteacher in two Hampshire schools. His main interest is in the management of schools, having taken part in the development of management competences with School Management South and being involved in both the Headlamp and NPQH initiatives. The current focus of his work is on Target Setting and School Improvement and he leads the primary team in the development of comparative information for schools. He is a Registered Inspector but his major role is in providing advice, training and inspection to a cluster of schools on behalf of the LEA.

Peter Earley works in the Management Development Centre at the Institute of Education, University of London where he is also an associate director of the International School Effectiveness and Improvement Centre. He has published widely in the fields of educational management, governance and professional development. He is currently co-directing research projects on improving governing body effectiveness (funded by the DfEE) and primary school inspection (funded by the Nuffield Foundation).

Brian Fidler teaches and researches at the University of Reading where he is senior lecturer and course leader for the MSc 'Managing school improvement'. He has published widely in the field of school management and his most recent book is *Strategic Planning for School Improvement* (Pitman, 1996). He is also editor of *School Leadership and Management*, the international journal of leadership and school improvement.

Helen Hosker is currently Primary Consultant and Manager for Services to Primary Education with Surrey Education Services Curriculum and Management Consultancy. She has been a headteacher of two primary schools. Her work involves supporting primary schools in developing school improvement programmes. She specialises in management development, working with new heads (through HEADLAMP) and aspiring heads as an NPQH (National Qualification for Headship) trainer.

Peter Johnson is Principal Inspector (Quality Assurance) for Gloucestershire LEA. He is responsible for management of the LEA's quality assurance procedures and the inspection of schools. He is the assigned inspector to half of the LEA's special schools. Prior to joining Gloucestershire in 1990, he was the headteacher of a special school in Cumbria.

Peter Lonsdale is currently deputy headteacher at Longhill School in Brighton. He is particularly interested in school improvement and methods of evaluating improvement. As acting head he took a school through an OFSTED inspection and subsequently started researching the inspection process as a tool for school improvement.

Geoff Lowe is a research associate at Sheffield Hallam University. Following eighteen years as the headteacher of a large 11–18 comprehensive school in Rotherham he took early retirement in 1995 to concentrate on doctoral research into the impact of OFSTED inspection on school development in a group of secondary schools. His interest is in exploring the factors which influence secondary schools' implementation of inspection recommendations over time. He is also tutor on the Open University PGCE course.

Margaret Mathieson is Emeritus Professor at the University of Leicester. She has long experience of preparing English graduates for teaching and has undertaken research into curriculum history. Her most recent publication (with Ros McCulloch) is *Moral Education through English* (David Fulton, 1995).

Jacky Metiuk has served as headteacher at Worplesdon County Primary School near Guildford in Surrey for ten years. In 1994 she was seconded as a Primary Consultant with Surrey Educational Services Curriculum and Management Consultancy for a year and she will be re-joining the LEA in a similar permanent post from September 1998. She is an experienced OFSTED inspector, having worked with LEA and private teams. She has worked as an associate adviser and trainer for the LEA, including work with governors and mentoring headteachers.

Janet Ouston is Senior Lecturer and Head of the Management Development Centre at the Institute of Education, University of London. A researcher in early school effectiveness studies, she has published widely and her current research interests are on the impact of inspection and the applicability of 'quality approaches' to schools.

Carl Parsons is Professor of Education at Canterbury Christ Church College. He has had a long-standing interest in school evaluation, particularly self-evaluation, and in the application of evaluation methods for educational improvement. He edited a collection of studies applying quality assurance approaches in a variety of educational settings: *Quality Improvement in Education – Case Studies in Schools, Colleges and Universities* (David Fulton, 1994). He is currently interested in how teacher professionalism may be reconstituted and sees OFSTED as a major impediment.

Sue Robb has been headteacher of Camberley Infant School, Surrey, for the last four years. Previously she was head of infants of a large British school in the Far East. On returning to the UK she took up deputy headship in Kingston upon Thames. She has a particular interest in the English curriculum, baseline assessment and the role of the manager within the school.

Mel Vlaeminke worked in a large comprehensive school for ten years, teaching history and holding a position of pastoral responsibility in the upper school. At the University of Leicester School of Education since 1982, she has taught PGCE students and researched and written on a range of topics, including the history of education, gender issues, citizenship, and moral and spiritual education.

Margaret Wood is a senior lecturer in educational studies at the University of Central Lancashire. Dr Wood was previously a teacher before moving into LEA work as an education officer and adviser. During her time as an adviser she worked as part of an LEA team on school improvement projects. She has worked extensively as an INSET provider and consultant to schools. She is a trained OFSTED inspector, undertaking inspections in both primary and secondary phases.

1

Introduction

PETER EARLEY

The inspection of schools carried out under the auspices of the Office for Standards in Education (OFSTED) is now an everyday fact of life in England and Wales.[1] The work of OFSTED and the process of school inspection, however, continue to generate much discussion and controversy. It seems that hardly a week goes by without either the popular or educational press commenting on some aspect of OFSTED's activity. The fact that the current Chief Inspector of Schools has adopted a high media profile and is prone to make announcements that are not always welcomed by the teaching profession may go some way to explain this high level of interest. OFSTED and the system of inspection associated with it have not gone unchallenged. This collection of chapters should be seen as contributing to the wider debate about the role and function of OFSTED inspection, particularly as it relates to the process of school improvement and the raising of standards.

The inspection system as it currently exists came about as a result of the Education Act 1992. This Act established OFSTED and provided it with funds, the bulk of which had previously been allocated to local education authorities (LEAs). A framework for school inspection was devised along with a four-year cycle of inspections which was later extended to every six years in 1997. This cycle of inspections marked a number of radical changes from previous systems and although the inspection criteria have been revised twice since their inception, the fundamental principles remain the same. All schools are inspected according to a specified format and an explicit framework. There are different handbooks for the inspection of secondary, primary, nursery and special schools but all are inspected against the four main areas of educational standards achieved; the quality of education provided; the effective management of resources; and the spiritual, moral, social and cultural development of the children at the school. The first round of inspections commenced with secondary schools in autumn 1993 and was completed with primary and special schools in the summer of 1998. Since autumn 1997 some schools have been inspected for a second time.

Schools are inspected by teams of inspectors, trained and accredited by OFSTED, and who are led by a Registered Inspector (RgI). The inspection of a school or group of schools is allocated to inspection teams by OFSTED through a bidding and contracting process. Inspectors and inspection agencies or consultancies tender for the contracts and, if successful, bring together a team of inspectors under the leadership of an RgI who arranges the inspection. A typical secondary school inspection involves about 12–15 inspectors and takes about one week with the bulk of the inspectors' time being spent observing lessons. The team will cover the main areas of the school curriculum and will also include a 'lay inspector' who has no professional background in education. A report, written by the RgI or lead inspector, and based on the record of evidence collected by members of the inspection team, will follow the inspection week (usually after one month or so) and will include a list of the inspectors' recommendations or 'key issues for action'. The school and its governing body are obliged to produce an action plan within 40 days of receiving the report which will outline how the school will address the issues identified. A summary of the inspection report and, at a later time, the action plan are also made available to all parents. The detailed action plan is sent to OFSTED, whilst yearly progress on the action plan is reported to parents at the annual parents' meeting arranged by the school's governing body.[2]

The purpose of regular, systematic inspections is to appraise and evaluate the quality and standards of education in the school in an objective manner making use of the inspection framework. But inspection is more than a mechanism to ensure accountability to government, the taxpayer and parents – most importantly, it is also about school development and the raising of standards. The main purpose of inspection, as stated by OFSTED itself, is to 'promote school improvement by identifying priorities for action, and to inform parents and the local community about a school's strengths and weaknesses' (OFSTED, 1993a, p. 17).

Now that the first round of inspections has been completed (in summer 1998), what do we know about the impact OFSTED is having on schools, particularly in terms of their development? Is the inspection process leading to school improvement as claimed by OFSTED in its well-known strapline or logo 'improvement through inspection'? There is no doubt that OFSTED has helped to identify the minority of schools that have serious weaknesses (about 10 per cent of all schools) and the small number which are failing to provide their children with an adequate education (about 2 per cent). There is a growing body of research and inspection evidence, much of it published, about the nature and characteristics of such schools and how some have improved sufficiently to be able to leave 'special measures' within two years or so (for example, see DfEE, 1997c; Earley, 1997; OFSTED, 1997a; Riley and Rowles, 1997; Stoll and Myers, 1997).

There has been less research interest in the impact OFSTED has had on the vast majority of schools, i.e. those not deemed to have serious weaknesses or to be in need of special measures. In addition, very little of the existing literature on inspection has been based on research that is independent of OFSTED. Over the last five years or so, OFSTED has published numerous documents (in addition to individual school inspection reports) drawing on its ever-growing database of inspection evidence. The most well known of these is the annual report by Her Majesty's Chief Inspector of Schools (HMCI), the publication of which, in February each year, is awaited with interest.

This book has as its central focus the impact of OFSTED inspections on schools. Its main concern is with what happens to schools *after* their inspection. Does inspection make any difference to a school's development? Does it contribute to the raising of standards or do schools, having got through what is commonly perceived to be a demanding experience, simply heave a huge collective sigh of relief and not worry too much about things until the inspectors are due to visit at some unspecified future date? For those schools who successfully come through the process – and success may be seen as simply no more than not being publicly labelled as 'failures' – what, if any, are the consequences of inspection?

All the contributors to this collection have, in one form or another, been researching the impact of OFSTED inspections on schools. The authors – academics, heads, teachers, LEA advisers, inspectors and a chair of governors – have been specially commissioned by the editor on behalf of BEMAS to draw upon their research or work as consultants to give accounts of how schools have responded to inspection. What results is an interesting collection of accounts which demonstrate the very different effects inspection can have on schools, governing bodies and LEAs. Their main focus of attention is the period between the post-inspection phase, from 12–18 months after the initial inspection, to the period when the possibility of reinspection appears (4–6 years later).

The various contributions are grouped under four broad headings: a national overview of school, governing body and LEA responses; case studies; critiques of inspection; and lastly, reinspection and the move towards school self-assessment or self-evaluation. A brief summary of the contributions in each section is given below.

A NATIONAL OVERVIEW

The three contributions in Section 1 attempt to give an overview of the effects OFSTED has had, nationally, on schools, governing bodies and LEAs. Janet Ouston and Jackie Davies' chapter is a summary of the ongoing research, based at the Institute of Education, into school inspection. This research, originally encouraged by BEMAS and latterly funded by the Nuffield Foundation, has also involved the editor and Brian Fidler of the University of Reading. The research focuses on the impact of inspection on secondary schools. (The team has recently secured a grant from the Nuffield Foundation to continue their research into inspection both in the primary sector and into secondary school reinspection.) Ouston and Davies' analysis of the experience of OFSTED is presented in six interlinked phases or stages, starting with the period before the inspection date was known, and continuing with the stage when the memory and impact of inspection may be fading – at least until the date of reinspection (stage 6) – was known. They argue convincingly that each of these stages influences the school's responses in the next stage and that, in turn, influences the next. The chapter focuses mainly on stages 4 and 5 from the implementation of the action plan to when the impact of the inspection has faded. (Stage 6 – reinspection – is examined by Fidler and Davies in Section 4.) Ouston and Davies examine how schools are developing post-OFSTED, particularly in terms of progress on the inspectors' key issues for action. The authors conclude that inspection has had a positive impact on the development of many secondary schools but raise questions about whether there could be other, more effective, ways of helping schools to improve. It appears that OFSTED may be performing its accountability function more effectively than that of 'improvement through inspection'.

The next chapter, on the effects of inspection on school governing bodies, also draws heavily on the Nuffield-funded project. It presents national data from questionnaire surveys, along with information from interviews conducted with LEA governor training co-ordinators, to argue that inspection has the potential to empower governing bodies and to involve them more in the work of their schools. The contribution is timely in the light of OFSTED's decision to inspect, from the spring term 1998, the extent to which a school's governing body is fulfilling its strategic role, and the Education Bill (currently before Parliament) which sees governing bodies as having a central role in raising standards in schools.

The final contribution in the first section centres on the role of LEAs. Again, this is timely given that LEAs are also now subject to OFSTED inspections (from spring 1998 and undertaken in conjunction with the Audit Commission). The focus of Margaret Wood's chapter is on how LEAs are supporting schools after their inspections, particularly in the light of recent legislation which gives the LEA a significant role in school improvement with the implementation of education development plans, and national and local targets. Wood, in a wide-ranging discussion, examines the role of LEA advisory and inspection services in developing quality in education. She focuses on the contribution of LEA personnel to the process of developing schools, highlighting the post-inspection action planning phase within the context of an LEA strategy for school improvement and a national target-setting agenda. From an analysis of the literature, particularly official documents, and her research interviews with LEA officers she identifies at least seven aspects of the LEA's role in the post-inspection phase. Several of the aspects of the LEA's role she documents can clearly be seen in action in the case studies outlined in Section 2.

CASE STUDIES

Section 2 consists of four case studies of individual institutions and describes how each has responded to its inspection. Two of the case studies are of primary schools, the third is of a special school that was subject to special measures and the last is an account of a secondary school's experience of working with their RgI on an improvement programme.

Tony Dimmer, an LEA primary consultant, and Jacky Metiuk, a headteacher, give a fascinating account of how one primary school responded to their OFSTED inspection and went about trying to develop a culture of 'restless self-evaluation'. In order to understand better the impact of the inspection and the evolving school culture, Dimmer and Metiuk met regularly with staff and governors to share observations about day-to-day developments. Their views were also gathered through individual interviews and discussions at meetings of all teaching staff after the follow-up inspection. The latter was undertaken by the LEA one year after OFSTED's visit in order to look at the progress the school had made, whether its direction was maintained and to give pointers to the future. The follow-up inspection, conducted by three LEA inspectors in spring 1997, was in part funded through the LEA's 'Self-evaluating and improving schools' project which allocates three days each year of consultancy time to supporting schools. As a result of the various strategies outlined by the authors, there is reported to be a greater enthusiasm amongst the staff for taking initiatives and in supporting the management of the school as a shared and collegial activity. They claim that the exchange of information and levels of reflection and evaluation prompted by the OFSTED inspection have been sustained and that the inspection can be seen as a staging post on the school's route to continued improvement. The school, in seeking to take a global view of school improvement (including the regular use of external perspectives) enhanced its ability to resolve the possible paradox between inspection and improvement. The case study demonstrates clearly that external perspectives made an important contribution to this primary school's improvement programme.

Riverside School is an 11–16 day special school for pupils with moderate learning difficulties and behavioural difficulties which became subject to special measures after its OFSTED inspection in autumn 1995. Chapter 6, co-written by the chair of governors (Vanessa Aris), the acting headteacher (Jim Davies) and the LEA adviser attached to the school (Peter Johnson), is an account of the school's recovery from failure. It explores the roles played by the staff, the governing body and the LEA in the school's recovery. The emphasis throughout is on the teamwork that developed between them and how this enabled the considerable difficulties to be overcome. The authors conclude that the process of recovery was time consuming and expensive as well as being painful and frequently traumatic. They are certain that the school needed to fail in order to secure the 'special measures' that enabled it to provide the quality of education its pupils deserved. They claim to have learned a number of lessons from the experience, most importantly: that recovery only begins when all parties acknowledge their responsibilities for the school's failure; that external support – in this case from the LEA – was essential (particularly in working with managers to improve their monitoring and with teachers to improve their teaching); that the partnership between the staff, the governors and the LEA is crucial to the recovery of the school; that a strong relationship between the chair of governors and the headteacher provides an effective catalyst for improvement; and, lastly, that real improvement only stems from improved teaching and learning. It is this they argue that should be the central feature of the work of senior managers.

In Chapter 7, Doug Close, ex-HMI and currently an educational consultant and RgI, describes how an LEA-maintained comprehensive school chose to employ members of his team, who were involved in the school's OFSTED inspection, in a consultancy capacity. Of course, this is perfectly legitimate – inspectors are permitted to offer their services to the schools they've inspected – it just means that the same inspection team will be barred from bidding for any future inspection of that school. It does not appear, however, to be a common occurrence. Even more unusual was the fact that Close and his colleagues were also involved in helping the school to prepare their post-inspection action plan. The headteacher viewed the inspection positively, seeing it as an opportunity to review the school's situation and to refocus development and improvement. The head, with the help of external advisers (the school's inspectors), has set an agenda for development, and the school has begun action which it believes will lead to the raising of standards. This account, three years on from the inspection, documents what happened, outlines some of the main constraints on improvement, and demonstrates how the school is able to look forward without fear to the next round of inspection. Close concludes by pointing to one of the main difficulties in school improvement by stating that whatever the leadership and management, whatever the supportive systems, any school remains vulnerable to factors outside its control. His contribution is a useful reminder that, in his own words, 'quality learning is delivered primarily by teachers, not by managers or systems – let alone inspectors or consultants'. At the case-study school, for example, one department carried a staff vacancy through temporary and supply appointments for well over a year and two of the four members of current staff plan to move to other posts in the summer. As Close concludes, in these circumstances simply maintaining quality will be very difficult: high quality cannot be guaranteed, it requires hard work and commitment – and, of course, a little luck.

The infant school which is the focus of Chapter 8 was one of the very first primary schools to be inspected by OFSTED in September 1994. This case study outlines the school's response to the inspection, particularly in relation to the need to raise standards in reading. The chapter is co-written by the head of the school, Susan Robb, who had been in post for one year at the time of the inspection, and the school's attached LEA primary consultant, Helen Hosker, who was also new to her post and to the school. They document how the very low staff morale following the school's inspection was addressed. With particular reference to reading standards and the monitoring and evaluating of classroom practice, they argue that teachers have become much more skilled and confident, and standards of achievement have risen. As a result of inspection the head, governors and staff, with LEA support, targeted improvement, achieved success and have identified further areas for development. Hosker and Robb claim that through the school's commitment to monitoring and evaluating the quality of teaching, a culture of improvement has developed which has enabled the staff to become skilled at identifying the need for change and development. Important factors underpinning the school's success were found to include the OFSTED findings themselves which provided an impetus for change; members of the OFSTED team had credibility and gained the respect of the staff; the action plan was carefully put together; a blame culture was avoided; the LEA supported the school with the action plan and training opportunities were made available; the school became involved in initiatives; LEA consultants provided support with monitoring and evaluation; the headteacher took a proactive role in the developments; the staff responded throughout in a positive way; and parental involvement in the school has been actively encouraged. Lastly, the commitment and support of the governing body were also found to have been crucial to the school's success.

SCHOOLS' RESPONSES: TOWARDS A CRITIQUE OF INSPECTION

In Chapter 9, Geoff Lowe, a recently retired secondary headteacher, discusses the extent of implementation of different types of inspection recommendation in seven comprehensive schools in seven LEAs, one year after inspection. He makes use of the notion of 'discourse', reflects on how various discourses have influenced teachers' responses to the schools' inspection recommendations and speculates on the prospects for real change in the classroom, i.e. in terms of pedagogy or teaching and learning. His investigation, which is ongoing and involves interviewing participants on seven occasions over four years, explores the perceptions of teachers at all levels about the prospect of inspection, the inspection process itself and the implementation of inspection recommendations. In order to promote a better understanding of the process of inspection-induced change, Lowe draws on the work of several social theorists to demonstrate that 'the employment of a discourse enables the speaker to deploy knowledge in such a way which claims to be the truth according to its own criteria and it can become the means by which power relations within a school and between the school and external agencies can be established and maintained'. In this way, he suggests, central government is seeking to take over or 'colonise' schools' discourses with OFSTED's view of the school. This is a view based on notions of standards, quality, efficiency, value for money and performance. Lowe sees headteachers and senior staff as transmitting OFSTED's values to their colleagues in managing the school's response to inspection. Schools are not the product of a single discourse associated with inspection, however, and Lowe states there can be a number of separate discourses with different origins (the example given is of each school's history and traditions, subject traditions and local communities). These differences, he suggests, may account for the variations in the degree of influence which OFSTED's thinking exerts on discourses within schools and between schools. Thus a measure of uncertainty is brought into the implementation of inspectors' key issues which impinge upon teachers' core educational beliefs, such as those concerned with teaching and learning.

Lowe's research reveals that headteachers and senior staff tended to have a more favourable view of the extent of implementation of inspection recommendations and were overly optimistic about their influence on what happens in the classroom. Perceptions of the extent of the implementation of the inspectors' key issues were found to vary both between schools and within the same school. Factors which either facilitated or inhibited the schools' implementation of key issues included the willingness of the staff; the responses of headteachers, senior staff and heads of department; the quality of the school's action planning; resources (including teachers' time); the availability and quality of advice from LEAs; the level of LEA funding; the conduct of the inspection; and the nature of the inspectors' recommendations. Lowe's investigation places these factors in the context of school discourses – the notion that central government is attempting to change the way teachers think and act through a process of top-down change is given support by his research. The various management-orientated initiatives promoted by central government over the last decade, e.g. local management of schools, school development planning, performance tables, OFSTED inspection and, most recently, benchmarking and target-setting, are said to have changed the beliefs which underpin the schools' discourses towards those of a more managerialist nature. This process can be viewed as the 'colonisation of school discourses'. Lowe's contribution shows that headteachers' attempts to colonise school discourses have resulted in degrees of 'decoupling' or separation of the discourses associated with school management from those associated with teaching and learning.

In a similarly, theoretically informed contribution, Peter Lonsdale and Carl Parsons present an interesting critique of OFSTED and its claim to effect school improvement. Drawing on their small-scale study of five schools (both primary and secondary) which has examined progress on action plans two years or more after they were first inspected in 1995, they suggest that the OFSTED strapline 'improvement through inspection' is an official deceit and that in an environment of individualism and 'marketisation', an accountability model of inspection, is more appropriate. A number of reasons for making this claim are put forward and the intentional lack of transparency is the justification for the authors referring to inspection as a hoax. They see the exercise of school inspection as one of improvement through threat and fear, an intentionally disciplining role. Their investigation focuses on the extent to which improvements could be attributed to the inspection, concluding that the accountability model of inspection is consonant with the created environment of individualism and the role of the market. The OFSTED inspection process is seen as part of the new public management in education and the new arrangements have, they argue, 'sought primarily to disempower and subordinate professionals, "police" the work being done and enable a punitive response to schools which the market alone cannot deliver'. Were improvement the prime goal, they continue, 'colleagueship would be retained, dialogue would be ongoing, and the inspection process itself would offer "solutions" rather than "issues" and empower front-line professionals not induce fear'. Lonsdale and Parsons conclude that the system is all stick and no carrot.

Furthermore, they claim that the inspection process does not represent good value for money – three quarters of the issues identified by the inspectors were already known by their research schools before the inspection – only in relation to a third of the issues was it judged helpful that OFSTED had highlighted them. In a time of shortage of resources (or at any time), they ask, should money be spent on a process that causes as much disruption as benefit? Interestingly, the lapse of time between the inspection and the time of the research did not lead schools to a more favourable view of OFSTED inspections. Heads spoke of feeling removed from the inspection process and disempowered; its morality was questioned in terms of waste, personal and institutional damage and fear. The purpose, in terms of improvement, was not evident. Lonsdale and Parsons conclude that the present process is subjugating, demeaning and deprofessionalising. In the future, they would like to see OFSTED concentrating on areas of known weakness in schools and focusing resources into the formative process of school development in partnership with schools and LEAs.

Interestingly, the next chapter, by Nigel Cromey-Hawke, a secondary school middle manager, comes to a different set of conclusions based on his research in 21 schools. The work reported in Chapter 11 draws on only a part of his ongoing research and inquires whether teachers themselves see inspection as facilitating school improvement. Teacher perceptions of the extent to which inspection has changed their own practices and affected their professional values are considered and some interesting differences identified, particularly (like Lowe) those between the views of teachers and their managers. Concerns that inspection, like other auditing devices, is itself conditioning the shape of what is being audited, are also explored. Cromey-Hawke suggests his research schools are beginning to moderate their attitudes to inspection and to OFSTED as an organisation itself. OFSTED and inspection are becoming institutionalised within the teaching profession and increasingly valued, albeit from a low starting base. The potential for 'improvement through inspection' is being recognised, it is suggested, by many groups within schools. He argues for the need for greater openness and recognition of the contribution all sides are making towards effective schooling, for schools to acknowledge inspection and to engage with it professionally, to temper it and to make it their own. Cromey-Hawke concludes by asking whether the need for both accountability and professional autonomy (and teacher creativity) can coexist in a relationship of mutual pressure and support based upon respect and trust. There is some evidence, however, that schools are reasserting their autonomy by their proactive participation in the inspection process.

The last chapter in this section, by Margaret Mathieson and Mel Vlaeminke, deals with an important part of the inspection framework, namely, school's performance in the promotion of pupils' spiritual, moral, social and cultural (SMSC) development. In an interesting account of this relatively unexplored and neglected area of inspection research they argue that the inspection of SMSC is undertaken with little official guidance, for either inspectors or schools, about what constitutes successful practice in this area. An analysis of about 100 inspection reports reveals a strange mixture of school features presented as evidence of SMSC alongside fairly relentless criticism, especially at secondary school level. The authors point to a further layer of uncertainty in the official rhetoric and execution of inspection in the wide-ranging interpretations placed on SMSC by OFSTED team members. Seen as 'the most important part of school life' and 'often dumped on the lay inspector', they claim that the judgements made on teachers' work in this area include some strange pieces of evidence. Also, they suggest that the frequent use of the term 'quality' in relation to pupils' spiritual, moral, social and cultural development is peculiar, implying that it is possible to be bad in this area and for outsiders to measure the deficiency. Their investigation suggests that many schools have struggled to determine how to respond to the inspectors' judgements in this important sphere. A common response has been to appoint new members of staff, often in religious education, sometimes in personal and social education (PSE), to co-ordinate and revitalise work in the school's provision of moral and spiritual education. Another response to the inspection has been to devote a training day or staff meeting to a discussion of moral and spiritual issues, often as a preliminary for an audit of provision across the curriculum. Mathieson and Vlaeminke's research shows that teachers are neither casual nor irresponsible in their approach to moral and spiritual education and they conclude by suggesting ways in which teachers are responding.

REINSPECTION AND BEYOND

The two contributions in the final section consider the reinspection of schools and the move to encourage a greater degree of self-assessment or evaluation by schools themselves. Brian Fidler and Jacqueline Davies' chapter examines reinspection – which will normally take place every six years and not four, as originally envisaged – and how schools are approaching it. It offers advice and examples based on research evidence accumulated over the last few years from the Nuffield Foundation-funded project on secondary school inspection (see Chapter 2 for further details of this research project). It also draws upon an ongoing small-scale study of reinspection, also funded by the Nuffield Foundation, which is following the progress of a subsample of schools first inspected in 1993 and reinspected in 1997/8.

Fidler and Davies commence by suggesting that a school's experience of the initial inspection is not necessarily a good guide to reinspection. To begin with, the inspection process itself has continued to change. The framework on which reinspections are carried out has a number of changes compared with the previous (revised) version in 1996, and is considerably different from the original framework that operated for the first two years of inspection. Particular features of the 1997/8 inspections include the grading of the performance of each teacher and the offer of feedback; assessment of the extent of progress on the key issues for action since the previous inspection; and more indication in the inspection report of what the key issues for action involve. Progress on the first inspection's key issues will be the starting point for the reinspection. Inspectors will examine documentary reports of progress since the last inspection (e.g. annual governor reports to parents, action plans, SDPs, etc.) as well as gathering other evidence of the school's capacity to manage change. Its central focus is on improvements since the last inspection and inspectors are expected to make judgements about changes that the school has made, whether they were an adequate response to previous inspection findings, how they have been made and, perhaps most difficult of all, if they have been sufficient.

Fidler and Davies point to the critical importance of the RgI – a further source of variation. They argue for a contingent view of the world, suggesting each school needs to work out an approach to reinspection which is appropriate for itself. They set out some of the factors that need to be considered in choosing and planning an approach to reinspection and refer to such factors as the reason for inspection (accountability or improvement?); the attitude to inspection; the school's previous experiences; the state of the school (e.g. likely to be 'failing' or 'satisfactory'); the state of the staff (e.g. innovative, coasting); and confidence in the inspection team. A case is strongly argued for paying close attention to preparing for inspection because in addition to its public cost, a great deal of school resources will be taken up by the process. They estimate that the cost to a school is at least as great as the contracted cost of inspectors; it therefore makes much sense to try to look upon this resource as an investment and to aim to generate a return that benefits the school. Fidler and Davies also suggest that inspection should be conceived as an opportunity to carry out some worthwhile developments which would be unlikely to happen without the arrival of OFSTED. It may be a number of years before a similar opportunity again presents itself.

The final chapter, by the editor, examines the move towards school self-assessment and self-evaluation. Drawing upon the various contributions to the book and other examples, particularly from the non-statutory sector, the notion of the accredited self-evaluating institution is raised as an alternative or complement to the OFSTED system. The importance of a culture of self-evaluation is stressed and it concludes that in the drive for school improvement there is a clear need for *both* internal and external approaches to evaluation and assessment. Each on its own is of limited value and neither is sufficient to bring about real improvement in schools. Although some commentators (e.g. Duffy, 1997; Fitz-Gibbon, 1998) suggest inspection is harmful to schools, there is a growing body of evidence that OFSTED inspection does lead to school improvement, broadly defined. The key question, however, which the final chapter begins to explore, is whether it is an appropriate or particularly cost effective way to effect change and raise standards in our schools. The debate no doubt will continue.

Notes

1.   The system of inspection is only slightly different for Wales, whereas the emphasis in Scotland is much more on school self-evaluation. All the contributions to this collection focus on English schools and the OFSTED system of inspection.

2.   For the reader unfamiliar with the specifics of the inspection process, further details can be found in numerous publications, both official (e.g. OFSTED, 1993/6b) and unofficial (e.g. Ormston and Shaw, 1994).

2

OFSTED and Afterwards?
Schools' Responses to Inspection

JANET OUSTON AND JACQUELINE DAVIES

INTRODUCTION

The research reported here was planned to investigate the medium and longer-term impact of OFSTED inspection on schools. It explored how secondary schools responded to their inspection and how they used the inspectors' findings to support their subsequent development. Information has been collected over a three-year period from 1994 to 1997. The research provides a complex but consistent picture of secondary schools' responses to inspection. It will be appreciated that this is inevitably a historical study. The OFSTED inspection framework has changed (in particular, reporting on individual teacher's performance) since the research programme was undertaken, but many of the issues that emerged remain as key concerns.

Information about schools' responses to OFSTED inspection was obtained through face-to-face and telephone interviews with staff and governors at 55 schools which were inspected in 1993, 1994 and 1996. Questionnaires were sent to all schools inspected in the autumn terms of 1993, 1994 and 1996 and response rates of between 60 and 80 per cent were obtained. This chapter outlines the findings from the interviews and the most recent set of questionnaires. The research was funded by the Nuffield Foundation and the final project report can be obtained from the first author.[1] Earlier findings are reported in Ouston *et al.* (1996; 1997a).

Most of the information included in this chapter has been obtained from headteachers; the research provided, in the main, a senior management view of inspection but some more junior staff were also included. Senior staff tended to have a broader and more 'managerial' view of the inspection process, while more junior staff saw the inspection in terms of their own experience of it, and their personal responsibilities. It should also be noted that many teachers working at the schools during the inspection had moved elsewhere and their replacements had no personal experience of it. Interviews included only those who had been at the school during the inspection.

STAGES OF INSPECTION

It is clear from the research that the impact of inspection should be seen as, at least, a two to three-year process, rather than a one-week event. It can be considered in six stages, where schools' and inspectors' attitudes and behaviour at each stage make an impact on the next stage. These stages are

1) before the inspection date is announced;
2) after the date is known but before the inspection;
3) the inspection, and writing the action plan;
4) the implementation of the action plan;
5) after the impact of the first inspection has faded; and
6) reinspection.

This chapter will focus on Stages 3, 4 and 5. Reinspection started in October 1997 and is the focus of our current research funded by the Nuffield Foundation. (Initial findings and thoughts on reinspection are presented by Fidler and Davies in Chapter 13 of this volume.)

Stage 1: Before inspection

Schools' responses at this stage were determined by their attitudes towards OFSTED inspection; their own success in terms of examination results and pupil recruitment; the extent of current internal change (which was often related to the length of time the headteacher had been in post); and by each school's culture and values. Some started inspection preparation at this stage but the majority waited until Stage 2.

Stage 2: Preparation

Schools in the research programme had between two and four terms' notice of the inspection date. The 1993 and 1994 inspected schools nearly all undertook extensive preparation, reviewed their practice and ensured that their paperwork was complete and well presented. But they varied in their overall approach to inspection: some saw it as 'free consultancy' while others worked extremely hard to conceal any weakness – they aimed for 'the perfect week'.

The least preparation was undertaken in schools with newly appointed headteachers where other changes were in progress. Nearly all those inspected in 1996 described themselves as 'fully prepared' with just over half presenting 'a highly prepared performance'. About one third saw this as making a 'major contribution to their development'. But the same proportion said that it slowed down developments not directly related to inspection. Many teachers found preparation the start of a very stressful process.

The inspection experience must be interpreted within the overall context of the school, and its aims, values and practices. Schools varied in the extent to which their management processes were in tune with what they perceived to be the OFSTED ideal. Other researchers (e.g. Lowe, Chapter 9) have commented on the extent to which this perception of the OFSTED ideal school has influenced the management of schools. It might be seen as a form of surveillance (Maw, 1996) where schools 'choose' to conform before inspection, rather than waiting until after the inspection. Some headteachers commented that the OFSTED framework was an excellent management manual, while others disagreed.

Stage 3: The inspection and action planning

The inspection itself was a critical time in determining schools' responses to the whole process. Schools valued inspectors who behaved professionally, and who were in tune with the schools' aims, purposes and values, and understood its context. Schools were critical of inspectors who behaved unprofessionally, and this coloured their view of the validity of the inspection and the extent to which it influenced practice subsequently.[2] They valued inspections which were seen as fair and accurate, and inspectors who contributed to helpful and supportive professional dialogue. A good inspection increased confidence in the whole OFSTED process and enhanced the validity of the report and its recommendations.

There were considerable anxieties expressed about the quality of some inspections, particularly concerning those undertaken in 1996. Practice may be diverging for two reasons: registered inspectors (RgIs) and team members may be becoming socialised into their own patterns of working. In addition, many inspectors were trained in the early years of inspection and the rigour required at that point may have faded. Headteachers were concerned about the number of inspections undertaken by some teams, about the commercial pressures on them and the lack of quality control. It should be noted that the research did not include inspectors so their perspectives on this issue were not explored.

The key importance of the school's perception of the professionalism of their inspectors is supported by findings from the 1996 questionnaire when schools were asked 'To what extent has your original view of the inspection team's professionalism changed as a result of the actual inspection?' Just over half said that it remained unchanged, 20 per cent were more positive and 22 per cent were more negative. While it is difficult to argue strongly for chains of causes and effects from data collected *post hoc*, the model is supported by both interview and questionnaire data. From the questionnaire data it is clear that schools' view of their team after inspection is more negative when they perceive their inspection report to be too negative, and when the headteacher reported that he/she was not able to speak openly to the RgI.[3] Interestingly, the perceived value of the inspection is highest when the report is perceived to be fair, rather than too positive. It is also highest in schools where staff agree that the majority of the inspectors' 'key issues for action' are important for their own progress.

Many of the reports included key issues which the schools were already aware of, but gave no suggestions about how they might be addressed. For example, at one school a key issue was 'develop effective strategies to deal with the underachievement of boys relative to girls'. The school agreed with the key issue but did not know how to enhance boys' performance. Often reports identified 'weaknesses' which the school had already started to make progress on. Again, advice would have been welcomed, but at that time it was not a requirement of the inspection process. This interpretation was confirmed by findings from the questionnaire. Eighty per cent of heads said that they had 'confidently predicted the outcomes of inspection' and 82 per cent would have liked the inspectors to give advice.

A third of the schools surveyed knew some of their inspectors before the inspection. Some teachers said that this was a positive advantage as the inspectors understood their school and the community it served. Others saw it as a disadvantage and that the school suffered by being inspected by people with whom they had a pre-existing – and possibly unproductive – relationship.

Headteachers, and teachers, varied in the extent to which they attempted to influence the agenda for inspection. In the early years the inspection process was intended to be identical in every school, but in practice some teachers saw inspection as 'being done to them' while others took a much more proactive approach guiding the inspectors' towards some issues and away from others.

SCHOOLS' RESPONSES TO OFSTED

It is proposed that the research schools can be placed into one of three categories according to their responses to inspection:

- *'Developing/reflective' schools* These schools were not at risk of failure; they were adequately managed and had acceptable levels of attainment. The inspection had little impact. Often they were confirmed in their existing direction and told to continue and extend current practice. Most of the schools in the research programme came into this category. These schools were likely to have a good understanding of their own strengths and weaknesses.
- *'Complacent' schools* These schools were popular with their communities. They had relatively socially advantaged intakes and above-average examination results. They were traditional in their approach and confirmed in this by

their enthusiastic parent bodies. They expected the inspectors to confirm their success.

- *'Struggling' schools*   These schools typically served a disadvantaged community and felt that they would never meet what they perceived to be the 'OFSTED ideal'. They felt constantly under pressure, and were generally negative about inspection. They knew they were at risk of failing the inspection and being placed 'in need of special measures'.

Progress at 'complacent' and 'struggling' schools particularly depended on their perceptions of the competence of the inspection team, and the extent to which the report and its key issues for action were seen as accurate and valid. They rejected, or were demoralised by, reports from teams which they perceived as less competent or professional and few changes in practice were subsequently implemented:

- *Complacent schools*, where staff were positive about the quality of their inspection, implemented the key issues for action which were compatible with their culture and values. They made little progress on implementing the key issues if the inspection team was not seen as competent.
- *Struggling schools* could benefit from inspection if they perceived they had a high-quality inspection team which took account of its context and culture. If not, they made little progress.

Once the inspection week is completed the inspectors prepare a written report which sets out their recommendations (the 'key issues for action'). Schools are required, within 40 days, to write action plans to demonstrate how they will implement the inspectors' recommendations.

In evaluating their inspection report, on average, schools considered 70 per cent of the inspectors' recommendations to be 'important' for the school (see Table 2.1). But some of these could not be implemented because they were beyond their direct control. Recommendations which were not congruent with the school's culture were considered as less important, and reports which were

Table 2.1   Heads' perceptions of importance of key issues and progress made 3–4 years later (%)

	Good progress made	Poor progress made
Important	55	15
Not important	15	15*

Notes:
n = 35.
* Two thirds of these issues concerned either the requirements for the corporate act of worship or school accommodation.

perceived as inaccurate could lead to complacency or to the undermining of initiatives for change. Poor inspection practice led to schools dismissing all or part of the inspection findings as invalid. In the questionnaire to schools inspected in 1996, headteachers were asked to say how many of the report's key issues for action were considered to be important. The average number of reported key issues was 5.6, and of these 3.8 (68%) were considered to be 'important' or 'very important', a similar proportion to that reported in the school-based interviews.

Some interviewees were clearly more satisfied with the experience of the inspection than others. There were wide-ranging perceptions of the thoroughness of inspection reports in different schools. Data from the questionnaire to the 1996 inspected schools confirm that 73 per cent thought that the report was 'fair', 19 per cent that it was too negative and 8 per cent that it was too positive. Seventy per cent were encouraged by the report, and 18 per cent discouraged. While the general picture is broadly positive, there was a sizeable minority who expressed reservations.

Stage 4: Implementation of the action plan

Schools varied in their planning of Stage 4 – the implementation of the inspectors' key issues for action. This depended on the perceived importance or value of each key issue to the school, and the ease with which it could be achieved.

During this stage schools' own 'important issues' were given priority and taken forward. Good progress was made in about two thirds of these (see Table 2.1). Implementation was most successful when the inspectors' recommendations and the school's own intentions overlapped. Here the inspection findings acted as a confirmation of the school's direction and could be used as a lever to ensure continued change. Most changes were made during the first year after the inspection.

Issues could be viewed as *important* in two ways. It was important

- that the school address the issue, and often this had already started; and
- for the school that the OFSTED report included the issue in the list of recommendations as it provoked action.

When good progress was reported to have been made on relatively unimportant issues these were usually straightforward matters that could be easily 'fixed'. Schools liked to have some of these issues so that they could 'tick them off' and see themselves as successful. Important issues where little progress had been made were often found in struggling schools. In these the inspectors often made a large number of recommendations, but implementation had to be phased. These were often very problematic, school-wide issues, such as the 'improving attendance' which schools may have tackled before with little or no success. The less important and less well progressed issues often concerned either accommodation (and therefore lay outside the remit of LEA-maintained schools) or the corporate act of worship which many schools had serious reservations about introducing. Both these issued tended to be 'reviewed' but little real action was taken.

How a key issue was addressed varied between schools. At some schools the headteacher took responsibility for addressing the key issues and change was planned using (as one head said) 'the imposition of my will'. At other schools the head shared the responsibility with senior management and at others reference was made to the role of the governors (see Chapter 3). For example, in some schools differentiation was addressed by consulting all teachers, but at others the headteacher made the decision and subsequently imposed it on the school.

At the schools inspected in 1993 and 1994 over half the reports included one or two issues which were valued because they pressed the school into addressing an issue that they knew they should be working on, but where they had not yet made any progress. Several headteachers commented that inspection 'made explicit something implicit'. The implementation of a school-wide assessment policy was the most frequently reported issue of this type, and was included in 37 per cent of reports. There was often considerable resistance to this from heads of departments. Heads, however, could see that this might threaten teachers' autonomy, flexibility and professionalism and valued the additional support provided by OFSTED.

SLOWED DOWN OR SPEEDED UP?

Schools were asked if OFSTED slowed down or speeded up change. Many staff felt they needed time to recover after inspection and development ceased for a short time (often depending on how close to a half-term or end of term the inspection was). Many schools reported slowing down while they recovered from the 'ordeal' of inspection – the 'post-inspection blues'. They then made a fresh start on implementing the key issues. However, some teachers expressed concern that inspection had slowed down development on other issues. Questionnaire data suggest that development was slowed down in one third of schools and speeded up in another third, with the remaining third stating that it made no difference to the pace of change.

Stage 5: Inspection fades

The impact of inspection appeared to have faded after about 18 months. But the recent announcement that schools will be reinspected from September 1997, and that they will be evaluated on their performance compared to that recorded in the previous report and their progress on the key issues for action, has led schools to reconsider the earlier inspection.

TENSIONS IN INSPECTION: ACCOUNTABILITY OR DEVELOPMENT?

There was a constant tension between what teachers saw as 'worthwhile' and 'not worthwhile' in OFSTED inspection because of its multiple purposes. An OFSTED report is a public document which can be used by the community and Her Majesty's Chief Inspector to assess the school. Naturally the school wishes to receive a report which says it is a good school which provides a good education, without too many 'key issues for action'. On the other hand OFSTED also has a developmental role: its well-known logo is 'improvement through inspection'. But can the dual purposes of accountability and development be met within the same process?

Schools must decide, for example, whether to assist the inspectors in finding weaknesses and must weigh up the benefits and disadvantages of doing this. If OFSTED is for accountability, then this would be an unwise strategy; if it is for development it would be an obvious first move. On the whole, however, the potential dangers were seen as greater than the benefits. Schools prepared extensively for inspection, and presented the most polished week they could manage for the inspectors. This had several negative outcomes:

- It distracted schools from 'normal' activities.
- It used time, money and human resources.
- It focused the school on conforming to the framework when this might not be in their best interests.
- Conflicts could become explicit.
- Stress built up in the school community as members worried about the damage to individual and collective reputations which might follow public criticism.

'Successful' preparation of a 'perfect week' led to weaknesses being hidden. At one school staff successfully persuaded the children to behave better than usual during the week of inspection. But subsequently the school lacked evidence to support their bid to obtain additional resources to work with students on their behaviour. Similarly, having 'poor-quality inspectors' had advantages and disadvantages. Weaknesses were not identified, so there was less public criticism of the school, but this made addressing the weaknesses subsequently more difficult. These issues can be seen as reflecting the conflict between inspection for accountability and inspection for development.

Inspection is intended to meet both these aims, but schools tend to take one perspective. This can range from seeing inspection as an audit and as 'free consultancy' – the developmental model – to those who consider that they are at risk of failure and possibly closure – the accountability model. Those who held the developmental model often presented weaknesses to the inspectors, while those who saw inspection as being for accountability concealed weaknesses and attempted to prepare for a 'perfect' inspection week.

Many of the complexities of OFSTED inspection can be seen as resulting from these two factors. Clearly the public face of OFSTED inspection is one of accountability and it is not surprising that schools saw it this way too. But some more confident schools argued that the process should be seen as an opportunity to examine critically their strengths and weaknesses. The approach adopted depended on the schools' assessment of their own performance, their attitudes to OFSTED before inspection and their experiences of the inspection itself.

Schools also varied in how much power they ascribed to the inspection process. For those at risk of failure (about 2 per cent nationally) it may have immediate and profound consequences, but for the majority this was not the case. Several years after their inspection, schools who saw it as being primarily for accountability, and as very powerful, were happy to have survived. They remembered the stress of the experience and they had often not made much progress on implementing change. Schools that saw inspection as developmental, and powerful, sometimes implemented change which they have subsequently realised was not in their overall best interests (e.g. the resourcing of religious education). The schools who saw the inspection process as less intimidating were more likely to have taken the inspection report as a starting point, made judgements about what was relevant to the school's needs and implemented change effectively: perceptions of their own professional power counterbalanced the power of OFSTED. Table 2.2 summarises this approach to conceptualising the outcomes of OFSTED.

Table 2.2   Accountability, development, power and the outcomes of OFSTED

Model	Ascribed power	Outcomes
Accountability	Powerful ➡	School adopts OFSTED model before inspection, overprepared, anxiety and stress, cover-up, the 'perfect week', avoided development, may fail *or* be relieved that they had survived
Development	Weak ➘	Pleased with confirmation, considered the report seriously, reflected on what is relevant for the school,
	Weak ➚	made informed decisions about change
	Powerful ➡	School too obedient, implemented inappropriate practices, regret and 'unpicking' of change

Some schools attempted to control the power of OFSTED by presenting the 'perfect week' to ensure they met the accountability criteria. But this reduced the value of advice and support about development. At one school the head organised a 'dry run' with a neighbouring LEA OFSTED team so that things could be 'put right'. Staff were concerned that much of the 'putting right' was superficial and hid real issues. But the strategy was successful and the report positive. On the other hand, some senior teachers hoped for an honest, and critical, report. They were disappointed when the OFSTED inspection fell short of this and little development followed.

Teachers who saw the OFSTED inspection process as less powerful were more likely to have reflected carefully on its value for the school and to have made professional decisions which led to appropriate, and positive, outcomes.

CONCLUSIONS

The impact of inspection began before inspection (Stage 1), and intensified during the preparation phase and the week of inspection (Stages 2 and 3). It continued during the implementation of the action plan (Stage 4) but faded after about a year to 18 months (Stage 5). The key issues were implemented most successfully when they were congruent with the direction already taken by the school and least successfully when they required the school to take a direction which did not fit current concerns, practices and values.

The main impact of OFSTED was to encourage the implementation of changes which were already seen as desirable. Headteachers used OFSTED inspection as a tool to facilitate change both during the preparation phase and in the years afterwards. When the inspectors recommended a key issue for action or a change that was not wanted, or valued, by the school, implementation was poor. Unwanted change was avoided by saying that the issue 'would be reviewed'; teachers also challenged the credibility of the inspectors or the inspection process. Most interviewees reported that there was something that the inspectors missed or misinterpreted and this was generally viewed as a lost opportunity. Developments planned before OFSTED but not supported by the report were usually continued, but without the catalyst provided by its inclusion in the list of key issues for action.

The impact of OFSTED inspection on a school varied depending on a number of variables, including:

Stage 1: Before the inspection is announced

- The school's culture, values and philosophy;
- the school's confidence in itself, its staff and its professional practice;
- the school's view of its own strengths and weaknesses;
- the state of the school before inspection, for example its position in the performance tables and in the local education marketplace;
- the history of innovation before OFSTED and the school's position in the 'cycle of change';
- the school's relationship with its LEA;
- the role of the headteacher and the number of years he/she had been in post;
- the style of management, autocratic or collaborative, established or new; and
- the quality and commitment of the staff.

Stage 2: Before inspection

- The school and its teachers' attitudes towards inspection; whether it was seen as primarily for accountability, or to support development;
- the extent to which these meshed with OFSTED's values;
- the extent to which the school felt under threat of 'failing';
- the length and use of the preparation period: perfection or good enough?; and
- the extent to which the school was proactive in contributing to the inspection agenda.

Stage 3: During inspection

- The quality, and perceived quality, of the inspection process and the inspection team; and
- the feedback, advice and support provided by the inspectors.

Stages 4 and 5: After inspection

- The extent to which the report was seen as accurate, fair, comprehensive, justified by evidence and relevant;
- whether issues that were important to the school were appropriately commented on;
- the extent to which the key issues were congruent with the school's context, aims, purposes and values;
- the extent to which the key issues were achievable;
- the extent to which addressing the key issues was under the school's control;
- whether financial and other resources were available to support change; and
- less controllable aspects of school life such as staff turnover, funding and changes in legislation.

The findings from this project on the impact are complex but consistent. Many themes recurred in each of the three groups of inspected schools included in the research, while others are particularly evident in early, or later, inspections. In the early inspections, in 1993, there was a concern that schools were often told to do things they were already doing. They were also told to 'review' certain activities, which led to nothing more than a review. Later on they were more likely to complain about poor inspection practice, which diminished the school's respect for the team and their perception of the validity of the report.

OFSTED inspection clearly had encouraged developments in practice in many of the schools taking part in the research. But its effects were patchy and very dependent on both school and inspection team. This conclusion is supported by data from the 1996 questionnaire. Headteachers of schools inspected in that year were asked to assess whether the preparation for inspection, the verbal feedback and the written report made a major contribution to their school's development. For 'preparation' 29 per cent said it had, for 'verbal feedback' 40 per cent and for the 'written report', 44 per cent. Only 17 per cent or about one in six were positive about the contribution of all three phases. The proportion saying that it had made little contribution were 21 per cent ('preparation'), 18 per cent ('verbal feedback') and 16 per cent ('written report').

Teachers and headteachers who made 'the most of inspection' were those who were as proactive as they could be given the nature of the inspection process. They

- maintained a professional confidence and did not allow the inspection to intimidate them;
- established a good relationship with the RgI;
- understood about the twin purposes of OFSTED: accountability and development;
- ensured that they met the accountability criteria;
- used OFSTED inspection as an audit of the school;
- used the opportunity to improve practice without creating excessive stress for teachers;
- noted poor inspection practice and brought it to the attention of the RgI;
- challenged the report if it was inaccurate;
- were realistic in deciding what should be done as a consequence of inspection;
- made informed and strategic choices about actions to be taken;
- integrated plans resulting from the inspection with their previous plans;
- used the OFSTED report as a lever for change within the school and outside;
- assessed what was feasible; and
- made professional judgements about what was right for their school at that time.

The research shows, without doubt, that OFSTED inspection did have a positive impact on many secondary schools, but questions remain about whether there could be other, more effective and less costly, ways of helping schools to improve their practice and outcomes. OFSTED's aim of accountability is clearly being achieved; that of development or 'improvement through inspection' is less clear cut or apparent for some of the schools involved in our research.

Notes

1. Dr Janet Ouston, Management Development Centre, Institute of Education, 55 Gordon Square, London WC1H 0NU.

2. OFSTED have recently (March 1998) acknowledged that there may be problems with some inspections by setting up a formal complaints procedure and an 'ombudsman'. Schools that feel unfairly treated will be able to appeal to this person for adjudication. This person will not be permitted, however, to order a reinspection.

3. The RgI (registered inspector) is the leader of the inspection team. RgIs are trained and accredited by OFSTED, as are team members.

3

Governing Bodies and School Inspection: Potential for Empowerment?

PETER EARLEY

INTRODUCTION

An interesting question which appears to have been relatively unexplored in the burgeoning literature on school inspection is the effect an OFSTED inspection has on the governing body. Does it have any lasting effects on the governors and governance of schools and if so what are they likely to be? Does inspection have the potential to empower governing bodies, particularly as they examine their role in relation to the post-OFSTED action plan? Similarly, is the process encouraging governing bodies to consider how they are currently performing their duties? With reference to relevant research findings, these are the key questions addressed in this chapter.

The initial question to be asked, however, is whether an OFSTED inspection should be seen as an inspection of the school *and* its governing body, or as being undertaken largely *for* the governing body – the post-OFSTED action plan is after all referred to as the governors' action plan? There is no clear-cut answer to this question other than to say that elements of both are likely to apply. The governor training organisation, the Institution for School and College Governors (ISCG, 1996), identifies a change of emphasis in the more recent school inspections from 'for' the governing body to 'of' the governing body and for the need for governing bodies to take cognizance of this development. It recommends that the inspection framework needs to state exactly what is required and expected of governors – and not only during inspection. The perception of LEA governor trainers too (see later) was that, although still variable, the more recent OFSTED inspections seemed 'to be hotter on governing bodies than before'.

The framework for the inspection of schools states that the registered inspector's (RgI's) report should include 'an evaluation of the strategic management of the resources available to the school, including an assessment of the work of the governing body and appropriate staff' (OFSTED, 1993/6b).

Similarly, the school is to be judged by the inspectors partly in terms of the leadership shown by the governing body and whether effective working relationships exist so that common goals can be achieved. In addition the OFSTED handbook notes that the inspectors' report should also include 'an evaluation of the effectiveness of the governing body in fulfilling its legal responsibilities' (OFSTED, 1993/6a).

The outcomes of the inspection – the report and the key issues for action – are an important source of evidence for governors and require the governing body to draw up the action plan and enable it to monitor the quality of education provided in the school. Certainly there has been no shortage of advice and information for governors on what the inspection of the school will involve and the nature of the governing body's main responsibilities which may be appraised (e.g. O'Connor, 1996; Stiles, 1996). Similarly, many LEAs have produced guidance documents for governors and provided training, either for individual governors or for the whole governing body, on what inspection entails and what will be expected of governors both during and after the inspection.

How governing bodies are able to cope with and respond to the inspection process both before it occurs, during the actual inspection and afterwards, will differ depending on the demands made on the governing body and its level of collective competence. The balance between the demands made on the governors by the inspection process and their overall competence to respond accordingly has been conceptualised by one of the governor training organisations (ISCG, 1996) and their model is reproduced in Figure 3.1. OFSTED inspection reports might usefully be able to categorise governing bodies in such terms. However, the range and extent of inspectors' comments regarding the operation of school governing bodies have been shown to vary considerably from one report to another.

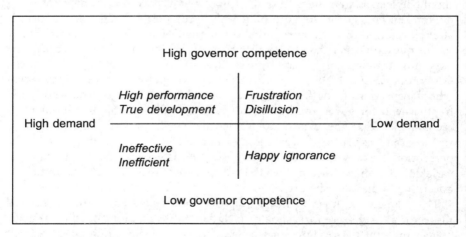

Figure 3.1 A model of the balance between governing body competence and the demands placed on it

A detailed analysis of references to governors in inspection reports has been undertaken by Creese (1997) who, following up an earlier analysis he conducted in 1994, found that the situation had changed very little, with again much variation in practice. Creese did note, however, that governors in the more recent survey were very much more involved in providing evidence on which inspectors based their judgements. Evidence was likely to be derived from interviews – probably undertaken by the lay inspector and usually with the chair and/or the chairs of committees. In both Creese's 1994 and 1997 analyses of OFSTED reports he found only one example of inspectors having attended a governing body meeting. His analysis of nearly 100 inspection reports shows that governors are becoming increasingly involved in the work of their schools and Creese makes the suggestion that OFSTED reports, partly in recognition of the time and commitment made by governors, should include 'at least one paragraph reporting on the work of the governing body' (Creese, 1997).

Creese's main finding (*ibid.*) was that 'there is still considerable variation in the length and detail of the section of the report devoted to the work of the governing body', although he notes that there is now a greater consistency in inspectors' expectations regarding governors' roles and the way in which an effective governing body will operate. Also there is (*ibid.*) 'a sufficient number of common themes and phrases which run through the reports to suggest that a clearer view of what is expected of an effective governing body is now emerging from OFSTED'.

The degree to which inspectors have reported on the governing body has been variable and perhaps for this reason OFSTED announced that for the spring term 1998, governing body performance would be specifically commented upon. Governing bodies were to be graded by the inspectors on a seven-point scale in relation to the degree to which they were fulfilling their strategic role – in Gann's view (1997) the only effective role that a predominantly lay group of people can play in schools. Inspectors were given no formal guidance from OFSTED on exactly how they should make their judgements, although broad criteria were offered for the achievement of grades 2, 4 and 6 (Upgrade 24, 1997).

It appears as though inspection is making it increasingly clear to governing bodies that they have an important responsibility to ensure that their school is operating successfully. Evidence from schools which have 'failed' the inspection and have become subject to special measures shows that their governing bodies have become more effective, making better use of the limited time available to them and assisting their school to come off the special measures register (DfEE, 1997; Earley, 1997; OFSTED, 1997c). But what of other school governing bodies – the vast majority – how has inspection affected them? What has been their response to the inspection process? In what ways and to what extent are governors involved in their schools after the inspection? An attempt will be made to address these questions with reference to research into school inspection and/or governing bodies.

INSPECTION AND GOVERNING BODIES: THE RESEARCH EVIDENCE

The immediate task of the governing body after the inspection is to attend the feedback session given by the RgI and then to work with the headteacher on the post-OFSTED action plan. Schools and governing bodies have approached this in different ways with the level of governor involvement varying considerably.

After the immediate euphoria, relief and celebration of 'having survived OFSTED' the notion of a period of 'post-OFSTED' blues or depression, frequently followed by a dip in performance, has been noted. The ISCG see this possible underperformance as needing to be dealt with through careful strategic planning in which governors have an important role. Not only does the governing body need to be aware of a possible dip in performance (which may last weeks, months or even terms) but also it needs to be 'ready to suggest strategies to deal with staff morale and absence, pupil unrest, lack of energy for initiatives and so forth' (ISCG, 1996). The notion of post-OFSTED depression was also mentioned by respondents in the Nuffield study of secondary school inspection.

Evidence from the Nuffield study

A summary of the main findings of the Nuffield-funded research into secondary school inspection is given by Ouston and Davies in Chapter 2. Evidence from this study shows that the level of governing body involvement varies considerably but for some it had changed since the school's inspection. This can be seen in relation to governors' contribution to their school's post-OFSTED action plan and to their general levels of involvement in the school.

Questionnaire surveys were undertaken of a large sample of secondary schools that were inspected in 1993 (the first year of inspection), 1994 and 1996 (the fourth and final year of the first round of secondary school inspections). The questionnaire was completed by senior school management (usually the headteacher) who were asked to indicate, on a six-point scale, the degree of governor involvement in the action-planning process. The results of three years of surveys are given in Table 3.1. The last survey in 1996 also asked respondents to note the extent to which governor involvement in the school had changed and these are given in Table 3.2.

Table 3.1   Extent of governors' contribution to post-OFSTED action plans (%)

| | No contribution | | | | Major contribution | |
	0	1	2	3	4	5
1993	9	36	20	21	8	6
1994	11	28	20	21	14	5
1996	7	21	19	28	16	9

Notes:
1993: $n = 170$ (60% response)
1994: $n = 252$ (60% response)
1996: $n = 305$ (80% response)

Table 3.2   The extent to which governor involvement in the school has changed (%)

	Decreased		No change		Increased
	1	2	3	4	5
1996	1	0	59	31	9

Note:
n = 305.

The data show that, over the years, governors have (at least according to heads) *increased* their contribution to the action-planning process and the percentage of governors making little or no contribution has been falling. In 1993, 45 per cent were reported to be making little or no contribution to the post-OFSTED action plan compared to 39 per cent in 1994 and 28 percent in 1996. Table 3.1 also shows that in 1996 one quarter of respondents reported that governors had made a major contribution compared with only 14 per cent in 1993.

The involvement of governors in the school generally was also said to have changed. In 1996 (the only year in which this question was asked) four out of ten heads reported that they considered the inspection had increased the involvement of governors. Also it is worth noting the large number of heads recording 'no change' (59% in 1996) and the fact that many of these heads – just over a quarter of all those providing written comments – explained that the governors were already heavily involved in their schools. Typical comments, for example, were: 'The governors are actively involved in school and have remained so'; 'the governors are already well involved'; 'the governors were fully active prior to inspection'; 'already heavily involved: ten full meetings a year and four committees every three weeks'; and 'already excellent involvement'.

It was reported that the experience of inspection had on occasions led to desirable or undesirable consequences and some heads noted how they had been able to use the report's findings to bring about change in the way the governing body operated. For example, one head noted that 'there has been an enormous increase in governor involvement, not only in implementing the Action Plan but also in the selection and interviewing for a new head'. Others remarked how the report's findings had helped to put pressure on the governors to increase their visits to the school or become more involved in monitoring policies. A direct result of inspection was that governors were said to be becoming even more aware of their responsibilities. As another head noted: 'Governors have used the report as a way of becoming fully informed of the work of the school, especially subject departments. I have welcomed this.'

Some respondents noted how inspection had either speeded things up or slowed them down. For example: 'the change was happening anyway but a criticism stung a few into greater involvement'; 'the report actually suggested that governors should be more involved but no action has been taken, they are if anything less involved'; and 'OFSTED's criticism of my governors made my two best ones leave – a disaster!'

Not all heads were welcoming of the increased governor involvement which inspection was said to have brought about. One head noted how his governors had moved 'from little direct involvement to attempting to be involved in almost everything. I personally view this as negative – a middle road would be better'. Another felt that the governing body was already overinvolved in the day-to-day management of the school and although OFSTED had commented on this it had, so far, gone unheeded.

The effect of inspection on the involvement of governing bodies was also an issue that was explored in interviews. Twenty follow-up telephone interviews were undertaken with the 1996 Nuffield sample with the respondents carefully chosen to represent a range of responses to the perceived effects of inspection.

Most of the heads described how governors had been involved in helping to draw up action plans, usually by setting up small working groups with staff who would draft the initial response. For example, in one school a small strategic group had been established consisting of four governors, the head, the two deputies and the bursar. Once this group had approved the draft action plan it went to the General Management Committee (made up of the chairs of various committees) and then, finally, to the full governing body. Governors were also involved in various capacities in monitoring progress made on the key issues for action. Some governing bodies were said to be working towards this – 'the governors have not asked yet which bits have been completed' – whereas others' involvement was quite developed.

One head whose governing body was described by OFSTED as 'outstanding', which he felt was 'well deserved and very pleasing', noted how he had been able to use the inspection very positively. A small committee, led by the chair of the Curriculum Committee, had been set up which liaised with the head over the action plan. Once formulated the action plan went to the full governing body. The head remarked that one governor (from a large petrochemical company) remarked that the school would never achieve all that was included in the plan but at the last meeting had to admit he was staggered at the progress made (the school was actually ahead of its target dates). The governing body was due to report on progress on the action plan to parents at the next annual parents' meeting in the autumn. This head when asked if the involvement of the governors had changed noted that it had increased a little as the group, which monitors the action plan, was now much more involved in curriculum issues. He went on to state: 'my governors have always been extremely supportive and very good – they don't just rubber stamp. But the curriculum areas I've always found a bit of a no-go area for governors' progress. The governors have got more involved in the action plan and many aspects of this are curriculum based.'

Another head noted how the governing body was involved in monitoring although this was mainly on the finance front. However, as the governors in this school were not involved much before the inspection any increase was seen by the head as an improvement. The head wanted the governors to be more involved and so had established a number of subgroups, whose meetings had minutes, which were circulated. The level of involvement had changed, governors had become more involved and interested but the head was concerned about asking too much from a group of volunteers and that 'we must be careful that we don't put too much demand on their time – they've all got their own lives and careers, so it's important to get the balance right'.

A grant-maintained school head, despite having had an excellent inspection from a first-class team, remarked that their criticisms of the governing body had led to the resignations of two governors. The governing body, on the whole, were 'an excellent bunch doing a hugely responsible job in a GM school for nothing' but in the inspectors' view it was not doing enough, being sufficiently proactive or monitoring. The head stated that this had led to some of the more conscientious governors resigning saying 'we just can't do any more'. This head was quite critical of the position governors had been put in by recent legislation and found it difficult to see how 'amateurs could be proactive in the running of a school – I wouldn't dream of advising my solicitor governor on how to run his firm...the school is doing well and the governing body is happy to let us get on with it'.

Another head claimed the school's governors were still operating in 'pre-86 mode' and that this weakness had been identified by the inspectors. But the inspection was said not to have made much difference (for example, not all the governors had attended the feedback). The governors were said to be 'good folk who mean well but were not competent to do the job'. Their passive role meant that they did not know what was going on in the school but as the head remarked 'it could be worse I suppose as they could be interfering!'

A very different picture of governor involvement was given by a head in a neighbouring authority. Governors had been involved in addressing the key issues in the action plan and through the committee structure they already participated in the school development plan and knew of the school's targets. This governing body had arranged two extra meetings in the week so the inspectors could attend. The action plan targets were apportioned to teams of governors so that they could look at what was being done and how it was to be achieved. In this school one of the action plan targets had been taken over completely by the governors who had been into the school to interview staff and work up ideas and suggestions. The key issue centred on the involvement of middle managers – post-holders were to be given more opportunities to be involved in whole-school decision-making. The head remarked that he had disagreed with the RgI over this issue so it was thought to be a good idea to give this key issue to the governing body: to enable them to go and talk to whomever they liked and to report back on what needs to be done to provide more opportunities to be involved in decision-making. Governors were also linked to other targets to make sure they were being implemented. As the head noted: 'it's a level of involvement that you don't often see in governing bodies.'

Levels of involvement did differ significantly and governing bodies were clearly operating at different levels; in some cases heads were content with this, in others they would have welcomed a greater degree of involvement. A head of a grammar school, for example, remarked that her governors had contributed little to the action plan but that did not mean to say they were not involved:

> My governors are very involved in everything but they say to me 'Right Mary you put it all together and we'll have a look at it'. So I dutifully do that and they pull it all to pieces and put their own stamp on it. We work well together and I enjoy talking to them – everything is talked through but it's my blueprint if you like in every respect. The governing body is effective – this was noted in the report – and we get on well but they leave me to get on to a large extent, perhaps more so than I would like. I don't want them to interfere but to get into classrooms more. We are appreciative of what is done and they have tremendous expertise but they are very busy people. Their own jobs keep them away from school during the day. So I would like them to have better first hand knowledge of what's going on in school.

Evidence from governor training co-ordinators (GTCs)

As part of another research project in which the author is currently engaged – into effective governance and school improvement – interviews were conducted with a small number (12) of LEA governor training co-ordinators (GTCs). Their comments are particularly interesting because they offer a view based on their work with a large number of governing bodies from across their local authority. It was apparent from the GTCs' observations that OFSTED inspections were seen as having the potential to empower governing bodies by making them much more aware of the nature and extent of their responsibilities.

There was agreement that governing bodies had found monitoring to be easier after an inspection but that did not mean that for some it was regarded as unproblematic. Inspection had the potential to empower governing bodies because for many they were, for the first time, involved in a meaningful way in the planning process. An LEA officer suggested that a change of culture in schools and governing bodies had been experienced in three ways:

1) The school had provided data to OFSTED which were also made available to the governing body.
2) The inspection report was available to the governors who were thus able to reflect on the main findings – this gave an entrée into the school, which some governing bodies had not had before.
3) The action plan had to be owned by the governing body and that this was the biggest step forward because it resulted in governors thinking about the key targets for their schools.

These three factors had been significant for many governing bodies and were likely to become even more important as governors took on their new legal responsibilities for target-setting, became more focused on school performance and encouraged a climate of self-review and continuous improvement. Governing bodies were beginning to talk about such things as benchmarking, baseline testing and 'added value'. But for the bulk of schools and governors it was new territory for both and they were learning together.

In a similar way it could be said that the OFSTED experience itself had led to a collective learning and of course there is nothing like an outside force to draw people together! An external threat can serve to unite the school and its partners. Most GTCs noted that inspection had had a positive effect – even though the experience itself may have been variable – as most governing bodies had to reposition themselves internally to deal with an external force.

Inspection had forced governors and heads to think more about the nature and the enactment of their respective roles. It had brought to heads' and governors' attention the fact that the governing body was part of the inspection and therefore governors would be interviewed or observed.

The experience of an OFSTED inspection has the potential therefore to bring both heads and governors together for the benefit of the common good. However, all the research into governing bodies agrees that the crucial factor in its effectiveness is the attitude of the head (e.g. Baginsky *et al.*, 1991; Earley, 1994; Creese, 1995; Esp and Saran, 1995). A governing body might rationalise its committees, share out responsibilities, be committed and so forth but if the head chooses to 'keep out' the governing body it is extremely difficult for it to operate effectively.

It was also suggested by LEA trainers that the obligatory nature of OFSTED inspection had contributed to 'tightening things up'. Governing bodies were said to be more aware that the inspection might produce some surprises, which they did not want – they did not want the inspectors to identify problems of which they should already be aware. One GTC gave the example of her LEA where a governing body had had concerns about the head and the lack of information they received. They were not sure what to do about this situation so the chair of governors approached the LEA's Governor Training Unit whose advice was to ask the school's link adviser to do a mini-inspection. There had been rumblings from both teachers and parents and the governors were not sure what was happening and why the school was making so little progress. The head's response to the governors was that the school did not need a mini-inspection and neither could it afford it. The governors had to really push for this and insist that it was their right. Eventually the LEA did the inspection without charge and as a result of its findings the head took early retirement!

In some LEAs inspection reports were being scrutinised for their comments on the operation of governing bodies. Inspection reports were said to vary from team to team in terms of both the detail and the accuracy of their comments about governing bodies. As one experienced governor trainer remarked:

> we look at all reports and what they say about governing bodies and we know that some of their comments do not match what we know about that governing body. Some of the less effective ones are said to be carrying out duties, monitoring, and so on simply because they've got structures in place. So they get a good report. Others are condemned when perhaps they are better governing bodies!

Another GTC, for example, explained that if an inspection report was critical of the governing body or a key issue focused on the governors, they would telephone the chair of governors and ask if the governing body would be interested in assistance, and in particular if they would like to undertake the effective governing body exercise which the LEA had developed. The exercise helped to identify areas where the governing body may wish to change. This LEA was also trying to be more proactive with its poorly performing governing bodies and had started to monitor participation in training to see if any governors were not taking advantage of the provision. The aim was to produce an annual printout for each governing body on its training participation.

Evidence from the National Foundation for Educational Research (NFER)

A third and final source of research evidence on inspection and its effects on governing bodies comes from a study by the National Foundation for Educational Research (NFER) on post-OFSTED action plans (Maychell and Pathak, 1997; Pathak and Maychell, 1997). The study consisted of a questionnaire survey of just over 200 schools (53% response) followed by case studies of five primary and five secondary schools where interviews were conducted with heads, staff and governors. An analysis of action plans returned from 177 of the responding schools was also undertaken.

The NFER research found that governor involvement in drawing up the action plan varied but over three quarters of schools made some reference to governors being involved in the process. Eighty per cent of action plans showed governors having a role in implementing parts of the plan, particularly in relation to school development planning and meeting statutory requirements. In the case studies at the very least governors were consulted for their views and these were taken into account before the final action plan was submitted for the approval of the whole governing body. Three of the ten case-study schools established working groups of governors and staff to construct the plan.

Governor involvement in action planning was also said to depend on the issue under discussion. Many governors felt they did not have the necessary expertise or knowledge and 'to a large extent look to the senior managers of the school for leadership and guidance' (Pathak and Maychell, 1997). However, where governors were involved, both the professionals and the (lay) governors were happy with this. They reported the major benefits to have been a sense of participation and increased knowledge and understanding of why certain action was taken in the school. Heads from the case-study schools reported that the involvement of governors had been worthwhile, particularly as it had made them 'examine fundamental objectives within their school and helped them think more clearly about addressing the issues' (*ibid.*).

In some of the case-study schools governors had also played an important role in the implementation of the action plan by, for example, providing moral support, allocating extra resources for implementation and taking responsibility for addressing certain key issues. These were not always concerned with non-educational matters; in some cases joint working parties were set up to revise or draw up curriculum policies. This was said to have enhanced governors' understanding of education and the potential contribution they could make to the school in the future.

Governors were also involved in monitoring the implementation of action plans. Where success criteria had been identified governors were able to visit classrooms, observe lessons and discuss the changes with staff. The NFER report notes, however, that as with the devising of the plan, some governors did not feel that they possessed the necessary expertise or knowledge to undertake these monitoring tasks. Governors were able, however, 'to get the flavour of the developments that have taken place' (Pathak and Maychell, 1997) and active involvement in the monitoring process was said to help keep governors informed about what was happening in school and improved their general understanding of factors affecting both pupils and staff. One of the NFER case-study heads referred to it as a form of professional development for the governing body. Governor visits in this school were now much more focused and closely linked to the key issues in the action plan. Therefore as a result of their involvement in action planning, some governing bodies had increased their participation in the school and this was seen as a very positive development by both governors and school staff.

GOVERNING BODIES – A NEW ROLE?

It is apparent from the research evidence that inspection has the potential to empower rather than weaken or emasculate governing bodies. For some it has meant, perhaps for the first time, that they have had a meaningful involvement in the school and its decision-making and planning processes. Prior to inspection there may have been an illusion of power but afterwards, given the right conditions and the support of the head, governing bodies have been able to become more involved in their schools, particularly in development and action planning and in the monitoring of progress.

Governing body reaction and response, however, have not been uniform. The ISCG notes how governing bodies have reacted very differently to inspection – both to its purpose and to the process: 'In many schools it has been used as an improvement *tool* or yardstick, whereas in others it has been viewed more like a *weapon* inflicting both pain and damage' (ISCG, 1996). In many cases inspection has been beneficial because it has forced the governing body to be formally involved and to be called to account. It has also helped to focus their efforts and to unite them against a common outside force.

But how are governing bodies responding not only to inspection but also to their increased roles and responsibilities since the advent of local management? An NFER study into governing bodies in the early 1990s claimed that progress was being made (Earley, 1994). More recently, Creese (1997) states that it is difficult to draw any general conclusions about governing body effectiveness given the variation in the amount of detail presented in OFSTED reports. He estimates (*ibid.*), based on his sample of nearly 100 inspection reports undertaken in 1997, that

> perhaps between five and ten percent of governing bodies are making a very significant contribution to the life and work of their schools. About five percent of governing bodies might be said to give cause for concern and one percent are so ineffective as to seriously prejudice the standard and quality of education received by the children in their schools.

If Creese's estimates are correct, this leaves a large number of governing bodies which are simply 'going through the motions' and perhaps gives credence to the claim of some heads that governing bodies generate a lot of work with little commensurate benefit or pay-off for themselves or their schools. At the time of writing the findings from those schools inspected in the spring term 1998 (when inspectors were requested to give particular attention to governance and grade the extent to which the governing body was fulfilling its strategic role) were not available. It will be very interesting to see how they compare with other work in this area.

For the ISCG (1996) it is apparent that OFSTED inspectors are making more demands on governors to explain how they fulfil their legal responsibilities and that the governing body's main roles 'are being closely examined and dissected'; yet they state many are 'neither ready for this scrutiny nor have the language and confidence to articulate what they do'. They also suggest that 'a realistic approach is needed about what governors should be expected to do for no financial reward'.

Nevertheless, inspection does appear to be encouraging more governing bodies to give serious consideration to how they are performing their duties. It has the potential to empower them. The focus on governors in the spring term, 1998 is likely to exacerbate this trend. Inspection in itself is unlikely to bring about improvements – either in the school or the governing body – but as both Creese (1997) and Gann (1997) have noted it can act as a powerful stimulus or catalyst for change. A credible and accurate audit of the school and its governing body can be most useful and 'provide powerful ammunition for those governors and teachers who are seeking to change for the better' (Creese, 1997).

Schools and their governing bodies are at different stages on the path towards improvement and the next challenge for both parties is that of benchmarking and operating in a target-setting culture (Earley, 1996; DfEE, 1997b; 1997d; 1997e). There will be a clear need for governing bodies to use their limited time carefully and to focus on the key areas of governance such as strategy and policy (Creese and Bradley, 1997; Gann, 1997; Walters and Richardson, 1997; Creese, 1998). Whether this is within the capacity of most governing bodies to achieve has yet to be clearly demonstrated (Corrick, 1996). What is clear, however, is that the effect of inspections on governing bodies is rarely neutral and that life after OFSTED is unlikely to be the same as it was before.

4

Partners in Pursuit of Quality: LEA Support for School Improvement after Inspection

MARGARET WOOD

BACKGROUND

This chapter examines the role of LEA advisory and inspection services in developing quality in education. More specifically, it focuses on the contribution of the professional support of LEA personnel to the process of developing schools, highlighting the post-inspection action-planning phase within the context of a strategy for school improvement. It draws on the author's background as a former LEA education officer and adviser, together with interviews and discussions with LEA personnel and makes reference to some of the literature in this field. The reshaping and redefining of the role of LEA advisory and inspectorial support are the backdrop against which this chapter is set and the changing political landscape and national policy initiatives inform the discussion of the nature of LEA and school partnership in taking forward improvement, especially in the post-inspection period.

INTRODUCTION

In setting out the background to the LEA role in quality assurance, the impact of recent policy initiatives on the scope and involvement of inspection and advisory services in the process of improving schools is considered with a particular focus on the post-inspection action-planning phase. This phase, following an OFSTED school inspection, has a clear emphasis on improvement through target-setting and this chapter explores the contribution LEA inspectors and advisers can and do make to this framework for the development of quality. The first initiatives of the new Labour government in education indicate a strengthening of the target-setting regime, as both schools and LEAs will be required to set clear targets for improved performance in National Curriculum assessments and GCSE examinations. Whilst the current OFSTED inspection arrangements are organised at national level, the contribution of support at local level in helping schools to evolve careful strategies to take forward inspection findings as a force for improvement is one which can be seen within the context of a planned framework of LEA support for standards and effectiveness. Indeed, the white paper *Self-Government for Schools*, (DfEE, 1996a), which is briefly considered below, included discussion of the functions of the LEA in quality assurance within the context of schools themselves having responsibility for demonstrating a capacity to improve. The white paper *Excellence in Schools*, (DfEE, 1997a, p. 27) recognises 'The main responsibility for raising standards lies with schools themselves. But they will be more effective in doing so if they work in active partnership with LEAs, OFSTED and the DfEE'.

Excellence in Schools describes a 'new constructive role' for LEAs in relation to support for school improvement and raising standards. It examines changes to the role of LEAs in recent years and redefines the nature of the new partnership with schools (*ibid.*, p. 69, paras 17 and 18):

> The role of LEAs has changed dramatically over the past decade. It is no longer focused on control, but on supporting largely self-determining schools. LEAs must earn their place in the new partnership, by showing that they can add real value ... The leadership function of an LEA is not based on control and direction. It is about winning the trust and respect of schools and championing the value of education in its community...

It is important to consider the LEA role in quality development through support for schools in post-inspection action planning, thereby contributing to the promotion of standards and effectiveness. The proof of inspection is intended to be seen in its effects on school improvement (OFSTED, 1994a, p. 39). The action-planning process is an important part of this drive forward and pursuit of self-improvement, and *Self-Government for Schools* (DfEE, 1996a, p. 55) recognised that 'All schools, no matter how high their current standards, have room to improve'.

The support to schools offered by LEA inspectors and advisers for taking forward inspection outcomes has perhaps been more widely debated in the context of 'failing' schools and schools with serious weaknesses. The discussion in this chapter includes consideration of post-inspection support for these schools but also takes a wider brief to encompass the pursuit of ever-improved standards of success in schools in general.

SETTING TARGETS FOR ACTION

The report *Setting Targets to Raise Standards* (DfEE/OFSTED, 1996, p. 5) surveying good practice in target-setting in schools, observed that:

> As the examples in this report suggest, target-setting is effective in schools which have taken a firm hold on school improvement matters generally while giving high priority in particular to *action* designed to raise pupils' expectations of themselves and hence their attainment. Some of the initiatives have arisen as a direct result of inspection and subsequent action planning; others are part of broader school improvement initiatives, promoted in some cases by LEAs.

The business of target-setting and the establishment of priorities for development in the context of post-inspection action planning can be a complex one. The targets must arise from the strengths and weaknesses identified in the school inspection report and need also to relate to the school's own priorities for development as articulated in the school development plan. Guidance for inspectors on good inspection practice and the characteristics of effective inspection reports was given by OFSTED (1994b). It stated (*ibid.*, p. 10) that useful reports, amongst other features, include 'Key issues that arise from the main findings, that are specific to the school and central to its development and improvement, and set clear and achievable targets at which to aim' and 'findings that advance the school's own thinking as well as those which confirm priorities identified in its development planning' (*ibid.*, p. 11).

Excellence in Schools (DfEE, 1997a) proposes a requirement that schools set challenging targets for improvement, particularly in relation to National Curriculum assessment and GCSE results, helped by benchmarking data and guidance provided by the LEA and DfEE. Whilst a range of improvement targets could be established by a school, there is a clear expectation that the benchmarking data supplied to schools will be used to set specific, numerical targets for improvement in the percentages of children achieving level 2 and above at Key Stage 1; level 4 and above at Key Stage 2; level 6 and above at Key Stage 3; and five or more GCSE passes at grades A* to C. Many argued during consultation on the target-setting arrangements that average levels at each key stage and average GCSE point score would provide targets that encouraged schools to develop inclusive improvement strategies. LEA advisers and others expressed concern that the targets as established would encourage a concentration of improvement energies on those groups of children just outside the target range: those likely to obtain grade D at GCSE, level 3 at Key Stage 2, etc., rather than a more inclusive improvement strategy focusing on the whole cohort. Each school's proposed targets would be discussed with the LEA which is there to help schools to set and meet their targets: 'The role of the LEA is to advise and, where necessary, challenge schools to set their sights at the right level' (*ibid.*, p. 27).

The National Literacy Strategy, unveiled by the government in late 1997, has been used to set targets for each LEA leading to 80 per cent of pupils reaching level 4 or above in National Curriculum English assessments at age 11 by the year 2002. As the LEA target, set by the DfEE in October 1997, has to be achieved by aggregation of individual school targets, the role of the LEA link adviser/inspector becomes crucial in negotiating these targets. Advisers/ inspectors are, therefore, immediately involved in the business of challenge and support for schools in the setting of targets and devising and implementing strategies to achieve those targets.

Target-setting can be seen as a way of ensuring that schools focus their energies on improving performance in line with the government commitment to raising standards. The DfEE guidance recognises that 'LEAs will play a positive role in supporting and guiding schools as they analyse data and set suitably challenging targets' (DfEE, 1997b, p. 4).

Many LEAs offer support for school self-improvement efforts through the provision and interpretation of assessment data, which can be utilised by schools as a source of contextual information, allowing comparisons to be made with the results of other schools in the LEA area. The provision of contextual analyses can be a valuable tool for schools when formulating improvement targets. A DfEE publication (1996b) offered examples of current LEA practice in the analysis and presentation of National Curriculum assessment results and reported that, in broad terms, LEA help can embrace: LEA-wide analyses; school-by-school comparisons; and help for individual schools to carry out and interpret their own analyses (*ibid.*, p. 2). Some of the issues and implications for development priorities which emerge from analysis of the data and which may inform the formulation of future improvement targets, may be highlighted by the LEA as issues upon which schools may wish to reflect. In this way the LEA plays an important role in helping schools to address the development needs which arise from the data. To 'provide clear performance data that can readily be used by schools' is recognised in *Excellence in Schools* as one of the key tasks of the LEA in helping to raise standards (OFSTED, 1997b, p. 6). LEA support for school improvement will be reviewed under Section 38 of the Education Act 1997, by which the work of LEAs will be inspected by HMI, and this is further discussed later in this chapter.

A SOURCE OF EXPERTISE AND SUPPORT: WORKING TOGETHER TO EFFECT IMPROVEMENT

LEA inspection and advisory staff often provide a continuum of support for schools to draw upon, in relation to the process of school inspection. This can include 'MOT health checks' offered to schools during the phase of pre-inspection preparation, attendance at the inspection team's feedback meeting to the school's governors and support for the requirement for post-inspection action planning. In addition, LEAs may provide formal training on inspection for schools and governors, examining issues pertinent to the period leading up to inspection, the inspection itself and the aftermath. The professional support of the LEA may be called upon by a school requiring subject-specific advice, from a subject specialist adviser or inspector, for example to offer guidance in the production of revised schemes of work, curriculum statements and policy documents. If it is management support that is needed, then the liaison or link inspector attached to the particular school may be the person best placed to respond.

The 1995/6 annual report of Her Majesty's Chief Inspector of Schools cautioned against what might be called the preinspection 'quick fix':

> This year, as last, there is evidence that LEAs are concentrating too much of their resources on pre-OFSTED preparation. Where this is a genuine attempt to assist the school to use the OFSTED Framework to evaluate its own provision and act on the

outcome of the evaluation, schools benefit substantially; where it is designed primarily to assist the school to present itself favourably in the inspection, it is unjustified'.

(OFSTED, 1997c, p. 42).

When responding to a request to work with a school to take forward its inspection findings, the type and extent of support will be appropriate to the school's own stage of development and internal capacity to engage in strategic planning. Support therefore needs to be responsive to the particular needs of the school. The school may feel quite confident in putting together its action plan and may draw upon the inspector or adviser for an external perspective and reassurance. The support may therefore be more at the minimalist end of the spectrum. This can often be the case in schools where the headteacher and governors have given some careful consideration in advance to how inspection targets link to future development targets and have begun to evolve strategies to achieve these. LEAs sometimes provide helpful written guidance and advice to schools and governing bodies on constructing an action plan, the requirements and nomenclature to be adopted and the characteristics of good action plans. The LEA inspector or adviser may also perform an important function in helping a school to set its inspection findings in a wider context. This can be through the provision of additional data such as value-added analyses to aid a school's reflection on its own strengths and weaknesses. LEA-wide school improvement initiatives can also make an important contribution in helping schools to evolve strategies to increase their effectiveness.

An important function the LEA can perform is to target support at the level that is needed while being responsive to the school's own stage of development. Practice in the process of self-review can place a school in a stronger strategic position when planning to integrate inspection findings with the school's own development targets. Experience of the GRIDS (Guidelines for the Review and Internal Development of Schools) initiative, for example, can be seen as making a contribution to the school's internal capacity for self-development.

Prior to the Education (Schools) Act 1992, some LEAs had implemented their own schemes of monitoring and evaluation, based on the principle of the LEA providing an external validation of school self-review within a framework for quality development. As a result the tradition of LEA and schools working together in partnership to effect improvement was established at local level. Evaluation, review, advice and support could be viewed as part of a continuum of provision within a unified system in which an LEA and its schools worked together to pursue a shared commitment to quality improvement. The inspectors' local knowledge and supportive relationships with schools could be seen as a cornerstone of this style of operation which actively sought to engage schools in the process of self-review.

The (Schools) Act 1992 can be seen to have drawn a clear functional line between inspection work and the offering of advice and support. The principle of impartiality contributed to this separation of the two functions, with inspectorial functions becoming divorced from those of advice and support.

It is perhaps in relation to 'failing' schools and schools with serious weaknesses that the importance of the LEA role has been more comprehensively charted. 'Wherever a county or voluntary controlled school is identified as "at risk", the Government will expect the governing body to work with the LEA to take urgent remedial action' (DfE, 1992, p. 49, para. 11.5). Here the LEA can be indispensable, having a central role in the action-planning and target-setting process. *Self-Government for Schools* (DfEE, 1996a, pp. 54–5) noted that 'Where a school is identified through inspection as failing or having serious weaknesses, the follow-up action should always include setting rigorous targets'.

The period following such a decision of the registered inspector and the inspection team can be something of a void for governors, especially when the leadership of the headteacher has been heavily criticised by the inspectors. Governors may feel naive and anxious about the drawing up of an action plan which will be scrutinised and closely monitored by HMI. The demands made on the school's LEA inspector/adviser can be great in terms of the level of expert professional support and guidance required in the preparation of an action plan and the subsequent guidance, monitoring and evaluation that are needed.

Amongst the factors helping schools subject to special measures to improve is that they have 'been well supported by their LEAs who have acted swiftly to provide good and timely support to schools' (OFSTED, 1997a, p. 6). In examining the factors that have played a part in helping schools subject to special measures on the path to improvement, the report recognises the role played by LEAs in this process. This has included, amongst other things, help given to schools in preparing their action plans and, often as part of the function of LEA inspection services, monitoring and evaluating the progress made.

Self-Government for Schools (DfEE, 1996a, p. 53, paras 23 and 24) considered the role of LEAs in quality assurance, whilst noting that

> Each school is responsible for its own performance. It is central to raising standards that the staff and governors of every school should feel that it is directly for them to monitor the quality of the education they provide, to identify ways of improving it, and to take the necessary action. There should be a presumption against any external intervention which detracts from that...The Government's priority is to foster the internal will and capacity of schools to generate their own improvement.

Excellence in Schools (DfEE, 1997a) outlines a clearly defined role for the LEA. This role involves the functions of both challenging and supporting schools, and the implications of exercising this enhanced remit are likely to include a higher profile for the work of the LEA adviser/inspector. Debate within LEAs is also centred on how to interpret the *Excellence in Schools* principle of 'intervention in inverse proportion to success' (p. 12). As the LEA role is defined as one of challenge and support for schools, it will be important for LEAs to ensure that this is provided for all schools, not just those that are deemed to have weaknesses. If successful schools are to continue developing, it will be important that they are included in the arrangements for 'challenge and support' to ensure equity of treatment for all schools; that success is built upon not dissipated; and that good practice is shared across the LEA.

Research studies have charted the changing role of the LEA and its transmutation in response to successive educational reforms and policy changes. The 'old' style LEA has had to reappraise its role in quality development in the light of the many changes to its position, powers and duties which have been reshaped and redefined by various legislative and policy developments. Riley *et al.* (1995) have examined the changing role of the LEA in furthering quality in the wake of many changes which have affected the *modus operandi*. In the LEAs studied it emerged that 'What mattered for schools was both the quality of the relationship with the LEA and the quality of the advice and support offered' (*ibid.*, p. 9).

ISSUES AND CHALLENGES FACING LEAs

After a period which has seen a reduction in levels of LEA advisory and support personnel, the provision of services to schools has been subject to the limitations of the prevailing resourcing levels. Schools may be heard to complain that their link adviser or inspector is rarely available for a speedy response to an issue that has arisen. Advisers and inspectors are compelled to spread their time too thinly in order to cover a multiplicity of tasks. A substantial part of this time is often devoted to a commitment to engage in OFSTED inspections which can take them away from the LEA and also is demanding in terms of the preparation and writing-up time needed for this work. Combining these commitments together with the other key tasks of the adviser/inspector role, including the targeted support which may be needed in the LEA's own schools following an inspection, can make heavy demands in terms of workloads. Prevailing constraints have sometimes necessitated difficult decisions about the levels of resources which can be sustained and the deployment of those resources.

The link inspector/adviser is a key player in focusing schools on improvement issues and this requires specialist skills and expertise. Schools sometimes expect their link adviser/inspector to have had headship experience him/herself, seeing this almost as a prerequisite for effective management advice and support. The effectiveness of LEA support to improve the standards, quality and management of schools will come under scrutiny as part of the new arrangements for the inspection of LEAs. How the LEA identifies priorities and deploys resources to meet them will be evaluated when judging the contribution made by the LEA's strategy to support school improvement as set out in the education development plan which all LEAs will be required to produce by April 1999 (OFSTED, 1997b).

LEAs differ widely in the level and extent of services they have been able to offer to schools, and the enhanced role envisaged in *Excellence in Schools* (DfEE, 1997a) and subsequent legislation are likely to make increased demands on resources. One LEA, which has committed itself devotedly to the pursuit of school improvement, has deployed resources to promote a range of support strategies, each with a central focus on improvement. These include: a programme of conferences and workshops with nationally and internationally recognised speakers focusing on the improvement process; sessions offered to schools on post-inspection forward planning and improvement issues as part of its programme of in-service provision; focused consultancy within schools on school improvement; training for school governors on the post-inspection action-planning process; strategies to facilitate networking between schools to encourage collaboration and the sharing of practice to enhance success; a series of planned networking meetings for schools to disseminate improvement initiatives; and specific school improvement projects into which schools might opt. In these sorts of ways the LEA has endeavoured to create and sustain a culture which is a force for improvement.

Inspection of LEAs will be carried out by OFSTED with the involvement of the Audit Commission. This would imply an inspection process which focuses not only on the educational effectiveness of LEA support for school improvement but also on value for money criteria across a range of local authority services which contribute to school improvement. Within this context, the targets for improvement set by individual schools and the aggregated targets for the LEA as a whole will need to be SMART (specific, measurable, achievable, realistic and time limited). This approach is likely to require LEA advisory and inspection services to think carefully about their role and their ways of working to ensure close connection with all relevant parts of the LEA in the determination of priorities and policies, and that clear evidence of progress towards targets is available.

The Audit Commission publication, *Changing Partners* (1998) makes it clear that LEAs will need to have clarity of purpose, competence across the range of services supporting school improvement and appropriate powers and responsibilities to deliver the role envisaged by government. In this respect, the code of practice for LEAs, which will follow the School Standards and Framework Bill's passage into law, will be an important indicator of government expectations and guide for LEAs on the role to be fulfilled.

THE LEA AND THE POST-INSPECTION PHASE

LEA support for schools in the post-OFSTED phase can be seen as an element of a continuum of support which is ongoing and often takes many different forms. From discussions with LEA officers and a study of the literature, it is possible to identify seven major aspects of the LEA role:

1) proceeding from shared values and established ways of working;
2) stimulating and fostering a development culture;
3) strengthening and sharpening the focus on improvement;
4) nurturing and enabling a wider strategic view;
5) a source of specialist advice and quality-enhancing strategies;

6) prompting a synthesis of targets for action and promoting evaluation; and
7) helping to take the strain.

It is to each of these roles and functions that attention is now given.

Proceeding from shared values and established ways of working

The relationship between the LEA and its schools is an important one and one which has undergone many changes in recent times. Having moved far away from what, in the past, may have been seen as rather a paternalistic role within a dependency culture, ways of working are now more commonly grounded in a commitment to partnership with schools. This partnership, which operates at local level, often proceeds from the basis of a shared value system which is at the heart of the relationship between LEA and schools. In this local context the LEA has an important role in promoting an ethos for school improvement and expectations of high standards. This ethos can be defined in terms of a commitment to consultation and shared decision-making and a continuous focus on strategies to nurture improvement and effectiveness within the context of partnership and respect for the autonomy of schools. Core values underpin a vision for education at local level, articulated through a belief in open and consultative ways of working in pursuit of an agreed goal, namely, that of educational provision of the highest quality. The LEA does not control schools, it works through partnership operating on the basis of mutual respect and trust and set within the context of local needs and concerns which are important to the community.

LEA advisers and inspectors are known to schools, particularly in smaller, more compact LEAs, and there is often a profound sense of allegiance felt in belonging to a community of schools bound together by strong local ties. The school's link liaison inspector or adviser can be a key figure through whom continuity of support is maintained.

Stimulating and fostering a development culture

LEA strategy for promoting quality in educational provision must be set in the context of the self-developing school. LEA strategy in this context and climate is therefore most appropriately one which can contribute to the formative processes of improvement, whereby the internal capacity of a school to engage reflectively in critical self-appraisal and self-scrutiny, as part of the culture of a learning community, is harnessed as a force for change and development.

This is an important backdrop to the process of LEA support for schools in taking forward post-inspection issues, and may best be viewed within the local setting, defined and shaped by shared core values. Within this setting, established and enduring relationships with schools, formed through dialogue and shared frameworks of understanding, can represent cohesive and powerful aspects of the dynamic at local level. This local setting may be one in which, prior to the Education (Schools) Act 1992, LEA monitoring and quality assurance strategies had operated effectively as mechanisms supporting school self-review and evaluation within a culture underpinned by a desire to stimulate and nurture improvement.

The LEA has to balance the functions of pressure and support by, on the one hand, not allowing schools to slide from achieving their development targets but at the same time providing a resource upon which schools feel able to draw for guidance and reassurance. *Excellence in Schools* (DfEE, 1997a, p. 27) sees a role for LEAs, acting as partners with schools, in combining support with pressure to improve:

> The LEA's task is to challenge schools to raise standards continuously and to apply pressure where they do not. That role is not one of control. Those days are gone. An effective LEA will challenge schools to improve themselves, being ready to intervene where there are problems, but not interfere with those schools that are doing well.

It may be seen by schools as a bonus to have access to support and advice from individuals to whom the school is known and with whom a relationship of trust has been formed over time. It is suggested that this relationship, cemented by shared values, agreed ways of working and strong local ties, can be seen to be an important part of a quality development model at local level. It is based on the notion of continued involvement and is a model in which the LEA and schools engage as active partners. However, at the same time the LEA must retain objectivity and ensure sufficient rigour if it is to serve schools well, to offer constructive support and to meet the wider purposes of public accountability. The LEA adviser or inspector fulfils the role of a critical friend, commanding the confidence and respect of staff and at the same time posing challenging questions.

Strengthening and sharpening the focus on improvement

Formulating clear criteria for improvement is fundamental if schools are to be able to measure progress towards specified action plan targets. It is important, therefore, to formulate improvement indicators which are measurable and this can be found hardest to achieve when considering, for example, demonstrable qualitative measures of improvement rather than quantitative measures. Here the support of the LEA advisers and inspectors may be sought in the formulation of criteria by which improvements (e.g. in teaching quality) can be shown. This support will be specific to the school but may also be placed within the wider context of LEA support for school improvement, particularly in those LEAs which have identified as part of a core purpose and mission, specific strategies for raising standards and increasing effectiveness. Such an orientation and resolve have led, for example, to LEA-wide school improvement projects, taking as their focus particular shared LEA and school concerns such as: differences in achievement related to gender; strategies to increase the effectiveness of teaching and learning; setting targets to raise achievement; and other such foci.

An LEA focus on strategies for improvement can merge with the post-inspection phase of taking forward inspection issues as part of a wider LEA approach to developing school effectiveness. This is particularly apparent where the LEA link liaison adviser or inspector role is defined in terms of school improvement work and, being thus grounded, their school visits are sharply focused on making a contribution to improvement. In such cases, the link adviser or inspector may incorporate into his/her support strategies: discussions with curriculum co-ordinators/subject managers about their own subject development plans in the context of the school action plan and school targets; monitoring of progress made against the specified action plan targets; visiting classrooms and offering feedback on teaching and learning; and examining attainment data. All this takes place within a climate and tone set by the LEA which expects ongoing improvement and which the LEA is sedulous in promoting across schools.

Nurturing and enabling a wider strategic view

Promoting a wider focus on school improvement can provide an antidote to those schools which may tend towards a limited and functional approach to progressing post-inspection issues. The LEA can help to set these issues in the wider context of school improvement and can nurture a longer term, more strategic view of planning. One LEA, as part of a planned school review strategy, deploys pairs of inspectors and inspection teams to visit at periodic intervals, as staging posts in a school's development. Each school's own link adviser or inspector represents the ongoing thread in a network of support, but this support is augmented with periodic paired inspector and team inspector visits to facilitate a more corporate look at longer-term, strategic issues, particularly progress with strategic planning in the context of the school action plan. Following the team visit, feedback is offered to the school governing body. This review strategy operates through an incremental approach, helping to move a school forward over time and encouraging a longer-term, strategic perspective.

A source of specialist advice and quality-enhancing strategies

It is important that the LEA presents its advice in ways which are enabling in the longer term. Thus the LEA needs to be able to invoke a range of strategies for school support to meet the individual and particular development needs of schools. The LEA can have an important role in offering specialist advice on personnel matters and finance in addition to that focused on educational issues. One very useful source of advice and support to senior managers has been the development of necessary skills to enable effective monitoring of classroom practice to take place. Where, for example, an LEA has worked with school senior managers on the application of OFSTED criteria for classroom observation, this has helped senior managers to gain an enhanced overall view of the quality of teaching and learning and to impact on learning outcomes.

Another important strategy which the LEA can employ is that of actively facilitating planned networking between schools, so enabling schools to work more closely together to effect improvement. In this way schools can be helped to draw on and share the successes and challenges they have experienced and to learn from one another. This can promote innovation and provide a stimulus to the development of practice, maintaining the momentum for ongoing improvement. Where the LEA organises a complementary programme of external speakers, raising and debating policy, research and strategy focused on improvement issues, then this can be a further factor helping to mitigate against a sense of parochialism and introspection. It can help schools to keep up to date with current initiatives and with changing political perspectives. It can contribute to a sustained focus on improvement, stimulated by informed debate and discussion.

Prompting a synthesis of targets for action and promoting evaluation

The formulation of the required action plan can help a school to focus on priorities for development in a structured and coherent way. The school's link adviser or inspector may be called upon to offer advice on adjustments to a draft plan or, in some cases, to help by working together with the school to devise a first draft. The targets for improvement section of the action plan is very important and advice and guidance are often sought in helping to formulate targets which are measurable, achievable and which can be monitored. It is important that progress towards the targets can be evaluated if improvement is to be demonstrated. Evaluation strategies can sometimes be a weaker feature in a culture which is task focused and concerned with getting things done. The provision of contextual data by the LEA may be helpful to schools for the purposes of self-evaluation and review, allowing progress to be compared against national expectations and also with that of other schools in similar situations. Analysis of value-added data can provide further material for reflection on the progress made by children.

The LEA can help schools to achieve greater clarity regarding the functions of monitoring and evaluation which can become confused. This has been termed the 'fattening the pig' syndrome, that is to say that just because inspection, monitoring and progress checks take place, improvement does not automatically follow. The pig is not fattened simply because it has been weighed and measured. What is needed is a coherent strategy for evaluation if improvement is to be effected and this may involve the reformulation of initial targets and a reconsideration of priorities.

The LEA inspector or adviser may be called upon to support the school in binding together the targets for action arising from the key issues identified in the inspection report and the school's own priorities for development, as articulated in the school development plan. Following the OFSTED inspection, the school may need to reflect on the impact of the key issues for action on its own development targets.

Helping to take the strain

Advice about monitoring and evaluating progress is important for all schools but particularly for those subject to special measures. The LEA inspector or adviser can be a source of support to the headteacher and senior management by monitoring progress against the action plan targets to compare with the accuracy of the school's own perceptions of the progress being made. The inspector or adviser can not only check the accuracy of the school's own perceptions in this way but can also be a valuable source of guidance and assistance to the school management team in helping to think issues through, in acting as a springboard for brainstorming possible strategies and in offering feedback following observation of classroom practice. The inspector or adviser can provide valuable feedback to classroom teachers following classroom observation, helping them to reflect on their practice and to formulate targets to effect necessary improvement in their skills as practitioners. Thus the link inspector or adviser can fulfil many valuable roles and functions in helping to share the pressures and demands.

The LEA adviser or inspector is often someone with whom the school has developed a rapport as part of a professional relationship. Where this relationship works well the adviser or inspector helps the school to refine its thinking and to maintain an impetus for continued improvement. This is an important focus for LEAs: conveying high expectations of improvement and nurturing a reflective, learning culture through which development work is stimulated and the momentum for which is maintained. *Excellence in Schools* (DfEE, 1997a, p. 28) envisages that a 'new constructive role will replace the uncertainty from which LEAs have suffered in recent years' and this role is focused on school improvement and raising standards. The proposed requirement for LEAs to formulate education development plans will be an important aspect of the focus on promoting school improvement and accountability for the achievement of agreed targets. The LEA partnership with schools is not one characterised by paternalism but rather one of professional support which is able to invoke a range of responses appropriate to the needs of each school. This strategy is one which seeks to engage with schools as active partners dedicated to the pursuit of improvement and success.

Arrangements to realise the principles of zero tolerance of underperformance, intervention in inverse proportion to success and operating as a partner with a commitment to raising standards all have important implications for the work of the LEA inspector/adviser. They are key players in promoting effectiveness and quality targeted at the specific needs of individual schools at the local level. The new regime of inspection of LEAs will ensure a sharp focus on getting this role right and the ability to deliver it effectively.

Section 2
Case Studies

5

The Use and Impact of OFSTED in a Primary School

TONY DIMMER AND JACKY METIUK

INTRODUCTION

The OFSTED strapline 'improvement through inspection' appears to many teachers and headteachers to contain a paradox. In the first instance it seeks to embody the notion of inspection as an externally imposed, 'one off' scrutiny of what is essentially a moving target; the term 'snapshot' is often applied to this kind of activity. In the second instance it brings in the idea of school improvement springing from within the culture of the organisation, a dynamic element involving constant self-evaluation. As Michael Barber (1996, p. 133) puts it: 'The most instantly evident feature of an improving school is that it is going places. It has a strong sense of direction.'.

When faced with the prospect of an inspection, this paradox can sometimes lead schools into confusion as they try to resolve the inherent contradiction between the two facets of the process. To quote Charles Handy (1994, p. 47): 'To live with simultaneous opposites is, at first glance, a recipe for indecision at best, schizophrenia at worst.'.

Handy's analogy of riding on a see-saw is well used to illustrate the importance of understanding and coming to grips with this notion of paradox which impinges in many ways on the professional lives of those who manage and teach in schools today. If neither participant on the see-saw understands the complex balancing process, then nothing much will happen and the result will be frustration. If both ends work in harmony, the result can be exhilarating.

While it may not be possible to resolve the paradox implied by improvement through inspection in quite such a tidy way, reflection on the nature of the paradox and its implications can enable the inspection to be managed to support the school's own agenda of improvement.

THE CASE STUDY

The subject of this case study is a primary school, which caters for 315 children aged between 4 and 11 years old in eleven classes. It serves an area about three miles west of a county town in Surrey, near a village, but focused on a private housing estate. This provides a mixed catchment area. The school has experienced a recent rise in roll but this has been stable for the last two years. The school's headteacher has been in post for ten years. During the academic year 1994/5, she was seconded to the LEA as a county consultant for primary education which enabled her to gain a broader view of primary education in the county, particularly as she had specific responsibility for supporting a group of 30 schools. One such area of support was with those schools which faced OFSTED inspections during the first year of the process. Upon returning to school in September 1995, the head had the task of leading her own school towards an inspection, which took place in February 1996. At the time, she was involved in writing her dissertation for an MA in education and had selected 'improving the quality of learning' as the main area of study.

This chapter is an account of how the school prepared for the inspection, managed the process itself and incorporated the outcomes into its own agenda for improvement. As Michael Fullan (1991) puts it, the school developed its role as a 'critical consumer of policy' in order to maintain the momentum and direction in its own development.

In order to gauge the impact of the inspection and to reflect the views of staff and governors, the authors have met regularly to share observations about day-to-day developments. The views of staff and governors were collected through individual interviews and discussions at meetings of the core team and all teaching staff after the follow-up inspection. At a meeting of the governing body in September 1997, the role of the governors in monitoring the work of the school was the main focus. The responses at that meeting formed part of the triangulation process in reaching the conclusions below.

PREPARING FOR THE INSPECTION

The school was informed about the impending inspection in June 1995. This enabled the head and deputy to discuss their strategy for managing the process of preparation before the autumn term. As the inspection was conducted under the original framework, the role of the school as an active participant and the notion of the actual inspection week being developmental were not yet enshrined in the OFSTED procedures. However, the spirit of the interim advice offered to inspection teams implied the importance of schools being involved as fully as possible.

In considering how best to prepare, it was felt important that all members of the school community should share a view of the inspection as a triangulation process. It would be an opportunity to gain a national perspective on the progress made to date and a benchmark from which to gauge the success of future development. Conflicting with this positive outlook was the anxiety which the news of the inspection engendered. This could have threatened to undermine confidence in what had been achieved and led to unproductive activity in the form of short-term preparations.

For the school to avoid this pitfall and the worst effects of the hiatus which could follow the inspection, it was decided that the main priority was to ensure that confidence and a truly collegiate approach were reinforced. This would be achieved through reflection upon the core values of the school and how these were implemented in the classrooms on a day-to-day basis. The aim was to ensure a robust ethos, which supported high self-esteem about the quality of teaching, and learning. This was to be combined with a sense of shared management of the curriculum based on a realistic view of the role of the subject co-ordinator and levels of subject knowledge. The latter point was further developed by each co-ordinator writing a personal summary sheet recording the point reached in individual subjects and which could be shared with inspectors when the time came. Teachers, therefore, had a greater sense of control over information being given, collected and subsequently reported on.

These considerations prompted a sense of cultural change within the school by stimulating the head to reflect on the way in which the school was managed. This hinged on the extent to which it was a 'learning organisation'; that is a place where all the stakeholders, head, teachers, governors as well as children are learning all the time. While the need for clear leadership had never been stronger, it was necessary to devolve management more widely through a respected 'core team' if shared management was to be achieved. It was essential to bring together a planning group with rigorous professional attitudes, humour, a deep well of collective experience, good communication skills and the authority that stems from the ability to listen. They needed to be able to share ideas and thoughts openly, actively encourage and offer practical support to others. Action research techniques were used when monitoring teaching and learning so that staff saw these as learning opportunities as well as a chance to carry out a management task. It enabled teachers to explore their beliefs, identify any conflicts between stated values and practice and to see these as dilemmas to be managed.

As Barber (1996, p. 144) writes: 'Turning a school into a learning organisation is partly a question of using resources well in order to make time for learning; and it is partly a question of exploiting the opportunities to learn that arise all the time in the course of a week at school.' This meant that meetings had to become keenly focused on the core activities of teaching and learning and that every opportunity should be taken to discuss these issues.

INVOLVING THE LEA

Having digested the implications of their deliberations, the head and deputy devised the programme for a two-day conference for the beginning of the autumn term of 1995. Both days were led by LEA consultants to ensure an objective standpoint. The first day was devoted to a close consideration of the aims of the school and the underlying values which it espoused. While these had previously been published, such an in-depth review into their precise meaning and implications, by staff and governors together, had not been carried out for some time. It began with a consideration about communication and shared understanding of the purposes and achievements within the school centred on the following poem.

> 'There is something that I don't know
>   that I am supposed to know.
> I don't know what it is I don't know and yet am supposed to know
>   and I feel I look stupid
>   if I seem not to know it
>   and not to know what it is I don't know.
> Therefore, I pretend I know it.
>   This is nerve-racking
>   since I don't know what I must pretend to know.
> Therefore, I pretend to know everything.
>
> I feel you know what I am supposed to know
> but you can't tell me what it is
> because you don't know that I don't know what it is.
> You may know what I don't know, but not
>   that I don't know it,
> and I can't tell you. So you will have to tell me
> everything'
>
>   (R.D. Laing, 1970).

The second day stimulated a similar review of the teaching and learning policy and practice. A further day's classroom observation, particularly of mathematics for more able pupils, gave more specific feedback on the quality of teaching and learning, across the school.

The impact of these inputs was to stimulate professional discussion, which both questioned and affirmed practice within the school so that the level of debate became more informed. This was seen as prerequisite to enabling all staff and governors to become actively involved in the inspection process and ready to receive the feedback from it. Plans to develop the 'core team' were delayed until after the inspection by the promotion of the deputy to a headship at the end of the autumn term.

In preparing for the inspection week, the head talked with others who had already experienced the process. This highlighted the importance of distinguishing between the stressful impact of such a period of intense scrutiny on individuals and the feedback and report contents which were mainly positive. The ability to view criticism in a similarly positive light had been a focus throughout the build-up and this was maintained during the immediate aftermath of the inspection. The staff and governors were as open as possible with the members of the inspection team in order that they had the best possible knowledge of the school and its complexities in coming to their conclusions. This was felt to be particularly important if the outcomes were going to be useful in enhancing the school's own improvement agenda. The team was rigorous and professional and the whole process was smoother because a good professional relationship developed between the head and the registered inspector.

USING THE INSPECTION REPORT

The report itself provided the school with a springboard from which to move forward. It both confirmed the school's own sense of direction and focused on specific routes to improvement. The key issues were detailed and there had been opportunities to discuss them with the inspection team so that the evidence which had led to these particular issues was clearly understood. The ownership of the report was greatly enhanced by the process of reading it closely, physically highlighting positive and negative statements to gain a sense of the overall balance within the text. Staff and governors read the report together enabling immediate discussion and resolution of negative responses. The physical process itself helped promote reflection about what the report said about teaching and learning. The various statements were then grouped and provided the starting point for classroom observations.

The main key issues focused on three areas. They were to

1) maintain the good provision for pupils' personal development and the good standards of work in mathematics, science, design technology, art and music throughout the school and religious education at Key Stage 1;
2) extend the structure of the curriculum to improve pupils' progression, by devising schemes of work for all subjects to provide clear expectations of the level of work to be covered at each stage; and
3) develop the use of teachers' assessments in all subjects to match tasks more precisely to the abilities of individual pupils.

Each key issue was carefully analysed, using all the information from the feedback, so that the implications could be set down as the basis for formulating the action plan. The plan showed clearly where the responsibility lay for the achievement of each action, it was fully costed to include funding from the post-OFSTED school improvement grant and the training budget and contained a realistic timescale with deadlines for achievement. Success criteria were included alongside each action so that staff, governors and parents would be able to tell how well the plan had achieved its objective. For example, where the need to identify clear objectives for pupils' learning within schemes of work to aid teachers' planning was identified, the success criteria state that that these should be present in weekly planning and that arrangements for monitoring would ascertain the impact of this on children's learning.

As a result of drawing up the action plan, the emphasis on teaching staff working together in a mutually supportive way came to the fore. A system for paired observations was devised which was intended to focus specifically on the success of planned learning objectives in supporting children's progress. This programme was sustained through the training grant and has allowed teachers to work together and support each other individually in developing the precision and effectiveness of their teaching. The work on learning objectives has also helped bring about the desired improvement in matching work more precisely to individuals and ability groups. These are now based on better day-to-day assessments of what children know, understand and can do. As a result, the records kept have increased in value as springboards for future teaching. This has stimulated teaching staff to reflect on the way in which they use the planning system to support and focus their work. As a result, they have devised short-term planning formats which, while giving a weekly overview, also enable them to consider the needs of individuals and groups of children on a daily basis. The success of this strategy relies heavily on the quality of the ongoing 'assessment dialogue' between pupils and teacher through which both can evaluate progress and plan the next steps.

MONITORING PROGRESS

As part of the initial strategy of managing the preparation, inspection and action planning, the school built in a follow-up inspection a year after the OFSTED inspection to look at the progress made, the direction maintained and to give pointers to the future. This contributed to the school's reprioritisation of schemes of work within the action plan. It was part of the culture of 'restless self-evaluation' (Barber, 1996) which is said to characterise improving schools.

The follow-up inspection took place in March 1997 and was carried out by the three consultants who had originally supported the school in the preparation phase of the inspection, one of whom is the attached consultant for the school and all of whom are accredited OFSTED inspectors. This was in part funded through Surrey's 'Self-Evaluating and Improving Schools' project which allocates three days each year of consultant time to supporting schools, and partly through the school's own devolved funding. The Self-Evaluating and Improving Schools project began in April 1996 and was designed to run for two years. Its expressed aims are to support all schools so that they

- set up a rigorous programme of self-review with a monitoring policy and schedule, linked to the school development plan;
- set specific target for improvement within the SDP, some of which are measures of attainment; and
- establish a systematic programme of benchmarking information using national information and Surrey's Strategic Information Service and Value Added data.

Initially much of the support was with headteachers and subject co-ordinators in developing monitoring strategies and classroom observation skills. More recently the monitoring role of governing bodies and target-setting have become foci.

As with the original inspection, a written report was produced and verbal feedback given to all staff as a group so that the implications of the findings could be thoroughly discussed. The opportunity was also taken to evaluate the staff's responses to the external monitoring of progress and the way in which the outcomes could be used. The main thrust of the findings was to confirm the progress which the school had made in moving towards the objectives specified within the OFSTED report. It also encouraged greater integration in the achievement of these by referring back to the initial reflection on teaching, learning and assessment as a holistic activity. This focused on the inter-relationship between the three main levels of curriculum planning and assessment recording and reporting.

The follow-up inspection report recognised the considerable progress made as a result of the school's response to the OFSTED inspection. However, it did raise the question about whether, in framing key issues, inspection teams always take sufficient note of the implications for school improvement of their findings. This is particularly so when issues such as curriculum planning and assessment are cited. If the close relationship between the two issues is made explicit, it can be supportive to schools when action planning, particularly in the sequencing of their actions. Without the constraints of the OFSTED framework, the team was also able to adopt a more advisory tone and introduce a practical note to the use of learning objectives in structured sessions so that they support pupils own understanding of the learning process and aid their own evaluation of progress. This underpins the idea of the 'diamond' shaped lesson (Brodie, 1995) or series of lessons in medium-term planning. This involves sharing the learning objectives as part of the sharp initial stimulus to a group or class, differentiated working on tasks in groups followed by a whole-class reflection or plenary when progress against the objectives can be evaluated. The model is exemplified by the 'Literacy Hour' promoted by the National Literacy Project and advocated by *Excellence in Schools* (DfEE, 1997a), the recent government white paper on education and recent legislation.

CHANGING THE CULTURE – TOWARDS A MORE COLLABORATIVE APPROACH

In referring back to the objectives set by the school at the preparation stage before the inspection, perhaps the major outcome of the reflection process was the growing realisation that cultural change was at the heart of what the school needed to achieve. This echoes Fullan's (1991, p. 67) tenth assumption about the management of change: 'Assume that changing the culture of institutions is the real agenda, not implementing single innovations. Put another way, when implementing particular innovations, always pay attention to how the institution is developing or not.'

In working out the action plan in practice, the staff have learned by experience. The importance of schemes of work, as foundations for planning across the curriculum, has been reinforced. Their completion has been brought forward in order to underpin tighter short-term planning and assessment. The role of schemes of work in the school's own monitoring has also been emphasised as the question of criteria and focus for subject co-ordinators was considered.

This change is evident in the way in which staff now see their own role within the classroom much more as part of an integrated whole. Individual post-observation discussions with teachers during the LEA follow-up inspection revealed an increase in teamwork across year groups and knowledge of the needs of groups of pupils. Discussion about the issue of progression, which the schemes of work have addressed, has given a clearer picture about the way in which teachers enable children to build up their knowledge, understanding and skills. Their planning and self-evaluation have improved and with it, the need for increasingly high levels of knowledge about subjects and pedagogy which detailed schemes of work can support. As a result of the initial paired classroom observations, which focused on objectives and learning, teachers have grown in confidence. There is now a greater enthusiasm for taking initiatives among the teaching staff and in supporting the management of the school as a shared activity. The exchange of information and levels of reflection and evaluation prompted by the OFSTED inspection and the preparation for it have been sustained.

SELF-EVALUATION AND MONITORING

This has had particular implications for the continuing development of subject co-ordinators as the middle tier of school management and their role in monitoring curriculum delivery and the quality of teaching. An example, which illustrates this, is the work done by the mathematics co-ordinator who was interviewed in September 1997 as part of this study. Her starting point has been the original LEA inspection report from before the OFSTED inspection. She has visited four classes to observe whether there has been progress in remedying the weaknesses identified. In planning and carrying out her visits, she has particularly commented on the good rapport and sense of trust and openness with colleagues. The visits lasted for about half an hour and involved observation of the teacher and discussion with the children to establish their capabilities and the extent of the challenge being offered. Within the observation, a specific focus was on the quality of questioning, intervention and support through coaching. Each visit has been followed by an individual discussion with the teacher to ensure that the process remained a mutual one. An overall feedback to staff was also delivered, highlighting the progress in areas such as differentiated group work and the quality of problem-solving. Issues for further training were also identified and reported, for example, the use of some structured materials to reinforce understanding. Where issues relate to individual classes, these are tackled separately from the main feedback but the school has now reached the stage where teamwork has grown more mature and such matters can be confronted.

As Barber, now head of the Standards and Effectiveness Unit at the DfEE, puts it: 'for self-evaluation to be effective, the difficult questions must be asked' (Barber, 1996, p. 137). Such questions as 'Is our teaching quality as reliable as it should be?', 'Does the head know about the strengths and weaknesses?' or 'Is there a culture which makes coaching of teachers possible?' are now part of the school's repertoire in a way which was not possible before the recent cultural shift. This monitoring process is now a key component of school development planning. Following the development phase, the school poses the twin questions, 'Do we do as we say we do?' and 'How well does it achieve our aims?' as part of its planned monitoring programme. The governing body has now become formally involved in the process and a policy and schedule for carrying out their role are being developed. Their views about the development of teamwork among both staff and governors were explored at a meeting in September 1997. A greater shared understanding and sense of involvement were very evident but there was also a strong feeling that the school should capitalise on the momentum gained over the previous two years.

This monitoring process has also spread into surveying parental opinion in areas such as homework and the reports which they receive about their children's progress. The questionnaire, which the school has used to collect parental views about homework, stems directly from issues raised at the parents' meeting before the OFSTED inspection. The school has reviewed its approach to the setting of homework and the success of the changes is reflected in the survey, particularly in responses from parents with children in years 3 and 4.

DEVELOPING COLLABORATIVE TEAMS

In terms of the developing team the school has moved from being collegiate, where there were good levels of mutual support, towards becoming collaborative, where issues are confronted more openly because an atmosphere of trust has also grown out of the closer working together. The progress has been from an 'experimenting team' towards becoming a 'mature team'.

The management 'core team', which it was not possible to establish before the inspection, has now been in place for a year and has been instrumental in devising and keeping the post-OFSTED action plan on track and evaluating progress. The response to the follow-up inspection grew from a team analysis of the findings. Their involvement has encouraged other members of staff to come forward and take on additional responsibilities.

The development of the 'core team', which is now known as the School Policy Group, as part of the management structure of the school, is illustrated by an increasing willingness to take the initiative in supporting development. Schools have access to an increasing amount of data, which can aid management in analysing performance, and the process of managing budgets and resources. In Surrey there is a measure of 'value added' available to schools in addition to a baseline assessment for 4-year-olds and the end of key stage assessment information. Schools also generate additional performance information through screening at year 3 and norm-related tests and National Curriculum tests at year 4. There is also a 'strategic information system' which enables schools to compare the way in which they allocate budgets, deploy resources and organise the curriculum to achieve their intended outcomes. The proliferation of such data offers positive advantages in benchmarking and target-setting but also adds an additional role for management. Members of the School Policy Group, realising the potential of such analysis because of their increased involvement, have brought forward an initiative to identify the data available and its possible uses, prior to establishing methods of storage and analysis using statistical techniques. Specific roles have been identified and included in job profiles for two members of the team. In the light of the recent Qualifications and Curriculum Authority publications on *Target-Setting and Benchmarking in Schools* (SCAA, 1997), and the issuing by OFSTED of performance and assessment data (PANDAs) from spring 1998, such innovations will be an asset to a self-evaluating and improving school. Greater knowledge about how the school is doing will help ensure that target-setting is seen as a process which involves staff, governors, parents and children in identifying areas for improvement and strategies to get there, rather than as an annual event to satisfy external demands.

IN CONCLUSION

The post-OFSTED action plan has now been assimilated into the school development plan and the inspection can be seen in perspective as a staging-post on the school's route to continued improvement. In fact this was exactly what was planned for from the outset. In seeking to take a global view of school improvement which included the use of external perspectives on a regular basis, the school's ability to resolve the paradox between inspection and improvement was much enhanced.

The decision to take a longer-term view and seek opportunities to develop cultural changes in the management of the school has been particularly successful. It helped provide mutual support during the run-up to the inspection and encouraged high levels of involvement which promoted ownership of the outcomes, both in terms of key issues and the report as a whole. Despite the inevitable delays in implementing plans which staff changes bring, the overall strategic plan to establish a school policy group of managers has sustained the momentum for improvement and minimised the lull in development which is sometimes the result of the inspection process. The involvement of all staff and governors from the outset has been a key to much that has been achieved. As Fullan (1997, p. 67) puts it in his second assumption about change: 'Assume that any significant innovation, if it is to result in change, requires individuals to work out their own meaning. Significant change involves a certain amount of ambiguity, ambivalence and uncertainty for the individual about the meaning of change.'

Charles Handy (1996, p. 17) echoes this sentiment: 'The acceptance of paradox as a feature of life is the first step towards living with it and managing it.' In a sense this could be said to be the challenge with which staff and governors have grappled over the past two years and, in doing so, they have demonstrated that external perspectives are an important part of school self-improvement: 'Though the current system of externally imposed inspections is often contrasted, usually deprecatingly, with a self evaluation model, the reality is that both are essential' (Barber, 1996, p. 38).

6

Brookfield Special School: Recovery from Failure

VANESSA ARIS, JIM DAVIES AND PETER JOHNSON

BEFORE THE INSPECTION

Brookfield school is an 11–16 day special school for pupils with moderate learning difficulties and behavioural difficulties. It is an urban school situated in an area of mainly private housing and located on a campus with two other maintained special schools and a large 11–19 grant-maintained comprehensive school.

Brookfield was inspected in October 1995. The team of OFSTED inspectors were experienced in special education and led by a highly regarded registered inspector. The school believes that the inspection was thorough and rigorous and that it exposed the weaknesses in the relationships within the senior management team and between it and the rest of the staff. Pupils' behaviour deteriorated during the week and it seemed that the pupils wanted the school to fail. The school was judged to require special measures. The school was found to be deficient in almost all aspects of the framework – standards, teaching, the curriculum and in particular leadership of the school and the behaviour of pupils were heavily criticised. Although many of the deficiencies were known to the staff, governors and LEA, the depth to which these were exposed by the inspection was a cause of some surprise. In particular, the behaviour of the pupils during the inspection led the deputy headteacher to suggest that they had deliberately misbehaved in front of inspectors because 'it was as if they wanted their school to look worse than it was'.

The school had been inspected twice by the LEA prior to the OFSTED inspection. In the summer term of 1993 a full team inspection was carried out by the LEA using the OFSTED framework. The main findings of this inspection contained many similar conclusions to the OFSTED inspection some two years later; in particular the quality of the leadership of the school and of the curriculum provided were judged to be poor. In contrast, however, pupils' behaviour during the LEA inspection was good and the quality of teaching observed was considered to be at least satisfactory. This latter point was confirmed by a pre-OFSTED audit carried out by two LEA inspectors in the month prior to the full OFSTED inspection.

So what went wrong? The most influential, though not the only factor for this seemingly rapid decrease in quality was, we think, the rejection, by the headteacher and the governing body, of the findings of the LEA inspection in June 1993. Neither accepted that the management of the school was poor, that the senior management team was ineffective or that the curriculum was inadequate. Consequently little was done to improve the situation. During the two years that followed, staff morale was eroded further and consequently pupils' behaviour deteriorated resulting in the situation where special measures were almost guaranteed.

AFTER THE INSPECTION

Autumn term 1995

The headteacher left the premises immediately after the feedback from the registered inspector on the Friday of the inspection week. He did not return to school and eventually, some months later, took premature retirement. The deputy headteacher did not feel confident enough to take on the role of acting head but agreed to do so for the remainder of the term until a temporary replacement could take up the position in January 1996.

So it was that the deputy, supported by the new chair of governors and the LEA, took the school through the critical period immediately following the inspection. The need for special measures was confirmed by HMI and the school set about the task of improving those things the inspectors had said were deficient. The report had not been sent to the school at this time and would not arrive until the end of the term. None the less the deputy head helped the staff to set priorities for their attention – high on this list was securing rapid improvement in pupils' behaviour and developing the senior management team into an effective unit that had the confidence of all staff. During the six weeks that followed the deputy head demonstrated effective leadership and provided a very high degree of support for his colleagues; the problems with pupils' behaviour were addressed by his immediate and personal attention to all incidents; and a firm line was taken with all such incidents, particularly with bullying – and slowly, gradually order began to be restored. Although staff morale was beginning to rise they still expressed anger at the outcome of the inspection and placed blame for the demise of the school on the headteacher, the governors and the LEA; at this stage they did not accept any responsibility for the school's failure and would not do so until some months later. For their part the governors and the LEA recognised that they had contributed to the failure and were working hard to support the staff in their quest for improvement; but it is probable that the support they provided was misguided and did not achieve the desired results because it promoted the dependence of staff rather than ownership of the problems and independence in the development of solutions. You can take a horse to water but if the horse doesn't know that it's thirsty...

Spring term 1996

In January 1996 the role of acting headteacher was taken up by the headteacher of a similar school in the county. He had been asked to take on the role soon after the inspection and his governors had agreed to his secondment. As a successful head of an effective school he had both the professional and personal attributes needed to secure the necessary improvements in teaching, the curriculum and the behaviour of pupils.

The inspection report had been received in the final week of the previous term and therefore the first job of the new acting headteacher was the compilation of the required action plan. The first draft of this document was produced by the acting head in consultation with the newly elected chair of governors. Subsequent drafts were produced by them after consultation with the DfEE, at a consultation meeting, the full governing body, LEA officers and the school's assigned inspector. Only much later, when the document was almost finalised, were the staff consulted on its content. Although this may seem, self-evidently, to have been a further mistake, it was considered to be an appropriate process at the time. With hind-sight it was a mistake which exonerated the staff of responsibility and delayed the recovery of the school for a significant period of time. This situation was also reinforced by the plan itself, an extract of which is included as Figure 6.1. For although it had been produced in accordance with OFSTED guidelines and had received approval by the DfEE, time and experience would reveal that insufficient responsibility for its implementation had been allocated to members of the teaching staff. As will be seen later in this account this situation changed as implementation progressed and staff became more confident in their quest for improvement.

Throughout the spring term the acting headteacher and the governing body continued to work hard to bring about improvement and were supported in this by the local education authority. Policy documents were written, timetables revised and efforts were made to promote the good behaviour of pupils. Progress was slow. The senior management team still did not function as a cohesive unit and teachers continued to experience difficulties with pupils. Towards the middle of the term teachers began to express dissatisfaction. Although they had not yet acknowledged their part in the school's failure they now felt excluded from the process of recovery and that things were being done to them without sufficient consultation. In short they became angry.

At the end of the term the acting headteacher was recalled to his school by his governors. This precipitated several days of crisis and confusion. The deputy head had previously stated that he did not want the job of acting headteacher and so the governors and LEA reviewed the alternatives – to parachute in

* Improve the quality of teaching and learning particularly in English and Mathematics and raise teacher expectations overall

PRIORITY	ACTION TO BE TAKEN	GROUP MEMBERS	RESOURCES	COMPLETION DATE	SUCCESS CRITERIA
Timetable	Review and revise timetable ensuring adequate time is available for the teaching of English and Maths.	SMT	From £5000 LEA support for funds 1995/96	Winter 1995/96	Suitable opportunity available for the teaching of English and Mathematics. Extra support and training for staff provided.
Staffing: Brookfield	Review staff deployment in the teaching of English and Maths using confident and competent staff.	SMT	Nil extra cost	Winter 1995/96	A rationalisation of staff and their strengths to improve the quality of teaching. Evaluated by LEA advisers and HMI monitoring visits.
Staffing: Additional	Negotiate with the LEA for additional staff to support teachers in the classroom and to offer further training in the teaching of English and Maths.	SMT, Governors and LEA	Additional resources from LEA GEST funds for school improvement	Winter 1995/96	A more efficient and competent teaching workforce. Suitable IEPs being introduced. LEA Special Needs staff to support teachers in the classroom.
Home-work	Introduce a homework timetable which involves parents.	SMT	Nil extra cost	Winter 1995/96	Closer relationships between home and school.

Overall the quality of teaching and learning in English and Mathematics to be improved by, e.g.:
a) Staff development with LEA inspectors to reinforce the characteristics of good teaching and learning.
b) Evaluation of quality by LEA inspectorate using OFSTED criteria.

* Improve leadership and management to ensure that the identified weaknesses are remedied

PRIORITY	ACTION TO BE TAKEN	GROUP MEMBERS	RESOURCES	COMPLETION DATE	SUCCESS CRITERIA
Management	Temporary appointment of acting headteacher.	Governors	£2500 paid by LEA	Winter 1995	Increase of staff morale and effective leadership and management, as evidenced by completion of staff questionnaire. Evaluated LEA support visits.
Senior Management Team	Consider role of SMT within the school with particular reference to effective leadership and decision making.	SMT and Chairman of Governors	Nil extra cost	Spring 1996 Summer 1996	A Senior Management Team which functions as an effective management body ie Monitors delivery of National Curriculum, supports staff in the classroom. Evaluated by survey of staff perception of SMT capability and effectiveness and review of management effectiveness by LEA officers using OFSTED criteria and feedback from HMI visits.
Review aims of the school	Review and restate the aims in relation to the desired ethos of the school.	All staff	Undertaken in Staff Meetings	Summer 1996 Autumn 1996	An environment more conducive to learning and personal development. Revised aims are known and understood by staff, parents and pupils (evaluated by survey).
Communication	Investigate and improve internal lines of communication.	1 SMT member and 2 teachers	Nil extra cost	Autumn 1996	Communications between staff improved, evidenced by collaborative work in cross-curricular groups. Formation of discussion groups. All staff familiar with and understand major priorities for development.

* Take immediate action to raise standards in English and Mathematics

PRIORITY	ACTION TO THE TAKEN	GROUP MEMBERS	RESOURCES	COMPLETION DATE	SUCCESS CRITERIA
GEST 95/96	Direct all remaining GEST monies (School Effectiveness) into resources for English and Maths.	All Staff and Governors	£2500	Winter 1995/96	An update, renewal and increase of resources for English and Maths, including purchase of new materials.
Timetable and Staff Deployment	Revise timetable and staff deployment to improve the teaching of these subjects.	SMT	Nil extra cost	Winter 1995/96	A more efficient and effective organisation of the teaching of English and Maths, with delivery monitored by SMT.
Specialist Staff	Specialist additional staffing made available by LEA to work along-side staff and offer support and training to teachers.	SMT, Governors and LEA	From £5000 LEA support for funds 1995/96	Winter 1995/96	Quality of teaching and learning enhanced. Evaluation by LEA inspectors and HMI visits.
Parents	Offer help to parents in supporting their child in the learning process.	All staff	From £5000 LEA support for funds 1995/96	Spring 1996	Raising pupil awareness and expectations, as evidenced by contents below.
Subject Action Plans	English and Maths co-ordinators to produce subject action plans.	English co-ord/Maths co-ord/SENARC	Nil extra cost	Spring 1997	Programmes of study which allow students access to KS3 & 4 Maths and English.

Overall success criteria determined by
● Increased performance as measured by KS3 SATS in 1997 and by progress from Key Stage 2 to Key Stage 3.
● Evaluation by LEA inspectorate.
● Random selection of individual pupil progress.

Figure 6.1   Extracts from the school's action plan

another headteacher or to give the job to an LEA officer who had previously been head of a similar school. For many reasons neither of these alternatives were viable and consequently the deputy head was appointed as acting headteacher. As it turned out, the best decision had been made, for all the wrong reasons, because the deputy became a leader and manager of substantial quality and it was the starting point of the staff regaining ownership of the school's recovery.

Summer term 1996

The term began in a conference room of a local hotel. Guided by a skilled counsellor from the LEA Youth and Community Service, the school staff and the school's assigned inspector went through a traumatic and frequently painful day. Anger and resentment were expressed openly and the air began to clear; responsibility for the school's failure began to be acknowledged and, most importantly, by the end of the day we began to see the way ahead. The new acting head played a very significant part in the success of the day by acknowledging that the school needed to change and that he was fully committed to bring about whatever change was necessary. The staff followed his lead and provided a similar commitment. For the LEA's part, the assigned inspector acknowledged that the support the authority had provided so far had been superficial and he committed the LEA to strong, interventionist support both at management and classroom levels. The following day the senior management team, now extended to include the chair of governors and an LEA representative, met to plan action for the term. So began a term which the acting head would later describe by the words 'Pressure, pressure and more pressure'.

It was clear from the lack of progress so far that the LEA needed to support teachers in classrooms as well as supporting the management of the acting headteacher. A rapid improvement in the quality of teaching was needed to promote improvement elsewhere. To do this the LEA formed a support team, the members of which had clear goals to achieve:

- the assigned inspector would monitor the progress of the school and work with teachers and the acting headteacher to set goals for further improvement – essentially an inspectorial role;
- a senior educational psychologist would work with teachers, and sometimes individual pupils, to promote better behaviour management and improved behaviour;
- an advisory teacher for SEN would work with teachers on the development of curriculum and assessment policies that were courses of action and not merely pieces of paper;
- an LEA officer would provide guidance on routine management and administration matters to the acting headteacher and governing body; and
- all members of the support team would seek to improve the quality of teaching and support the development of the senior management team.

It was also clearly stated that all members of this team were 'inspectors' and would be continuously evaluating the progress made by the school and would report this to the LEA's Chief Education Officer and Chief Adviser – there was no hidden agenda. The deployment of the support team and other LEA personnel, who were drafted into the school to carry out specific tasks, meant that during the summer term at least one LEA officer was in the school every day of each week. In addition to this the LEA increased the school's budget to enable the appointment of an additional teacher so that teaching groups could be reduced in size and aid the management of difficult behaviour. The commitment of the LEA in personnel and finance was significant and therefore improvement was not desirable. It was essential.

The extended senior management team decided that teachers did not really know what was expected of them when their teaching was being inspected. Though most were perfectly sound teachers and some were very good, many had performed badly in front of a critical audience and would continue to do so as close scrutiny of their practice continued to be a feature of the recovery process. What was needed was a teaching policy – not the definitive, highly polished type but a working document that would enable:

- teachers to analyse their teaching and set targets for improvement;
- the support team to make judgements about the quality of teaching against an set of criteria which teachers recognised as theirs; and
- teachers and evaluators to agree the findings.

This policy was achieved simply and quickly. At a staff meeting, the assigned inspector used the eight OFSTED criteria for teaching and asked the teachers to answer the question: 'What features of your teaching and classroom would you want a visitor to see that would show that you had good knowledge and understanding of the subject, that you set high expectations . . . ' and so on for all eight criteria. The answers given were simple, straight-forward and helpful. They enabled teachers to:

- know what was expected of them;
- begin to realise the things they did well;
- recognise the things they needed to improve; and
- begin to acknowledge that they held some responsibility for the school's failure.

The teaching policy was formulated quickly and modified only slightly during the course of the term. It proved to be a powerful tool to aid the recovery process for it became the focus of much discussion and a catalyst for improved teaching and for curriculum development and assessment. It also provided the instrument used by inspectors during lesson observation, by teachers for self-evaluation, and a slightly modified version of this instrument was used by teachers, in negotiation with the assigned inspector, to set targets for improvement. Much later in the recovery process the same instruments were used by the acting headteacher to monitor progress independently of the LEA support team. The eight headings of the modified lesson observation form are included as Figure 6.2; the small print is a synopsis of the teaching policy.

One of the first tasks of the extended senior management team was to review and rewrite the action plan. The new version took account of the progress made so far and reallocated responsibilities so that the plan became the new senior manager's plan and through this it became the school's plan. The regular presence, in the school, of the chair of governors became a strong feature of the recovery at this stage. In her weekly meetings with the acting headteacher she was able to suggest ideas and actions that he could take to the staff. Although she was frequently present in the school, staff were wary of her, because she was also an inspector, in the independent school sector, and therefore visits to classrooms were conducted by other members of the governing body. This increased the involvement of all governors and ensured that they were aware of the difficulties and the progress being made. The governors met regularly to receive progress reports, accept new policy statements, often offering amendments, and to plan further action.

As the term progressed it became a very stressful period for the staff of the school. They felt that the LEA was 'pushing too hard' and that the daily presence of an inspector or adviser was 'overbearing.' None the less teachers supported each other well and began to talk candidly about their teaching demonstrating a commitment to succeed – even if it was only to get the LEA off their backs. Under the leadership of the acting headteacher staff began to see the action plan as 'theirs' and they started to work diligently on the completion of policies. A new curriculum model was designed and a timetable for its delivery in the autumn term was drafted; policies for assessment, recording and reporting, behaviour, and spiritual, moral, social and cultural (SMSC) development were written. The major focus on the quality of teaching was aided by the design and implementation of a standard format for lesson plans and medium and long-term planning was improved by the redesign of schemes of work and half-termly forecasts. Monitoring of teaching had revealed inadequacies in the format, content and use of individual education plans so these also were redesigned making them more precise and more able to guide the development of teaching and learning.

Throughout the term the role played by the governing body increased. The chair of governors became an active participant in senior management meetings and met weekly with the acting headteacher. The partnership which developed between the acting head, the chair of governors and the assigned inspector was a crucial aspect of the recovery at this stage and was undoubtedly the catalyst for the rapid progress made throughout the remainder of 1996. Although the partnership was initially concerned with getting the basic tasks completed, we were constantly aware of the need to build a new culture in the school; team-building at all levels was vital to the success of the school and so we focused on building a strong senior management team so that they could weld the staff, as a

QUALITY OF TEACHING   **GRADE** _____

Teacher .... *Subject* .... *Date*................ *Time*........

1. **Secure knowledge and understanding of the subject taught**
    (Does teacher show depth of knowledge of subject; provide accurate and
    appropriate information for pupils; give clear instructions; use a range of
    approaches; use and display stimulating material; ensure that the content is
    accessible to a lay person; do pupils understand their work, can they talk about
    it; does the teacher use an appropriate range of questions?)

2. **Set high expectations that challenge pupils and deepen their knowledge
    and understanding**
    (Are the aims, purposes and expectations of the lesson clearly stated; is
    assessment used to improve teaching; do pupils engage in self-assessment
    and review of their own work; do pupils have a knowledge of their own learning;
    do teachers have a good knowledge of their pupils; is the lesson well prepared;
    does lesson plan reflect individual needs and IEPs; is homework set; are
    resources of a high standard?)

3. **Effective planning**
    (Is a lesson plan available; does content of lesson match NC; does planning
    take account of NC PoS; does planning influence pupils' work; is the process
    and structure of the lesson clear; are time and resources used effectively; is
    lesson part of a series; does content enable assessment of learning and lesson
    evaluation?)

4. **Methods and strategies which match curricular objectives and needs of
    pupils**
    (Do methods used match needs of pupils; evidence of appropriate group work,
    independent learning; whole class teaching; are pupils on task, interested and
    enjoying work; are methods based on an assessment of need; do methods take
    account of NC programmes of study?)

5. **Are pupils managed well and are standards of discipline high?**
   (Good relationships; behaviour management in accordance with school policy; high expectations of good behaviour; clear ground rules, understood by pupils; positive, supportive atmosphere in the classroom; clear sanctions applied consistently; all aspects of lesson managed?)

6. **Use time and resources effectively**
   (Prompt start; lesson proceeds according to plan; enough activity/content for the time allowed; pace appropriate to the task; lesson concludes promptly and on time with expectations and purpose achieved; consideration of pupils' performance according to time of the day?)

7. **Assessment used thoroughly and constructively and to inform teaching**
   (Are records of pupils' progress available; do records inform lesson plans/IEPs; does assessment inform pupils about their improvement; is there a common assessment format; does assessment comply with statutory requirements?)

8. **Is homework used effectively to reinforce or extend what is learned in school?**
   (Regularly set; regularly marked; builds on class work?)

Figure 6.2   Modified lesson observation form

whole, into an effective team. We did not take them away for a 'management weekend' of 'ice-breaking' and 'team-building' as it would have been a waste of their time and energy. Instead we focused the development through the jobs that needed to be done, setting deadlines for their completion, sometimes ridiculously short, and monitoring progress to make sure they were met. The acting head quickly gained confidence; he earned the respect of the governors, the LEA and the staff and began to make difficult decisions when faced with questions about the competency of teachers.

As the term progressed teachers became more involved in the recovery process. They were beginning to respond to the twin approach of advice and inspection. They clearly appreciated the advice from advisers who worked with them on the development of policies and procedures and they were beginning to recognise the benefits of having their teaching monitored on a regular basis – though sometimes they expressed open hostility when faced with the results of this exercise. The support group had adopted, without intending to do so, the classic 'good cop/bad cop' approach – and it was beginning to work.

At the end of the term the support team carried out a full 'inspection' of teaching. Thirty lessons were observed over the course of a week. The results were positive:

- overall, the quality of teaching had improved slightly from the baseline of the OFSTED inspection;
- planning was uniformly better;
- teachers were now more aware of pupils' individual needs and were making better use of individual education plans;
- there was a higher proportion of good and very good teaching than in the OFSTED inspection;
- there was a small proportion of excellent teaching; and
- classrooms were more settled and pupils' behaviour was generally good.

Some problems still remained, however:

- the quality of teaching in English and mathematics, a key issue, was still too low; and
- the range of teaching was too wide – from excellent to poor.

At this point the action plan was again revised to improve the teaching of English and mathematics by reducing the numbers of teachers who taught the subjects even further. In addition, each teacher completed an individual action plan for improvement of their teaching, to be implemented in the autumn term. At the last senior management meeting of the term the acting head reported that teachers were very tired but were appreciative of the progress they had made and they acknowledged that the strategies 'imposed by the LEA' were working and were 'turning the school around'. The icing on the cake was provided by the publication of the results of the Key Stage 3 National Curriculum tests which showed considerable improvement over the previous year.

Academic year 1996/7

The first HMI monitoring visit was scheduled for mid-autumn term. We were quietly confident that we could demonstrate improvement, but support, encouragement and monitoring continued. The acting head reported that teachers were still intimidated by the LEA presence in the school but recognised that it was a very necessary evil! The close partnership between the senior management team, governors and LEA continued to provide the direction for improvement. The senior management team was boosted by the appointment, from its ranks, of an acting deputy headteacher and the co-option of a teacher to

SMT status. The latter move was particularly beneficial as the teacher concerned was recognised by all staff as a consistently very good teacher and this emphasised further the importance of good teaching. The traumas of the previous term were showing benefits:

- the policy statements were becoming working practices;
- teachers stated that the paperwork was useful and that it was theirs;
- communications in school and with parents were improved;
- staff expressed a high degree of confidence in the senior management team;
- the modified timetable provided for more specialist teaching and consequently teachers' confidence in their own abilities increased;
- pupils understood that there was a zero tolerance of bullying and so behaviour improved and the more vulnerable pupils felt secure; and
- parents began to work more closely with the school when behaviour difficulties occurred.

By October 1996 it was clear that the school had regained the initiative. The will to succeed expressed by the acting headteacher was now embodied in all staff. As a result the role of the LEA needed to change. The support for the senior management team, advice to teachers, especially for English and mathematics, and the monitoring of progress continued – but the LEA presence was less frequent and the touch a little lighter.

A member of Her Majesty's Inspectorate visited the school in November. The results of this inspection were very encouraging. Teaching quality had improved, curriculum planning and other policies were judged to have improved. The school was making sufficient progress. The staff, the governors and the LEA were elated but not complacent. We knew that there was still much to do.

As the year progressed the school continued to improve. Behaviour difficulties became fewer and through application of an accepted set of procedures those that did occur were managed well by a more settled and confident staff. The acting headteacher continued to grow in stature and authority. He now assumed full responsibility for monitoring quality with the LEA now playing a supportive role. Importantly he focused the development of the school through leadership of teaching and the curriculum and led the senior management team in this direction. The partnership between the acting headteacher and the chair of governors continued to strengthen and they became the driving force as progress and improvement increased. By the end of the spring term it was clear that the senior management team was functioning effectively and LEA representation was reduced to occasional attendance.

The school was now in charge of its own destiny. The new member of the senior management team brought organisational strengths to the team and the features of her very good teaching became features of the management structure. The team set new, even higher expectations of the school and there began the drive towards higher accreditation for pupils as a means of raising standards. The year ended very positively:

- Key Stage 3 test results showed further improvement with pupils achieving level 4 in mathematics and science for the first time; and
- a second visit by HMI was very positive – 'sound or better progress in all respects' and the promise of a full inspection on the next visit.

Academic year 1997/8

The school was now functioning independently with staff and governors operating just like any other school and the involvement of the LEA at a level similar to other schools. Self-evaluation had taken over from external evaluation as the norm and although the LEA continued to monitor the progress of the school it was undertaken to confirm the judgements of a now confident and very capable acting headteacher and senior management team. The quality-assurance procedures of checking plans, observing teachers and writing action plans for improvement were now an accepted part of school life. School improvement had taken place and we awaited the, it was hoped, final visit of HMI with considerable confidence. In January 1998 two of Her Majesty's Inspectors visited the school. They observed lessons, scrutinised documents and interviewed staff. Their judgement was that the school had improved significantly and that they would recommend the removal of special measures. This was confirmed a short time later and in February 1998 the acting headteacher and the chair of governors attended a parliamentary reception for schools which had succeeded in moving out of special measures.

THE FUTURE

Throughout this time a separate but not unconnected process has been played out. The LEA has, for some years, planned the slow integration of pupils with moderate learning difficulties. This has resulted in falling rolls in special schools for such pupils. It is not intended to close such schools, however, but the result has been the proposed amalgamation of Brookfield with its partner primary special school which is situated on the same campus. Neither the intended integration or amalgamation are connected in any way to the 'failure' of Brookfield but this did create a background to the process of amalgamation and an additional source of stress for the staff of the school. Because of this we felt that it was crucial that the school should come out of special measures before the amalgamation took place so that the 'new school' could begin life unblemished by history. According to the acting headteacher, with the support of the LEA the school has:

- a senior management team which provides strong leadership;
- a very positive ethos;
- a high standard of teaching and learning;
- a culture of self-evaluation;
- a readiness to implement initiatives; and

- a determination to improve still further.

The proposals for amalgamation were accepted by the Secretary of State and the two schools became one in April 1998.

CONCLUSION

The process of recovery was time consuming and expensive; it was painful and frequently traumatic. But we are now certain that the school needed to fail in order to secure the 'special measures' that would enable it to provide the quality of education its pupils deserve. We have learned that:

- recovery only begins when all parties acknowledge their responsibilities for the failure;
- an LEA 'support team' is needed to provide effective support;
- LEA support should be decisive and interventionist and should focus on all levels of the school. But it should especially seek to improve the quality of teaching by working with managers to improve their monitoring and with teachers to improve their teaching;
- the partnership between the staff, the governors and the LEA is crucial to the recovery of the school;
- a strong relationship between the chair of governors and the headteacher provides an effective catalyst for improvement; and
- while policies and procedures may need writing, real improvement stems from improved teaching and learning and this should be the central feature of the work of senior managers.

7

Responding to School Inspection: Focusing on Development

DOUG CLOSE

INTRODUCTION

This is a case study of a comprehensive secondary school in the London area which was inspected in 1994. The headteacher welcomed the inspection as an opportunity to review the school's situation and to refocus development and improvement. The inspection was carried out by a team of independent educational consultants. The inspection was thorough and was well received by most staff. The key issues identified by the team set an agenda for school development. With the help of external advisers, including members of the inspection team in a consultancy capacity, considerable development has taken place, leading to improved standards. A further round of supportive consultancy has just taken place. This focused on five key areas of the curriculum and will help the school to prepare for inspection in the autumn of 1998.

BACKGROUND OF THE SCHOOL: UXBRIDGE HIGH SCHOOL

The school is a self-governing day school for boys and girls aged 11–19. It has almost 1,100 pupils. The school is located on an open greenfield site on the edge of Uxbridge, one of the main urban areas of the outer London borough of Hillingdon. The local area is one with evidence of social deprivation and low income but with pockets of affluence and economic growth. Pupils come from about 30 primary schools in the area and ethnic minority groups constitute an increasing proportion of the population. In 1989 the school was one of several named for possible closure under the LEA's reorganisation proposals. This led to a period of uncertainty until the school became grant maintained in 1992. Intake numbers dropped significantly between 1989 and 1992, with pupils going to several other more popular comprehensive schools in the area. The school was inspected in November 1994.

BACKGROUND TO THE INSPECTION TEAM: CLOSE ASSOCIATES

The inspection was conducted by a small independent team of educational consultants. Its members are mostly former members of HMI or LEA advisers, plus former headteachers, deputy heads, a chief education officer and so on. Members have considerable experience of secondary schools and particularly those in the London area. Since OFSTED inspection began, the team has undertaken two or three inspections each term and over half of these have been in the London boroughs. Many of the team are active as consultants in schools and colleges. Consultancy in schools includes headteacher mentoring; pre- and post-OFSTED support; strategic and action planning; management and team development; quality and performance management systems; and value added.

BEFORE THE 1994 INSPECTION

The identification of the school for possible closure led to a significant drop in its pupil intake. This was halted when the school became grant maintained. In 1993 the number of applications for places exceeded the intake capacity. At this stage school examination results were showing little improvement and were worse than several neighbouring schools. Behaviour, exclusions and attendance were acknowledged problems. A report on financial management published by the National Audit Office early in 1994 included several critical comments. There were a number of specific indicators of weakness:

- in 1994, 21 per cent of the pupils gained five or more higher grades (A* to C) in GCSE. This compared to a national average of 40.5 per cent;
- the proportion of pupils attaining five or more pass grades was 75 per cent compared to the national average of 87 per cent;
- the standard attainment test (SATs) results in English and mathematics were very weak (for example only 34 per cent of pupils gained level five or above in mathematics, against a national average of 57 per cent);
- these results should be taken in the context of a weak attainment on entry. For example in the national standardised (NFER) non-verbal reasoning tests, almost half of the pupils entering in 1994 gained grades significantly below the average and only one sixth gained grades significantly above the average;
- average attendance was 87 per cent against a national average of 91 per cent;
- the number of fixed period and permanent exclusions from the school was about twice the national average;
- the sixth form was small and uneconomic and;
- the pupil:teacher ratio was about 15:1; about 10 per cent below the national average.

The headteacher, particularly, welcomed news that the OFSTED inspection was to take place late in 1994. Much of the school's management effort in 1992/3 had gone into setting up financial and other systems following the school's move to grant-maintained status. By 1994 attention was being returned to school improvement in the knowledge that the school had a stable future. The school development planning process was reviewed and the format of the school development plan was amended and improved. The new plan enabled senior management to develop and display a long-term and a short-term view of the school. A number of valuable initiatives were started, for example on monitoring pupils' progress, a revised timetable, an extension of the programme of extracurricular activities and work to improve attendance. The head felt that the OFSTED inspection was an opportunity to review the situation with the help of external advisers. The key issues from the inspection would set an agenda for development and would enable the pace and breadth of development to be increased. The expectation was that this would lead to further improvement in standards.

THE INSPECTION: NOVEMBER 1994

The inspection itself was effectively organised and as relaxed as possible. The inspection team included specialists in all the subject areas, most of whom were respected for their national perspective. Five of the team were former HMI and one was also a registered inspector for secondary schools. Most of the team had already worked together on eight OFSTED inspections including four in Hillingdon. There were no major glitches during the inspection week and good professional relationships were quickly developed between each of the heads of department and their subject inspectors. Relationships between the head and the registered inspector were fostered by regular frank meetings which exposed any day-to-day difficulties and allowed discussion of the main findings and key issues as they emerged. The inspection was monitored by an HMI from OFSTED. This overt monitoring helped school staff to perceive inspection as a more coherent and fair national system.

The main findings of the report included the following key statements:

the school is a well run, caring community with a high level of staff commitment. Appropriate policies supported by good documentation and effective communication are already in place to enable the school to continue to move towards sound standards... Standards of achievement in relation to pupils' abilities were sound or better in 80 percent of the lessons seen... In 1994 the proportion of pupils gaining five or more higher grades (A* to C) in GCSE showed some improvement though this proportion is still only about half the national average... Pass rates... in English, mathematics and science remain significantly below national norms... Teachers are hard working, committed, energetic and caring... The quality of teaching was good or very good in 43 percent of the lessons seen and sound in a further 38 percent... The requirements of the National Curriculum are met though the time allocation to some subjects in some years is tight... The school development planning system is effective but could be further strengthened by linking targets to resource allocation... The school manages its finances well and generally uses its staff and physical resources efficiently... The library is inadequate and there is also a need for continued expenditure on information technology (IT).

Key issues for action were

- maintain the caring ethos and strong pastoral support for each pupil;
- continue to focus on improvement of standards for all pupils;
- continue to focus on improving attendance and classroom behaviour;
- ensure that all teachers have sufficiently high expectations of all pupils; review their approach to differentiation;
- ensure that the good practice in particular areas and by individual teachers is spread across the school; continue the support for new staff;
- review the detailed implementation of setting and of the curriculum through the timetable;
- develop a strategic plan for development of sixth-form and vocational provision;
- improve provision for collective worship, and for religious education in the sixth form, in order to meet statutory requirements;
- monitor the implementation of all policies, ensuring that appropriate resources are allocated including management time and staff professional development; and
- continue to press for improved accommodation, library and IT provision.

During the inspection the team met regularly in order to come to a corporate view of the main findings and key issues. Following the inspection, the senior management team were able to read the first draft of the report in detail and this was followed by a discussion with the registered inspector. There was also a presentation of the main findings and key issues to governors. School staff were mostly pleased with a thorough and fair inspection which they felt was a very positive and constructive experience. Even so, the inspection team gained valuable feedback from the school on how its processes could be improved. The monitoring letter from HMI was also supportive but also gave useful pointers to how the team could improve its inspection procedures. Later on, the inspection report itself was monitored by HMI at OFSTED and the result of this too was useful comment on possible improvement.

FOLLOWING THE 1994 INSPECTION

The senior management team involved governors, staff at all levels, and the registered inspector in producing a detailed action plan. This was structured on the inspection key issues and reflected the format of the school development plan. It detailed responsibilities, resources, success criteria, targets and monitoring strategies for each agreed action. This action plan formed the agenda for initial change. In subsequent years, the remaining action targets were subsumed in successive school development plans and target planners. Additional priorities, notably literacy development, have been introduced.

Since the inspection, appropriate members of the inspection team and other external advisers have been used by the school. They have helped in training and mentoring and have supported action at many levels. Specific topics have included value added; a review of the sixth form; subject monitoring; support in mathematics; and the introduction of a lesson observation scheme involving the senior management team and heads of department.

Consistent, detailed and focused school development planning and feedback; subject monitoring; and lesson observation have all been crucial elements in moving steadily towards internally driven quality assurance. As this is achieved, the use of external consultants can become more and more positive. Supported by school-based coaching and mentoring, middle managers can gain the power and the ability to foster improvement in their areas and more widely across the school. This is happening already in some but not all teaching and support teams.

ACHIEVEMENTS SINCE 1994

(*Note*: The following achievements follow the order of key issues from the 1994 inspection report.)

The strong pastoral support for pupils has been reinforced by appointing heads of year and resurrecting the house system. This has also allowed some improvement to the management structure of the school overall. The range and volume of extracurricular opportunities have been extended, particularly through lunchtime clubs and other activities. House assemblies have been introduced and merits, for good attendance and so on, are rewarded within the house structure.

The school is developing a 'school standards unit'. This is collecting school and national comparative data and is doing some work on value added. The work is also acting as a focus for staff professional development. The value-added system intends to link SATs results at Key Stage (KS) 2 and data on intake testing with results at SATs at KS3, GCSE and A-level or General National Vocational Qualifications (GNVQ). Some of the comparison also looks at estimated against actual grades for each subject. Termly grade recording for parents shows the profile of grades as they build up. Predictive reports for pupils are also being brought in.

Table 7.1 External examination results 1994/7

		1993/4	1994/5	1995/6	1996/7
5+ A*–C GCSE %		21	29	32	31
5+ A*–G GCSE %		75	80	77	89
1 or more A*–G GCSE		90	90	89	94
A-level average points		10.7	10.7	8.2	11.2
L5 SATs %	EN	39	n/a	56	42
	MA	34	n/a	53	54
	SC	55	n/a	42	45

There has been some improvement in the external examination results over the last few years (see Table 7.1). Specific achievements have been

- the proportion of pupils gaining five or more higher grades at GCSE has increased from 21 to 31 per cent;

- the proportion gaining five or more pass grades has increased from 75 to 89 per cent;
- the proportion gaining one or more pass grades has increased from 90 to 94 per cent;
- the proportion of merit and distinction grades in GNVQ has increased; and
- the number of pupils taking A-level and the A-level pass rate have increased.

Mathematics was the weakest of the three core subjects in 1994 and so was the subject of a full senior management team audit and a supportive post-OFSTED inspection. This exercise led to a variety of improvements including much more detailed schemes of work, which included differentiated worksheets at many levels. Setting arrangements have been refined; new systems and procedures for homework have been introduced. Most of the departments have improved to some extent in the last few years, but the improvement in mathematics has been the greatest. The proportion of pupils gaining higher grades in GCSE mathematics rose from 23 per cent in 1994 to 32 per cent in 1997. At the other end of the attainment range there were 21 pupils in 1994 who were not entered for GCSE; this number has been reduced to seven in 1997.

Attendance has been a focus of attention and has improved to some extent. This is counter to a trend of increasing absence in many of the London boroughs. Overall attendance has increased from 87 per cent in 1993/4 to 88.4 per cent in 1996/7. Unauthorised absence has reduced from 3 per cent to 1.2 per cent in this time. New procedures on attendance have just been introduced which attempt to involve parents more in improving their sons' and daughters' attendance. For example new school rules will ban holidays during term time. The number of exclusions has remained fairly steady which is creditable in view of the national trend of increasing exclusions and the increasing school numbers.

The expectations of all teachers have been raised. The proportion of pupils entered for at least one GCSE has increased from 92 per cent in 1994 to 97 per cent in 1997. Achievement for higher-ability pupils has also increased and almost 20 per cent of students achieved the higher grades in seven, eight or nine subjects. Sixth-form results continue to improve slowly with 100 per cent pass rate in all but one of the GCE A-level subjects and the majority of students in GNVQ intermediate and advanced programmes achieving merit or distinction grades. The approach to differentiation has been improved particularly in mathematics and arrangements for setting have been completely reviewed.

The school has worked to spread good practice through consistent monitoring. This has followed specific training of the senior management team and heads of department in lesson observation. There is a freer exchange of information between departments. For example, individual heads of department give talks to other heads on good features of their work, such as the homework system in mathematics. Displays around the school have been significantly improved and include some displays featuring extensive individual projects completed at home.

The setting system has been reviewed and is now working well. Setting is the norm. Pupils are set at the start of year 7 as a result of reports from the primary school, KS2 SATs and result of standardised tests. Setting occurs independently for most subjects and movement between sets is based on results and effort. There is retesting in years 8 and 9 which results in some movement between sets. The timetable has been restructured into a two-week, one-hour block timetable. This has enabled some more flexibility and a better balance across the curriculum, with improved time allocation to some subjects.

The school has developed a strategic plan for the development of the sixth form and vocational provision. Vocational programmes have been enhanced. The sixth form has increased in numbers from about 60 in 1994 to almost 100 and further increases are anticipated. Enrolments to almost all courses are economically and educationally viable. There is a sixth-form induction programme and performance of all students is monitored against targets which are exposed to the students and to staff. A-level pass rates have improved; GNVQ results are good. An evaluation of some of the sixth-form course provision is planned.

The arrangements for assemblies have been changed, with collective worship included specifically in one assembly each week and connected themes for tutor periods for the rest of the week. Registration and form times have been changed and the use of this time improved. RE in the sixth form is based on day conferences, tailored from input by various outsiders. Together with preparation and follow-up, this probably meets the statutory requirements in the sixth form.

Monitoring has been enhanced. There is formal monitoring of classroom practice by the senior management team and heads of department. There is also monitoring of a variety of statistics, for example, on examination results, assessments and attendance. Professional development has been highlighted and is now properly monitored. For example, the school knows that in addition to its five training days last year, 73 per cent of the staff took part in a specific training event and all participated in a variety of twilight and on-the-job development.

There have been some accommodation changes including four new classrooms, a new demountable classroom and improvement to two laboratories and sixth-form areas. The school is currently bidding for additional accommodation for its sixth form. IT has been enhanced so that there are now four rooms of modern personal computers. A fifth room is designated and will be equipped as soon as funds are available. Almost all machines are to a common specification with common, industry-standard software but the school is not yet networked. The use of the library has increased and a sixth-form library has been designated. There is an agreement with another local authority's library service to lease or hire all books, plus videos and other materials. An extensive section of books and materials has also been developed for staff and management.

The popularity of the school has been considerably increased. A completely new school prospectus and a new school song were introduced in 1995 as part of a public relations push. The improved perception of the school in the community can be seen from detailed figures on the number of applications for entry (see Table 7.2). There were 290 applications for entry in 1993 and this has steadily increased to 480 in 1997. The increased popularity of the school means that admissions criteria have to be more stringently applied. This has reduced the geographic area of intake to some extent. It has also improved the overall ability of the pupils. The intake in 1997 included some pupils with very high scores in standardised tests as well as some with very low scores. The spread of ability on intake is now almost in line with the normal national distribution.

Table 7.2   Applications to the school 1993/7

	1993	1994	1995	1996	1997
Y7 intake numbers	185	180	202	206	208
No. of applications	290	350	410	440	480

FURTHER DEVELOPMENT

Recently, five departments were identified through the school's internal monitoring for further supportive consultancy. Several of these departments have not yet made the improvements seen in many other areas. Among the main reasons for this have been rapid changes in staffing and/or statutory requirements. Close Associates provided the consultants in March 1998, continuing the link between the inspection team and the school. Each of the consultants spent two or three days on site with the department, meeting staff, observing classes, looking at pupils' work and reviewing documentation. Each review included a concluding meeting with the head of department and the appropriate member of the senior management team. There was a brief report on the area, including a list of issues for action. In line with the new inspection requirements the consultants also provided appropriate feedback to each teacher. The departmental reports and action plans have been drawn together and will be aligned with the school development plan. The more important, supportive aspects of each of the consultancies will, it is hoped, have left staff feeling positive and able to contribute to the school's preparation for the next round of inspection.

CONCLUSION

Since 1994 the school is much more firmly established as a successful community comprehensive. The first-round OFSTED inspection was a mainly positive experience. Structured school development was put in place and is continuing. The school is now popular and well regarded in its local community. Examination results have improved and the improvement sustained. The school now has a firmer base from which to face the second-round OFSTED inspection which is scheduled for Autumn 1998.

However, the identification of some areas which need specific support at this stage points to one of the main difficulties in school improvement. Whatever the leadership and management, whatever the supportive systems, any school remains vulnerable to factors outside its control. Quality learning is delivered primarily by teachers, not by managers or systems, let alone inspectors or consultants. At Uxbridge, in IT, for example, the department carried a staff vacancy through temporary and supply appointments for well over a year. Two of the four members of current staff are moving on in the summer. In these circumstances, simply maintaining quality will be very difficult.

This is a report which reflects well on the OFSTED approach and the way in which inspectors, consultants and schools can work together. Even so, consistent, high quality cannot be guaranteed. It requires hard work and commitment – and a little luck.

8

Raising Standards and Raising Morale: A Case Study of Change

HELEN HOSKER AND SUE ROBB

Camberley County Infant School was one of the very first primary schools to be inspected by OFSTED in September 1994. This chapter seeks to examine the school's response to the inspection, particularly in relation to the need to raise standards in reading. The chapter is written by the headteacher, who had been in post for one year at the time of the inspection, and the school's attached LEA primary consultant, who was also new to post and to the school.

In the course of looking back over the three years that have passed since the inspection the authors have used some of the key questions from *Inspection and Re-inspection of Schools from September 1997* (OFSTED, 1997d). The reinspection of schools focuses on improvements since the last inspection and inspectors are charged to make judgements about changes the school has made, whether they were an adequate response to previous inspection findings, how they have been made and, perhaps most difficult of all, if they have been sufficient. In order to test out their views the authors have consulted the teaching staff through a brief questionnaire and informal discussions, interviewed the chairman of the governing body, and held conversations with parents and the headteacher of the junior school that some of the children move on to.

The school was opened in 1987 and is situated near to the centre of a medium-sized town. The school has a highly regarded nursery class attached to it, admitting 42 children on a part-time basis. At the time of the OFSTED inspection the school roll stood at 123, and there were 6.8 teachers, mostly long serving including a non-class-based special educational needs co-ordinator (SENCO) and a music specialist, a nursery nurse and five special needs/teachers' assistants.

Children attending the school reflect a broad cross-section of the immediate community with one third from housing association accommodation and a further two thirds from private and military homes. A proportion of the children come from economically advantaged homes but there are also a significant number from disadvantaged homes. At the time of the inspection 20 per cent of the children were entitled to free school meals and, alongside the children on statements and on the SEN register, the headteacher and SENCO had identified a number of children of low to average ability who were underachieving in the acquisition of basic language skills.

BEFORE THE INSPECTION

Prior to the OFSTED inspection, as a result of an initial audit of the school, the new headteacher had expressed concerns over several issues to the governing body, but it was the standards of reading throughout the school that she found most worrying. The chairman recalls that the governors had begun to realise that the school's results were poor in comparison with other local schools and his discussions with parents had reinforced this view. He was pleased that the headteacher was prepared to voice her concerns to staff and parents and that she had discussed them with the LEA team drafted in for a pre-OFSTED health check. However, there was insufficient time before the inspection to agree and implement a new policy and structure or to begin to put in place a training programme.

Members of staff still subscribed to an inherited attitude that good schools correlated directly to stimulating, celebratory, child-orientated display. Some of this stemmed from the LEA support in the past for aspects of good primary practice which placed a major emphasis on the classroom environment, the ethos and on developing children's creativity. Its roots also lay in the fact that staff and governors had been protected from previous LEA inspection reports, that raised areas of concern, which had been edited before being disseminated. As a result staff worked very hard to create an attractive working environment and, in the weeks before the inspection, focused more attention on preparing the physical surroundings than on their roles as teachers. Curriculum planning was based around whole-school themes and classroom practice was often characterised by children pursuing a wide variety of low-level tasks with teachers predominately involved in organising rather than teaching once each group had been introduced to its activity. Alma Harris and colleagues (1996, p. 15), writing about school improvement, notes that it 'nearly always starts with a view or an evaluation of some aspect of the school's functioning'.

It can be seen then that two of the areas for improvement that were to be firmly evidenced during the inspection were known to the headteacher and she was to some extent prepared for what was to follow. The OFSTED report was to give credence to her own judgements and open the way for improvement.

The pre-OFSTED review confirmed the unknown quality of the real inspection. Inspectors had only recently been trained and were approachable and supportive and gave credit for planned changes rather than basing their findings solely on the hard evidence of daily practice. In retrospect whilst the report echoed many of the findings of the OFSTED inspection the style of the feedback and the encouragement provided did not prepare the staff for the reality of what was to follow.

THE INSPECTION

During the week of the inspection great respect was felt for the registered inspector (RgI), an early years specialist, based to her secure knowledge base and sincere attitude and it was agreed that the team of five inspectors was thorough. Throughout the week the team was monitored by an HMI. The teachers found the whole process difficult, particularly since it was unrelated to anything in their previous experience or to the experience of colleagues in neighbouring schools.

During the week the inspectors were, in the words of one teacher, 'amazingly unobtrusive [but] people felt flat, there was no feedback, it was very alien and demoralising – just some little comment would have helped'. It was evident at the full feedback to governors and senior management at the end of the week that the inspection team had collated a sound evidence base for their findings. There was mutual agreement and confidence that the RgI had reported an accurate analysis of the school and that she was convinced the school would flourish under a focused action plan.

IMMEDIATE POST-OFSTED PERIOD

In the immediate post-OFSTED period the most significant factor was the low morale of the staff. The main findings of the report included:

> The overall standards in the school in the majority of subjects are sound or better, although many able pupils are underachieving. Standards in English and in particular reading need to be improved.

> The quality of education is generally sound and pupils have good attitudes to school and their work. Pupils' progress is variable although mainly sound apart from in English.

The paragraph for English, whilst commenting favourably on the introduction of Reading Recovery, was critical of other aspects of the teaching of reading and of the silent reading times: 'A lack of guidance or monitoring of pupils' reading books is leading to the use of unchallenging reading material or pupils struggling to read unsuitable text.'

Further comments in the paragraph on teaching were disappointing and found a high proportion of unsatisfactory teaching in English and mathematics. Thus there was a feeling amongst the staff of having let the new headteacher, the school and the children down. Consequently they had to find ways to come to terms with the report and to recognise the cultural change that would be needed to achieve the first two key issues – to raise standards of achievement, particularly reading, and to widen the range of learning skills to raise standards. This would mean that displays would no longer be the focus of a 'good' school, that teachers would have to have high expectations of all children and that they would have to be far more actively involved in teaching than before. The role of the teacher would have to be re-established and the process of doing this would have to make teachers feel confident about their teaching. There would also need to be a school way of working which was proactive in identifying future needs and areas for development in order to avoid complacency in the future.

The greatest immediate hurdle facing the headteacher was the raising of staff morale and the bonding together of a professional team who would be sufficiently strong and open enough to take on board the necessary action plan. She was helped by the report's recognition of her as a strong headteacher who was beginning to introduce systems of monitoring and evaluation through classroom observation and feedback and had put an effective development plan in place: 'There is positive leadership by the headteacher who has been in post for one year and there have been significant developments in the school during this period.'

A member of staff thinking back to that time commented that it was also helpful that, amongst the staff, 'there was no sense of denial, people accepted the report, they were conscientious and realistic enough to acknowledge the need for improvement [even though] they felt drained with nothing left to give.' Furthermore, this teacher pointed out that as a staff they exhibited a very strong team spirit which was to stand them in good stead as they approached the necessary changes.

Another important factor in the post-OFSTED period was the attitude of parents. Parents had been told prior to the inspection of concerns about the standards achieved in reading – and had been listened to when they had raised similar worries. They were unanimously supportive of the school's proposals at the open meeting held by staff and governors to discuss any aspects of the report. The PTA pledged funds for new reading materials and to promote a major book/reading week.

ACTION PLAN

The first two days of the spring term 1995 were earmarked for the staff and governors to formulate the action plan. Prior to this discussions took place between the LEA attached consultant, the headteacher and the deputy head aimed at identifying staff training needs and strengthening the headteacher's planned approach to classroom observation. The discussions enabled the formulation of clear aims for the action plan and also the development of strategies to try to make the staff feel nurtured and valued as well as providing opportunities for reflection and development.

It was decided that the two planning days would be held away from school in a small country hotel. Included in the programme were sessions by LEA consultants who facilitated discussions on the skills needed to teach reading and practical ideas for the monitoring of reading. As hoped, everyone responded to the atmosphere and the amenities and the headteacher welcomed the beginnings of a glimmer of determination towards 'getting it right for the children', as one member of staff put it. The end result of two intensive days was that the staff were mentally drained but enthused to teach reading and a powerful action plan rigorously aimed at improving standards had been formulated for which everyone felt ownership.

One of the strengths of the action plan was that it focused on immediate action and was crystal clear in describing what was to happen. Very little time was allowed for recovery and the timescale for implementation of the key action points was tight (within two terms). Monitoring was inbuilt and linked to achieving the success criteria.

The success criteria and actions were greatly influenced by the beginnings of the national and LEA emphasis on the need for improved standards, and included:

- a commitment to improve national test results;
- liaison with the junior school to begin simple benchmarking;
- in-school monitoring of reception baseline screening, middle infant screening (MIST) in year 1, and year 2 national tests to evaluate progress and the impact of teaching; and
- the use of LEA consultants to evaluate progress and give external validity to the school's programme of monitoring.

THE PROCESS – IMPLEMENTING THE ACTION PLAN

In order to ensure strong curriculum leadership in the area of reading the headteacher decided to become the co-ordinator. This was a key factor on the road to improvement. The previous, very able, co-ordinator had obtained a post elsewhere so there was a vacancy but had she remained the headteacher would have worked in partnership with her. This decision ensured a high status for reading, quick responses both internally and externally, efficient and effective oversight of strategic and day-to-day developments. It also enabled the headteacher both to demonstrate and develop her own knowledge base in a vital area of the curriculum while the rest of the staff and the future co-ordinator were involved in in-service training and focusing on their skills as teachers. A further important factor was the role of the deputy headteacher who was fully involved in all the planning and able in her teaching to put ideas and theory into practice and lead by example.

Harris and her colleagues (1996, p. 35) recognise the need for headteachers to be proactive in this way: 'leaders of effective schools know that they must invest in the continuous development of their staff. For leaders this means that they must spend time on the following: acting as coach, counsellor, educator, guide and champion in encouraging their staff and setting high standards.'

Instrumental to improving the teachers' skills in the teaching of reading was the in-school training from the school's Reading Recovery teacher. Over a series of three twilight sessions she explained simple, practical and easily applied teaching techniques such as word cutting and matching; child finger pointing; word building using magnetic letters; running records; the necessity of child-owned time (i.e. no adult prompts) for decoding; and the use of picture, context and word cues. All staff observed the 30 minute intensive one-to-one Reading Recovery session and commented on its pace and structure.

Teachers recognised the importance of the running record component of Reading Recovery. They agreed it was a vital diagnostic monitoring method for actually identifying children's reading problems and informing the next teaching step, which must be included in their teaching of reading.

Gradually the training filtered through into daily practice with focused and planned reading sessions evident and a consistency in the teaching and monitoring of reading throughout the school. Silent reading was cancelled immediately and teachers recognised the need for structured reading sessions which were planned to include phonic work, reading games and group reading. Many of the Reading Recovery techniques were to prove useful in these sessions.

An audit of reading materials identified gaps at all stages which were rectified. A particular focus of the audit was the variety of reading materials for reluctant readers and boys. This was to prove invaluable for later research by the school into boys' reading standards.

The school's reading policy was overhauled to include aims, structure, a well researched colour coding system linked to the National Curriculum levels, phonological progression and the development of a home and school reading partnership.

This partnership with home was viewed as an opportunity to involve parents fully with their child's learning, and included:

- a detailed information booklet;
- parent workshops to make reading games, big book/group-reading;
- supplementary materials;
- the active inclusion of parents helping with reading in the classrooms, which included training in the skill of listening to children read and the use of individual recording sheets; and
- parent information meetings and workshops to keep them up to date with developments.

Parents soon recognised the need for more resources and the money was quickly raised for their purchase.

An important new resource was 'the big book'. These large editions of popular stories such as 'Goldilocks and the Three Bears', 'The Tadpole Diary' and 'The Lighthouse Keeper's Lunch' enabled a group or class of children to be taught such skills as intonation, use of question marks, sight vocabulary, picture clues and word building, in an effective, efficient and fun session.

HEADTEACHER MONITORING

Paramount to the implementation of the action plan and resulting strategies was the headteacher's realisation of the importance of continuous monitoring and evaluation of the teaching and learning in the school, and her role in this vital area. The headteacher became committed to implementing a system of classroom observations followed by detailed feedback. A termly plan of dates and times, which were rarely changed, was agreed between the staff and the headteacher. She planned one detailed observation a week which meant that on average each teacher was observed twice a term. Teachers had to recognise that during the observation the headteacher would be in a monitoring role. She would have scrutinised their planning prior to the observation. In addition the headteacher made it clear that she would be looking at work, noting the levels of attainment, children's comments and attitudes as well as observing the actual teaching session.

In response to teachers' comments about the lack of feedback during the OFSTED inspection the headteacher provided feedback about her observations immediately after them. A form of negotiated agreement and discussion evolved which led to the identification of areas for development which would be referred to at the time of the next observation. Comments were recorded on an OFSTED-style proforma. A copy of the proforma was kept by the headteacher in her confidential monitoring file whilst the original was kept by the teachers in their own portfolios. In the beginning most of the teachers found it extremely threatening but now they recognise it as a routine and supportive part of the school's culture.

Although the teaching of reading was the initial focus of the observation, the headteacher has been able to collate a strong evidence base concerning the general quality of teaching and learning and has also expanded the focus to relate to ongoing developments and current school development plan initiatives. In addition, she feels it has empowered her to make informed management and staffing decisions as well as giving governors an accurate account of the quality of teaching and learning in the school and the rationale behind future areas for development.

Throughout the implementation and continuation of the monitoring and evaluation programme the headteacher was supported by the LEA through monitoring visits from the attached consultant and through joint observations (headteacher and consultant) which provided an opportunity for sharing perspectives. Two terms after work on the action plan began two consultants spent a day in the school evaluating the progress that had been made towards improving the quality of the teaching of reading and the standards achieved by the children. They noted a real improvement in the children's reading ability, which was reinforced by the SATs results for that year and were able to make further recommendations to support teaching.

In spring 1996, when the LEA launched a 'self-evaluating schools' project the school was identified as one which already had many of the characteristics of effective self-review in place and the headteacher was invited to share her approach to monitoring with newly appointed headteachers.

THE LEA READING PROJECT

Running parallel with the school's action plan was the Surrey Reading Project – a 16-month project centred around action research in individual schools with support through in-service training activities. Camberley Infant School was successful in its application for inclusion in the project on the theme 'An in-depth study of reading in reception'. This resulted in a new injection of energy to help the staff fulfil the aims of the action plan. The reception year was purposely chosen for this focus as it was felt that it would instil a positive attitude to reading at an early age and that the skills the children gained would consequently enhance the teaching in years 1 and 2.

From July 1995 to January 1996 the school worked with the project leader to bring about a reception year reading programme which would focus on a basic skills approach of quality, whilst ensuring a balance of activities and fun. The headteacher decided to visit reading projects in inner London schools on her own in the first instance. This resulted in her filtering the broad aims and possible activities to the reception year team. It was then left to the team and project leader to identify the training and development required for devising a daily reading programme which would include procedures for monitoring and assessing progress.

On reflection, the staff involved in the project acknowledge that this approach was a key issue in its success as it resulted in a unique programme tailor made to the needs of the children and school. The current reading co-ordinator feels that if she had observed the project elsewhere in the early days she may well have rejected it. She would not at the time have been able to separate out the useful elements and would have been swamped and worried by the less useful aspects. By the time she did visit the London schools she was able to make informed judgements based on experience.

The programme that has been developed is a daily dedicated literacy hour known as CIRI – Camberley Infants' Reading Initiative. The hour is planned on a weekly basis around a set text. Central to the session is a 'Big Book' input followed by phonic activities including a sing-along slot. The children then rotate, as appropriate, around such activities as group reading, word building, reading games and practical activities in the water, art and design technology areas.

Assessments from September 1996 to July 1997 indicate improvement in book knowledge, phonic acquisition, key words and an enthusiasm and motivation to read. Parents are delighted with the results and, as one parent said: 'If this had been in place for my older daughter when she was in reception she would have enjoyed learning to read.'

Naturally this programme took much teacher-time to implement and made heavy demands on resources. It also involved much discussion over whether it was appropriate for such young children. There are no longer doubts about this. The chairman of governors from his regular networking with parents at the start and the end of the school day is confident that they feel their children are not only making progress but enjoy school and have a rich range of experiences. When asked to reflect on the project one teacher wrote: 'The children's enthusiasm, burgeoning independence and co-operative working has created a very positive environment...because it is so constructed and predictable children feel they have ownership and it gives them security.'

Parent questionnaires and individual comments praise the school for its commitment to developing its approach to reading. Typical of the comments are the following:

> CIRI is wonderful...my son comes home talking about the author, illustrations and exclamation marks.

> Jamie wants to go to the library...my older son didn't.

MOVING ON

It is only now that the three-year action plan is completed, and further plans are being developed, that real improvements can be claimed. The school's national test results (see Table 8.1) indicate continuing progress even though they dipped in 1996 when there were more children than usual with severe learning difficulties. In-school comparisons between correlated aspects of the school's reception screening and later MIST and national test results indicate continual improvement in reading standards.

Table 8.1   National test results

	Pre-Level 1		Level 1		Level 2		Level 3		Level 4		Level 2 and above	
	Nat'l	CIS	Nat'l	CIS	Nat'l	CIS	Nat'l	CIS	Nat'l	CIS	Nat'l	CIS
1997	9	5	16	15	49	51	26	29	0	0	84	85.5
1996	3	9	18	14	48	49	30	28	0	0	78	78.0
1995	1	0	14	11	62	53	23	34	0	2*	85	89.0
1994	*2*	*1*	*18*	*24*	*51*	*59*	*29*	*16*	*0*	*0*	*80*	*75.0*
1993					No results entered							
1992		2		23		50		25		0		75.0

Notes:
1992: no national results available.
1996: dip year – due to revised curriculum.
In addition CIS high percentage of pre-level one exempted pupils due to special educational needs.
*Post-OFSTED year.

The school's commitment to Reading Recovery, which has been viewed by some as an expensive gimmick, has ensured a highly skilled member of staff able to lead by example as a year-1 class teacher, share her skills with colleagues and aid the development of the teaching of reading within the school. In the last three years Reading Recovery intervention has also had a positive effect on the lives of 18 children by helping them to become enthusiastic, average readers for their age and by raising their self-esteem.

Through the school's commitment to monitoring and evaluating the quality of teaching a culture of improvement has developed which has enabled the staff to become skilled at identifying the need for change and development. The headteacher is especially proud to be leading a staff-team which is motivated to develop new initiatives and to respond to training and development opportunities. This was further recognised when the school became one of the first in Surrey to gain the Investors in People award. During 1997/8, CIRI has been extended into years 1 and 2, ahead of the National Literacy Strategy, and target-setting linked to specific groups within each year has become established within the school development plan. Plans were being formulated to develop the school library in partnership with parents to celebrate the National Year of Literacy. Staff, in their co-ordinator roles, have become extremely involved in the monitoring and evaluation of the school.

REFLECTIONS

When OFSTED revisit Camberley Infant School they will be able to see what has changed in response to the findings of the original inspection and able to track the strategies, training and developments undertaken to bring about improvement. Whether that improvement is sufficient is a question that the school, staff and governors continue to ask. In future this should become clearer as they will be able to use the LEA value-added analysis and data for benchmarking alongside teacher assessment and test results when determining targets for improvement. At this stage the school is proud to claim that improvements have taken place and that these have had a qualitative impact on what is on offer to children as well as raising achievements in national test results.

In analysing what has underpinned the success it is possible to suggest the following:

• The OFSTED findings supported and reinforced areas for development that had already been identified by the headteacher and some governors, but not fully accepted or understood by the majority of teaching staff. The findings provided an impetus for change.

• All members of the OFSTED team had credibility and gained the respect of the staff – judgements were accepted.

• The action plan was thoroughly planned and rigorously implemented. It was well paced and well led by the headteacher. It included who was responsible for what, success criteria and was set within a challenging time frame.

• A blame culture was avoided. The focus was on moving forward and supporting teachers' abilities to implement the plan.

• The LEA supported the school with the action plan. Training opportunities were made available, the school became involved in initiatives, and LEA consultants provided support with monitoring and evaluation in order to validate the school's view of achievements and areas for development. The LEA's 'self-evaluating schools' project fully supported the approach taken by the headteacher, and latterly the co-ordinators, to monitoring and evaluating the quality and effectiveness of the provision on offer.

- The headteacher took a proactive role in the development, making it one of her key priorities. Sheila Russell (1996, p. 33) sums up the approach: 'One skill of leadership is balancing pressure and support. A school which demonstrates confidence in its teachers creates a climate of collaboration and creativity where each person can contribute new ideas, and new energy to the development of the school as a whole.'
- Full use was made of an expert subject teacher through her involvement in leading staff training and workshops and through enabling her to develop her skills as a Reading Recovery teacher.
- The staff responded throughout in a positive way, supporting each other, trying things out and making careful assessments of what worked and what did not, reflecting on their practice in an increasingly open way and as one said 'by continuing to work very hard'. Developments were not without pain but the strength of support for each other has been a powerful force in moving things forward. Staff now plan and refine the next stages of development.
- Parents have been informed, given practical advice about supporting their children and their involvement in the school has been actively encouraged.
- The commitment and support of the governing body.

At the beginning of 1998 the school is in a position to look towards the implementation of the education reforms and the National Literacy Strategy with confidence and in the knowledge that instead of facing something new they can feel they are well on route to tackling fresh challenge and managing change successfully as an improving school.

Section 3
School Responses: Towards a Critique of Inspection

9

Inspection and Change in the Classroom: Rhetoric and Reality?

GEOFF LOWE

INTRODUCTION

This chapter describes the extent of implementation of different types of inspection recommendations in seven comprehensive schools one year after inspection, reflects on how various discourses have influenced teachers' responses to the schools' inspection recommendations and speculates on the prospects for real change in the classroom. The term discourse refers to 'all that can be written or said about a particular area' of school activity (Layder, 1994, pp. 97–8). The employment of a discourse enables the speaker to deploy knowledge in such a way which claims to be the truth according to its own criteria and it can become the means by which power relations within a school and between the school and external agencies can be established and maintained. In this way central government is seeking to take over or 'colonise' schools' discourses with OFSTED's view of school, based on the notions of standards, quality, efficiency, value for money and performance that are contained in successive OFSTED handbooks and inspection frameworks (OFSTED, 1993/6), through the programme of school inspection. It is headteachers and other senior managers who transmit OFSTED's values to their colleagues in managing the school's response to inspection. However, schools are not the product of a single discourse associated with inspection but a number of disparate discourses which have different origins – for example, in the school's history and traditions, subject traditions and local communities. These may be underpinned by values different from those associated with OFSTED's 'multi-level, performance, process, context' model of the school (Gray and Wilcox, 1996b, pp. 66–8) and this may account for the variations in the degree of influence which OFSTED's thinking exerts on discourses within schools and between schools. As a consequence this brings a measure of uncertainty into the implementation of inspection recommendations which impinges on teachers' core educational beliefs such as recommendations concerned with teaching and learning.

THE INVESTIGATION

The investigation, which is ongoing, explores the perceptions of teachers at all levels about the prospect of inspection, the inspection process itself and the implementation of inspection recommendations. Seven comprehensive schools, situated in different LEAs with a range of pupil intakes and a variety of local communities but thought to be typical of the majority of the schools inspected during 1996/7, are participating in the research. Data have been obtained from interviews with 60 teachers who are involved in a range of school activities, together with observations and an analysis of a range of school documentation and activities. The participants are being interviewed on seven occasions over four years. The first series of interviews took place within two weeks of the inspection; the second within three weeks after the inspection; and the third and successive interviews are being conducted at intervals of six months. An analysis of the interim data forms the basis of the descriptions in this chapter. The schools' anonymity is preserved by the use of alphabetical identifiers. Characteristics of the schools and their inspection teams are to be found in Table 9.1.

Table 9.1   Characteristics of the seven comprehensive schools

Characteristics	Inspection						
School	A	B	C	D	E	F	G
School type	11–16	11–16	11–18	11–18	11–18	11–16	11–18
Type of control	County	County	County	County	GMS	County	County
Gender of pupils	Mixed	Mixed	Mixed	Mixed	Mixed	Mixed	Mixed
No. of pupils	i*	iii*	iv*	iv*	i*	ii*	iv*
No. of teachers	S**	V**	X**	W**	T**	V**	V**
OFSTED team	Non-LEA	Non-LEA	Non-LEA	LEA	Non-LEA	Non-LEA	LEA
% free meals	1.5 x nat. av.	2 x nat. av.	= nat. av.	= nat. av	< nat. av.	< nat. av	= nat. av.

Notes:
* Size of pupil population: i = 800–999; ii = 1000–199; iii = 1200–399; iv = 1400–599.
** Full-time equivalent number of teachers: S = 40–49; T = 50–59; U = 60–69; V = 70–79; W = 80–89; X = 90–99.

THE IMPLEMENTATION OF THE KEY ISSUES ONE YEAR AFTER INSPECTION

The investigation relies upon the participants' accounts of the extent to which inspection recommendations have been implemented. There was a large degree of consensus amongst the participants about the extent of implementation of recommendations relating to changes in the curriculum, the level of resources, accommodation/facilities and health and safety procedures. There was less agreement about the extent of implementation of those inspection recommendations concerned with teaching and learning as well as the monitoring of the curriculum by senior and middle managers. Headteachers and senior managers tended to take a more favourable view of the extent of implementation of inspection recommendations, an attitude that may be explained by their overview of the school. It appeared that senior teachers had been overoptimistic about the degree of influence they had exerted on what happened in the classroom. The participants' perceptions of the extent of implementation varied both by school and within the same school. This suggested a need for a five-point scale which would match the extent of differentiation and a five-point rating scale has been adopted.

Table 9.2 Extent of implementation of inspection recommendations one year after the school's inspection

Area of school activity	Extent of implementation				
	Full	Substantial	Some	Limited	None
Curriculum		A6, C1, C6, D2, E5, F2 F5, G5	E6, F1	B1, B3, G2	A5, D6
Curriculum monitoring/evaluation		A2	A3, E3, G3	C3, F4	
Teaching/learning		D1	A1, C2, E2, E4	F3, G1	B2
School development planning			D5	E1	
Pupil attendance/punctuality			B5	B4	
Accommodation		D4	C4	B7	
Resources		C5, D5	A4	B6	
Health and safety		A7, E7			
Assessment of pupils' work			G4		

Note:
The capital letters in each cell designate the school in question and the attached numeral relates to a numbered inspection recommendation.

One year after inspection none of the inspection recommendations had been fully implemented. The schools made the most progress with the inspection recommendations concerned with modifications to the formal curriculum, for example by plugging gaps and removing duplication, changing spending priorities and providing more effective health and safety procedures. Least progress had been made with those recommendations concerning learning and teaching and monitoring the curriculum.

THE SCHOOLS' RESPONSE TO THE INSPECTION FINDINGS

The headteachers of schools A, B, C and D believed they had a 'good inspection'. The headteachers of schools E, F and G were dissatisfied with the conduct of the inspection but, with the exception of the headteacher of school E, viewed the process as fair overall. All headteachers, including the headteacher of school E who had reservations about some of the inspection's findings, were able to use the inspection report to good effect with their own staff, the local community and the local press.

School A was described by the inspectors as an improving school with many strengths, which was successful in meeting its aims of raising pupil expectations and standards. It had made substantial progress with implementing three of the seven recommendations that related to the statutory requirement for a daily act of collective worship, monitoring the work of departments and various health and safety issues. Some progress had been made with recommendations to improve monitoring of the pupils' performance by form tutors, to increase spending on books and equipment and to be more consistent in marking and day-to-day assessment. The school had incorporated a requirement for heads of subject to provide the headteacher with information about 'good teaching practice' in the annual review of the progress made by the department to raise the standards of pupil attainment. The headteacher did not intend to take action about an inspection recommendation to do with increasing the pupils' ability to access other cultures and the spiritual dimension of the school's curriculum which he believed was based on inadequate inspection evidence. He intended to pursue the school's own programme for raising the pupils' awareness of European cultures.

In its inspection report school B was described as a sound school which was showing much determination in combating low educational expectations in the local community. The quality of teaching was 'good overall'. Both the school's governors and the senior management team were praised for giving 'clear direction' to the school. With the exception of an improvement in the level of the pupils' punctuality, brought about by ensuring that the schools' buses arrive on time, the school had made little progress in implementing its seven inspection recommendations. Something about the school's circumstances had prevented it from responding to the inspectors' recommendations, yet these circumstances pertained during the school's inspection. This raised doubts about the inspection report as a basis for taking action to improve to the school.

The inspectors viewed school C as a good school where pupils achieve standards in line with, or above, those expected for their capabilities. They praised both the quality of teaching and the leadership given by the headteacher and governing body. Immediately after the inspection the school set about implementing its inspection recommendations. One year later it had made substantial progress with implementing three inspection recommendations concerned with improving the pupils' access to information technology, complying with the statutory requirements for the curriculum and developing the school library as a support for learning. The headteacher had persuaded the LEA to implement a programme of improvements to the accommodation and to the science facilities. Limited progress had been achieved with establishing formal monitoring of teaching and learning and there had been discussions about replacing the school's own arrangements for monitoring the work of teachers in the classroom.

A successful school where pupils attain very high standards and where racial harmony is a strength was the description given to school D in its inspection report. The inspectors praised both the quality of teaching in the school and the leadership afforded by the headteacher and the senior management team. In their judgement the school had made substantial progress with implementing four of the six inspection recommendations. This school was the only one in the research to have made substantial progress with a recommendation to identify and disseminate good teaching practice. However, the school was experiencing difficulties with bringing its own, idiosyncratic, procedures into line with OFSTED's recommendations for school development planning.

The inspectors viewed school E as a 'successful community school' where the standards of achievement are 'overwhelmingly sound and very often good'. The headteacher and the senior management team were said to be giving strong leadership. Notwithstanding these comments the staff had very little confidence in the inspection process. Factors in the conduct of the inspection had negatively influenced the school's response to the inspection recommendations. Relations between the headteacher and registered inspector had been strained because the head believed that the lead inspector had brought his own views about the school's management to the inspection, leading to some poor quality inspection findings. Two of the school's seven recommendations concerning the pupils' access to information technology and safety had, nevertheless, been substantially implemented a year later. Some progress has been made with implementing inspection recommendations dealing with extension of the pupils' opportunities for spiritual development, encouraging the sharing of 'good teaching practice' and assisting pupils to assume more responsibility for their own learning. The headteacher was not intending to implement an inspection recommendation to improve strategic planning in one area of the curriculum which had been the subject of disagreements between the headteacher and lead inspector.

The inspectors of school F had taken the view that the school's standards of attainment were 'above average' and the quality of teaching was good overall. They praised the 'effective educational leadership' given by the headteacher and governors in pursuing the school's aim to be a caring community. However, the head was disappointed with what he perceived as the lukewarm tone of the inspection feedback about the school's spiritual, moral, social and cultural development, which he had taken as severe criticism of his own leadership. He transmitted negative views of the inspection to the staff and had thus influenced the staff's response to the inspection findings. A year later the school had responded by making substantial progress with implementing two recommendations concerned with the school library's contribution to the work of subjects and the provision of a more structured programme of homework. Little or no progress had been achieved with three recommendations: to increase the level of the pupils' participation in the learning process; to monitor the work of teachers in the classroom; and to extend differentiation.

School G was described as 'providing a good education for its pupils' in its inspection report. The pupils' levels of attainment were said to be in line with expectations and the pupils had been making 'satisfactory and sometimes good progress'. Teachers were assessed as hardworking, and the governors, head and senior managers were praised for their commitment to improving standards. The headteacher considered that the school's inspection was fair overall. However, he was dissatisfied with the outcome in the case of three subject departments. OFSTED had not confirmed his view of the quality of management, standards of attainment and state of staff morale in these departments and he was unsure what to do with inspection recommendations which seemed to be inappropriate for improving these departments. He was not ready to implement the school's inspection recommendations and he needed to consult with the school's liaison adviser and his senior colleagues about how to ensure that the school's middle managers take more responsibility for implementing the school's inspection recommendation. After nine months, one inspection recommendation concerned with improving the pupils' access to information technology had been largely implemented. The school had made some progress with a recommendation to continue improving its assessment practice by better use of target-setting. Plans to broaden perceptions of good management practice among the schools' middle managers through a programme of training, presentations and staff discussion to take place in the autumn term in the following school year had been drawn up and were to be communicated to the staff towards the end of the current school year.

FACTORS INFLUENCING THE IMPLEMENTATION OF INSPECTION RECOMMENDATIONS

The research has revealed the factors which either facilitated or inhibited a school's implementation of inspection recommendations which could be related to the school itself, could be external to the school or pertain to the inspection process. They include the following:

- the willingness of the staff to implement the inspection recommendations;
- the responses of headteachers, senior staff and heads of department;
- the quality of the school's action planning;
- the direction of resources including teachers' time allocated to areas needing improvement;
- the availability and quality of advice from LEA advisory services;
- the level of LEA funding;
- the conduct of the inspection; and
- the nature of the inspection recommendations.

THEORETICAL CONSIDERATIONS

This investigation has attempted to place these factors in the context of school discourses to promote a better understanding of the process of inspection-induced change. What had been accessed and understood in each school is the effect of the interplay of various school traditions, myths and history, the more immediate traditions of managerialist thinking and the school's OFSTED inspection. The school's discourses – collections of knowledge, truth claims and the means of establishing and maintaining power relations – influenced teachers' responses both to the inspection process and the school's attempts to implement their inspection recommendations. The cultures of the schools were not of a piece. They were 'complex, contradictory and somewhat incoherent organisations' and, like other 'values organisations', had inherent tensions in their work practices, values, and attitudes of teachers (Ball, 1997, pp. 317–36). It was clear that these schools did not fit neatly into the model of a school in the OFSTED handbooks (OFSTED, 1993/6a), nor did they fit OFSTED's technocratic approach to school evaluation in fully describing features which had a bearing on the school's future development.

The notion that central government is attempting to change the way teachers think and act through a process of top-down change is given support by the research, and this can be viewed in terms of Habermas's (1984; 1987) 'theory of communicative action', especially his idea of 'colonisation of the lifeworld'. The research is not intended to develop this singularly complex social theory but will identify and develop concepts which will contribute to a better understanding of how inspection affects school development. The various management-orientated initiatives promoted by central government such as the local management of schools, the trend to formulate school development plans, performance tables, OFSTED inspection and, most recently, target-setting, appear to have changed the beliefs which underpin schools' discourses towards those of a more managerialist nature. This process can be viewed as the 'colonisation of school discourses'. The main 'carrier' in colonisation at the level of the school is the headteacher and thus it is unsurprising that the trend towards managerialist thinking seems to have had its greatest impact on the headteacher and senior staff. It appeared that the headteachers' attempts to colonise school discourses have resulted in degrees of 'decoupling' or separation of the discourses associated with school management and teaching and learning. Decoupling of discourses has been described elsewhere in the public service: Broadbent *et al.* (1991) have observed the effects of decoupling in the health service as a consequence of central government reform. The effect of the decoupling of discourses about school management from teaching and learning has been to minimise the number of occasions when headteachers become involved in questions of pedagogy. It appears that headteachers have restricted their involvement in pedagogical matters to the approval of recommendations made by middle managers to change the curriculum, for example by giving their consent to the introduction of new courses such as the General National Vocational Qualification (GNVQ). Thus the decoupling of discourses may account for the schools' difficulties with the implementation of inspection recommendations, such as:

use a wider range of teaching styles to encourage students to think for themselves.

provide more opportunities for pupils to take responsibility for their own learning.

extend the pupils' capacity to think for themselves.

increase the monitoring of the work of teachers in the classroom . . . to identify good practice . . . identify weaknesses.

establish formal procedures to monitor teaching and learning in the classroom.

(Schools' OFSTED inspection reports)

The schools' OFSTED inspection was used by headteachers and heads of subject covered to validate their own agendas for action and to prepare the schools for inspection. It was also an opportunity for headteachers to influence teachers' thinking with the notions of performance, standards, quality, efficiency, pupil progress and behaviour. However, once the school was no longer under OFSTED's immediate gaze, these attempts to achieve shifts in teachers' thinking appeared to be only partly successful. It can be argued that in some cases teachers absorbed OFSTED's language of reform but not the substance (Mclaughlin, 1991). Thus it was not surprising when the schools in the investigation had difficulty in handling recommendations concerned with changes in pedagogy. These findings seemed to confirm the conclusions of other studies that focus on the implementation of inspection recommendations (e.g. Gray and Wilcox, 1995b).

RESPONSES TO INSPECTION – THE DECOUPLING OF DISCOURSES

The headteacher of school A was a firm believer in, and a fervent exponent of, the values which underpin the OFSTED discourse. Immediately after being appointed he set about imposing on the staff a technocratic discourse based on notions of performance, standards, value for money, efficiency and accountability. A new, simplified management structure, under the headteacher's direct influence, replaced the more traditional hierarchical structure. A collegiate approach to decision-making was replaced by competition for resources and an emphasis on how to achieve the school's objectives. In his view the system of OFSTED inspection had more to do with making schools accountable and was less to do with school improvement. The school's inspection was merely a snapshot evaluation which compared unfavourably with the school's more rigorous system of self-review. He was also unimpressed with the quality of the school's inspection findings. A recommendation to increase the degree of rigour of the monitoring of subject departments to identify more clearly weaknesses and areas for improvement which was in line with his own plans was met by the introduction of a system of 'daisy-chain evaluation' – one department reviewing another. The inspectors had also recommended the sharing of good teaching practice with the intention of increasing the range of teaching styles to encourage more students to think for themselves. However the headteacher's interest in this matter was confined to which teaching styles would lead the school to achieve the national average for 5 GCSE A–C grades. The staff seemed to share the head's single-minded approach to improve the school's examination results.

School B's performance on a range of school indicators had fallen below OFSTED's benchmarks and the headteacher had been convinced the school would fail its inspection. Her strategy for improving the school had been first to impose OFSTED's thinking about schools on the staff and then to introduce a series of initiatives designed to improve the quality of teaching. This had the effect of decoupling school management from teaching and learning, leading to divisions between the headteacher, the senior management team and the rest of the staff. The resultant differences of opinion fitted neatly into a long-standing tradition of 'them and us'. Teachers retreated from the headteacher's views about school into various traditions associated with two sites, subject departments and local community ideas about industrial relations and, as a consequence, the school failed to have its own discourse on school self-improvement. To everyone's surprise the school's inspection team praised both the quality of teaching overall and the quality of the headteacher's leadership. However, the inspection may have contributed to the school's dysfunction by appearing to vindicate mutually opposed views of the school. Twelve months later school B had failed to make progress with the implementation of six of its seven inspection recommendations, notwithstanding a well crafted post-inspection action plan and advice from LEA subject advisers. Two inspection recommendations concerning respectively the need for a school language policy and to encourage the pupils to take more responsibility for their own learning, were perceived by the senior management team as 'impractical' and 'buckets' for a number of problems which were already dogging the school. A newly appointed headteacher is seeking to recouple school management with teaching and learning by working closely with the staff to raise standards of literacy and oracy.

The headteacher of school C had used an evolutionary approach to colonise the school's discourse with managerialist thinking during the eight years of his headship. His strategy had been to involve teachers fully in the school's system of development planning to influence their views about how the school should be managed. Gradually teachers associated the new discourse with 'the way we do things around here'. The OFSTED handbook was used to audit the school's strengths and weaknesses, to review the school's priorities and to prepare the school for inspection. Heads of subject viewed the school's inspection as an opportunity to confirm both their opinions about the quality of teaching in their areas and to validate their agendas for change. Despite their perception that the school had a 'good inspection' and that the inspection was fair overall, teachers expressed some reservations about the validity of the process to assess the quality of their teaching. They had been disturbed by the discrepancy between the inspectors' and their own views on the quality of teaching. Nevertheless the school set about implementing four of its six inspection recommendations in the immediate aftermath of inspection. However a year later the school had achieved the less progress with the two inspection recommendations dealing with the establishing of formal monitoring of the work of teachers in the classroom and developing strategies for pupils to take more responsibility for their own learning. Notwithstanding the fundamental changes in teachers' views about how to manage the school which had occurred, OFSTED's views about the quality of teaching and learning had not penetrated the classroom and teachers still maintained their right to determine the scope of teaching and learning. It appeared that if the school were to attempt to change thinking about teaching and learning it would need to recouple the discourses about school management with teaching and learning. However, the initial response to the two inspection recommendations has been to view them as technical/managerial procedures rather than anything which could question teachers' beliefs about teaching and learning.

The headteacher of school D was encouraging his colleagues to achieve an understanding of 'good teaching practice' by means of a school-wide debate about the school's discourse on teaching and learning. Teachers had been engaged in discussions on questions of pedagogy during visits made by the senior management team to observe a cross-section of lessons. A programme of classroom observation was directed towards disseminating good practice with subject departments. This revealed degrees of confusion and uncertainty about key terms such as standards, attainment and performance – confusion which stemmed from the interweaving of various discourses. The headteacher responded by attempting to recouple the school's discourse on school development and improvement with the various discourses which influenced teachers' work in the classroom, to achieve a shared understanding of these terms. The school's plan was for teachers to observe teaching outside their specialist areas and for them to create a school code of good practice which would be used to inform judgements about the quality of teaching throughout the school. In this way it was hoped that the school could break away from the parochialism which influenced the thinking about teaching in some subject departments. The school intended to eschew what it perceived as OFSTED's narrow view about teaching quality for its own much broader vision about what constitutes good teaching.

The headteacher's approach to school development planning had bemused the inspection team and its response was to recommend that the school should have fewer priorities, more success indicators and a more formal process of assessing costs. The headteacher had sought to reconcile his own idiosyncratic approach which was flexible, responsive to change, sensitive to opportunity and embedded in humanistic values, while accommodating some aspects of OFSTED's rational technical approach. The outcome was a plan which was a point of reference for individuals seeking to take initiatives instead of a rigid framework.

Schools E and F were very successful in the educational marketplace. It was perceived that parents were in favour of these schools because of their firm commitment to traditional values, their orderly environments and their reputation for excellent GCSE results. OFSTED inspection was perceived as the means of making schools more accountable, to be unrelated to questions of school self-improvement, and a threat to the status of the school in the community. Although the schools received 'good inspection reports', factors in the inspection itself, such as the conduct of the inspection, meant that teachers had a negative view of the inspection and one inspection recommendation in particular – which suggested that the pupils be made more responsible for their own learning. Action on this recommendation was initially confined to amending the school's objectives for teaching. However, after a period of reflection, the headteacher of school E decided to encourage the pupils to participate more fully in their own learning by broadening the pupils' opportunities for investigation, research, group work and problem-solving by forming a group of senior colleagues, including himself, to act as change agents. No arrangements had been made to have a formal review of the group's work and it was not clear how it intended to disseminate its ideas.

Six months after the inspection, school F's acting headteacher had taken a small step to implement a recommendation – to increase the level of monitoring of teachers in the classroom, to identify good practice and weaknesses and to provide more appropriate professional support – by attempting to clarify heads of subjects' expectations about monitoring the work of their colleagues. This was a sensitive issue and he feared there would be a 'collision of disparate discourses' (Ball, 1997, p. 318), leading to conflict, confusion and uncertainty in the school's response to an OFSTED inspection recommendation. His view was that a headteacher alone could question the validity of views which were widely held in the school. The governors had made only a passing reference to the school's inspection report in the process of appointing a new headteacher and it appeared that they attached little importance to inspection recommendations. This had created more uncertainty about the school's future response.

MAKING THE BEST OF INSPECTION FEEDBACK

Although the headteachers had placed their schools in the managerialist discourse of planned development and had invested in OFSTED's model of school quality, performance and pupil progress, an analysis of their responses to the inspection process suggests that such notions were only part of a balance of these newer and established views of management. As a consequence each school was a brew of managerial surveillance, subject traditions, corporate culture, hierarchies, degrees of willingness to act on inspection advice and adherence to the school's own values. In spite of these different situations the schools had experienced less difficulty with the implementation of those inspection recommendations concerned with management, administration and school documentation. Much less progress had been made with transforming teaching and learning in line with OFSTED's thinking. The perception was that the recommendations in this area were difficult to achieve. The headteachers of schools A, B, D and G responded by attempting to recouple the discourses about management and teaching with varying degrees of success. Each headteacher employed a different strategy which varied by the extent to which the headteacher's views about improving the quality of teaching were imposed on their colleagues. In school B this achieved precisely the opposite of the desired effect – a complete decoupling of school management and teaching and learning leading to splits between the headteacher and many sections of the staff. As a consequence this school was unable to respond to the recommendations of the inspectors. In the other schools the headteachers encouraged their colleagues to commit themselves to the school's managerial discourse in exchange for a sense of being involved in something which realised their own sense of worth and which optimised the school's success or, at the least, guaranteed its survival. It was interesting to note that teachers in these schools spoke proudly of their schools and how they compared favourably with other schools in the local area. However, teachers were sceptical about the school's efforts to transform teaching in line with OFSTED's recommendations for the school. Such recommendations were perceived to be impractical and inappropriate, inspired by OFSTED's desire to increase surveillance and a source a great deal of additional paperwork. The prospects for transforming teaching and learning appeared to be at their best in school D which was moving towards a new view of good practice in teaching and learning – a view which would take account of various factors including those of a managerialist orientation, teachers' own beliefs and any future unforeseen circumstances. The school was thus attempting to grapple with teachers' lack of trust in the moves to limit their freedom of action in the classroom and the proposals to cast middle managers in the role of the controller of teacher quality. It was clear to all that the headteacher and the senior management team were trying to inform the school's discourse by seeking teachers' views on the principles and practice of teaching in exchange for an acceptance, by teachers, of the need for a school view of good teaching practice. The school appeared to be moving towards quality assurance and away from OFSTED's preoccupation with quality control. The investigation will be examining the school's claims for the transformation of teaching.

MOVING THE SCHOOL FORWARD AFTER INSPECTION

An overview of the investigation suggests that there is no single recipe for achieving the transformation of the seven schools. Those headteachers who were dependent on managerialist tactics, including OFSTED inspection, to prompt change and who came to believe that the school's version of managerialism was the lingua franca of reform, soon found that teachers had absorbed the language of reform but not the substance. This was most evident in matters which were affected by teachers' core beliefs. It appeared that those headteachers who were aware that they could lead the school through a clearly articulated school discourse had seen a need to recouple the various views about management and teaching. Their actions were persuading teachers to review their own thinking about a range of key ideas underpinning good teaching practice. For their part, the headteachers had begun the process, moving away from notions of control which have influenced the development of their initial ideas on school management. It remains to be seen if this is to be translated into real reform.

10

Inspection and the School Improvement Hoax

PETER LONSDALE AND CARL PARSONS

INTRODUCTION

This chapter fundamentally questions the ability of OFSTED to fulfil its mission of 'improvement through inspection'. There are three grounds for asserting this, and the intentional lack of transparency is the justification for calling it a hoax. First, the position occupied by OFSTED in the educational administrative and political structures of England and, with small differences, Wales, and the remit given it by DfEE, render the inspection process illegitimate and disqualifies the agency itself from playing a supportive and developmental role. Secondly, the content of reports and the reporting requirements, as set out in the handbook for inspection, are oppositional in character despite their claim to represent best practice and high standards. Thirdly, the stretched chain of responsibility – from national government to school – and the purposely emasculated mediating potential of the LEA make the exercise of school inspection one of improvement through threat and fear, an intentionally disciplining role.

Evidence is drawn from the experience of five schools which drew up their action plans after their inspections. Their experience of the action planning required by OFSTED soon after the inspection, and reflections on the impact of that action planning two years later (autumn 1997), provide a longer-term view of development inspired by inspections of this type in this sociopolitical context. In particular the investigation focused on issues identified by the inspection and the extent to which improvements in the schools could be attributed to the inspection. This is part of a broader set of inquiries into the bases of the OFSTED inspection programme (see Field *et al.*, 1998). The final conclusion reached in this study is that this accountability model of school inspection is consonant with the created environment of individualism and 'marketisation', and it is an official deceit to claim an improvement agenda or effect.

A POLITICISED BACKGROUND

OFSTED inspection has been in full swing in both primary and secondary schools since September 1994. 'Improvement through inspection' has been a catch-phrase OFSTED has attached to the whole enterprise; indeed, the corporate plan produced in 1993 had this as its subtitle. It is, therefore, appropriate to ask if the process lives up to its mission. Huge amounts have been written about it already (Gray and Wilcox, 1995a; *Cambridge Journal of Education*, Vol. 25, no. 1, 1996; Earley *et al.*, 1996b; Ouston *et al.*, 1996a).

There are two background matters which are of particular interest before setting out the methodology and findings of this study. First, there is the interesting paradox, not unusual in the development of government policy, that much time and documentation were earlier devoted to promoting the notion of schools producing their *own* development plans as a consequence of the diagnosis of their *own* needs. Two publications (DES, 1989; 1991) and considerable in-service work went into promoting this voluntaristic approach to institutional development now superseded, and thus devalued, by the imposition of the blanket OFSTED process. Secondly, though there has been no overt participation in this movement from the DES/DfE/DfEE, the whole quality movement has infiltrated school management. Numerous publications have recommended and illustrated the practice of quality improvement (Parsons, 1994), total quality management (TQM) (West-Burnham, 1992; Sallis, 1993) and the management of change (Fullan, 1991). A key message from the industrial and academic quality assurance corner is that inspection as a quality-control measure occurs too late in the production of a product or the delivery of a service; it is processes earlier in the enterprise which need to receive support and attention. With the intrinsic antipathy between external, hierarchical inspection on the one hand and TQM, the school effectiveness and school improvement movements on the other, it is naive of HMI Frost (1995, p. 3) to write: 'no serious mention of inspection is made in the literature on school effectiveness. Even more emphatically does the literature on total quality management (TQM) eschew the notion of inspection'.

Inspection is regarded as a punitive process unlikely to motivate workers to achieve higher standards; quality gurus are strident in their recommendations for a supportive, developmental and threat-free approach to quality improvement. Fullan (1991) suggests that support without pressure leads to waste and pressure without support leads to stress. Serious questions are begged about whether support and encouragement to move forward – the carrot – are present in the inspection process and whether, despite the rhetoric, it was ever intended that they should be there.

A related question is about where accountability for, and democratic control of, education and education improvement now lie (Ball, 1996). The distinctiveness of the new public management in education is delineated by Bottery (1996, p. 183) and affects teacher autonomy through specific policies amongst which are performance indicators, content control, tightened and targeted resourcing and quality assurance. The OFSTED inspection process is part of this and its impact can be analysed in terms of *distance*, *purpose* and *morality*.

Distance

The new public management (Bottery, 1996; Clarke and Newman, 1997), hived off agencies, subcontracting and targeting in a marketised, 'informing the public' environment, have attenuated the link between government policy and school and classroom practice. There is a sense of 'remote control' (Hoggett, 1994) and insulation from blame on the part of government and government departments. The DfEE has been privileged in this way, and continues to be so under the new government. Distance, and levels of insulation, are laid out in Figure 10.1.

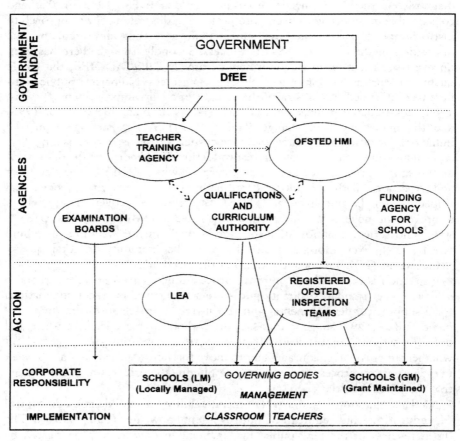

Figure 10.1. Mapping school inspection in the new management of education

The distance is evident in government operating through the DfEE to mandate OFSTED which subcontracts to inspection teams which work on schools. Other potential centres of (relatively) autonomous power have been brought firmly under department rule or emasculated: the Teacher Training Agency (TTA) has functions once performed by the National Advisory Board (NAB); the School Curriculum and Assessment Agency/Qualifications and Curriculum Agency can be traced back to the Schools Council with its control dispersed amongst government, LEAs and teacher unions; LEAs have seen their funding and power greatly diminished by grant-maintained schools, local management (LMS) and the requirement to devolve a minimum of 85 per cent of the education budget to schools. The DfEE sets the curriculum, assessment framework and inspection criteria, and schools, as individualised entrepreneurial units, must respond. Consultation has been minimal and schools are subject to control and direction. The dotted lines crossing the diagram are dividing lines of varying permeability. Between classroom teachers and management there is more exchange and negotiation than between school and OFSTED inspection teams. Higher, the divides have further strength in establishing distance, filtering, isolating responsibility, empowering the higher entities and disempowering those below (see Figure 10.1).

Purpose

The purpose of this structure can be read most easily as establishing a non-negotiable, deprofessionalising accountability system, punitive in intent and practice ('naming and shaming'), driving up standards by fear. It excludes teachers' claims to valid collective judgement, and the surveillance by inspection teams from the outside has prompted greater monitoring within schools by senior management. Examples given later show schools fulfilling requirements without judging that this is useful. There are also profound messages about impotence and fear in the face of future inspections.

The idea of driving up standards is aggressive and does not bring with it a sense of support and joint effort in what can be seen as an increasingly difficult job with young people. As discussed above, numerous writers have held forth on the most successful methods of bringing about improvement, and inspection is not a prime tool.

Morality

Morality is used broadly here to include the way people are defined and valued, particularly the 'workers'. The morality is now devoid of collective principles save those of compliance and competition. To misuse Ball's (1997) polarities, we witness social efficiency supplanting social justice and critical discourse overridden by incorporated simplicities. Partnership has been replaced by competition and a professional community riven by segments of the education workforce hired to be the paid inspection force, the prime instrument of a punitive accountability machine. The imposition of the surveillance regime is itself given as proof of the legitimate lack of trust and as a justification for silencing teachers' voices in educational debate.

The arrangements established have sought primarily to disempower and subordinate professionals, 'police' the work being done and enable a punitive response to schools which the market alone cannot deliver. Were improvement the prime goal, colleagueship would be retained, dialogue would be ongoing, and the inspection process itself would offer 'solutions' rather than 'issues' and empower front-line professionals, not induce fear.

The system is all stick and no carrot. To extend Cerny's (1990) notion of the architecture of politics, it is evident that the OFSTED inspection process is part of a 'policy architecture' such that, no matter what the claims made for it, its purposes are coherently built into a much larger edifice, the hierarchical, non-negotiable, distrustful, deprofessionalising new public management.

QUESTIONING THE RATIONALE FOR THE OFSTED INSPECTION PROCESS

From its inception the clear purpose of OFSTED was to 'improve the quality of education offered and raise the standards achieved by the pupils'. The inspection report should 'communicate effectively... the emphasis throughout should be on judgements and evaluation' (OFSTED, 1993/6a, pp. 16–17). A later document states: 'The central purpose of the report is to identify the strengths and weaknesses of a school, the overall quality of education provided, the standards pupils are achieving, and what should be done if improvements are needed' (OFSTED, 1994e, p. 8).

The muted yet still punitive tenor of the above confirms a perception most people have, both within and outside education, that OFSTED's prime *raison d'être* is 'sorting out difficult schools'. To date they have been successful in highlighting schools that are having difficulties. In these 'special measures schools' or 'schools giving grounds for concern' rapid changes have occurred. An OFSTED inspection passing this judgement cannot be ignored by governors.

Laar (1996, p. 24), himself a registered inspector, writes: 'Inspection carried out by skilled professionals can be a positive force, enhancing the performance of teachers, and thus the education of pupils, and improving public understanding. For those who do it well – the majority – inspection is a worthy occupation.' Earlier phrases he uses about 'informer' and 'collaborating with the enemy' are nearer the mark. Kogan (1986) long ago emphasised the necessity of a personal and emotional commitment to the accountability system if it was to be meaningful and productive in terms of improvement. That has not been sought, nor is it forthcoming, in the accountability imposed through the OFSTED inspection system. It is a mark of professionals that they have some control over their work lives, that their expertise is recognised in the execution of their work and that motivation is intrinsic because of this. The idea of a vocation is underpinned in part by the more general respect that these features bring. Inspection brings a lack of trust which Richards (1997, p. 7) refers to in his damning judgement:

> The very large sums given to OFSTED and taken away from local authorities are part of the enormous price central government has had to pay for not trusting the education service... The size of the sums devoted over the last decade to assessment, inspection and regulation rather than to educational development beggar belief.

Power's (1997) analysis of the 'audit society' points both to the cost of the 'regulatory state' and to the fact that inspection does not solve the problem of trust so much as displace it. Teachers are demeaned by the lack of trust placed in them, their judgements have been comprehensively usurped and the nature of the job of teaching has been stripped of its complexity. Gilroy and Wilcox (1997, p. 3) write of 'OFSTED's naive nineteenth century belief in the ability "objectively" to observe facts'. This, and other theoretical problems, are ignored with the result that 'the practical act of judgement by OFSTED is disguising very real practical problems that are generated by them [the theoretical problems] and to which OFSTED and its inspection teams seem oblivious' (ibid., p. 35). The imposition of an incontestable framework is part of the distance, the subjugation of a public service ethic and the relegation in prestige of front-line educational professionals. The very architecture of inspection is like a criminal trial without counsel for the defence and where the best hope is for an acquittal.

METHODOLOGY

Five schools were visited following an examination of their inspection reports. These schools consisted of three secondary schools, one primary and one infant school. Two of the schools were in county LEAs, two in London and one in a metropolitan LEA. The inspection reports were largely satisfactory and none indicated a school which was failing or with serious weaknesses. The reports themselves were analysed and the action plans were examined. Interviews were carried out in the five schools with the headteacher, governors and, in secondary schools, with a selection of heads of department. In all, 19 interviews were conducted.

The analysis of the first set of interviews sought to determine the benefits and costs to the school of the inspection experience. In particular it sought to identify the action plan points that had arisen as a direct result of inspection and to find out whether there had indeed been 'improvement through inspection'. Table 10.1 sets out in abbreviated form the inspection issues for the five schools and each school's reactions to the issues. The second set of interviews took place two and a half years later. These were intended as a longer-term follow-up from the inspection with the intention of finding out if, with the lapse of time, a more considered and perhaps positive view of the inspection process emerged. Respondents were quickly drawn to report their views on the next inspection.

Table 10.1   OFSTED inspection key issues for action and school impact

OFSTED inspection issues	Identified prior to inspection	Subsequently in the action plan	OFSTED highlighting of issue felt to be helpful to the school
School 1: Secondary			
1) Maintain the present thrust of policies that are proving successful	Yes	?	No
2) Articulate more clearly key areas for future development	?	?	No
3) Undertake review of post-16 provision and other aspects of curricular organisation with a view to reducing the amount of teaching time lost	Yes	Yes	Yes
4) Extend the monitoring of the development of finance and resources...	No	Yes	No
5) ... meet the requirements for collective worship	Yes	No	No
6) Take action on the health and safety issues identified in the report	Yes	Yes	No
7) Continue the good start made to implementing policy for pupils with SEN	Yes	Yes	No
School 2: Infants			
1) Provide a richer range of teaching strategies matched to pupils' different abilities...	Yes	Yes	No
2) Identify areas of existing good practice in teaching and learning and incorporate those throughout the school	Yes	Yes	No
3) Develop a more rigorous and consistent approach to assessment ...	Yes	Yes	Yes
4) Further develop the skills of middle management to improve curriculum monitoring	Yes	Yes	Yes
5) Monitor and improve the co-ordination of opportunities available across the curriculum which provide for PSE	Yes	Yes	Yes
6) Address the provision of a daily act of collective worship and the requirement to provide an annual review of statements of SEN	Yes	Yes	No
7) Undertake the targets in the school development plan relating to the improvement of the learning environment	Yes	Yes	No
School 3: Secondary			
1) Plan for the further development of the skills that support individual inquiry and study	No	Yes	Yes
2) Extend current good practice in matching work closely to pupils' abilities and in responding to pupils' work by giving specific subject feedback to them	Yes	Yes	No
3) Raise standards of achievement in geography Key Stage 3	Yes	Yes	Yes
4) Refine schemes of work especially in those subjects...	No	Yes	Yes

OFSTED inspection issues	Identified prior to inspection	Subsequently in the action plan	OFSTED highlighting of issue felt to be helpful to the school
5) Support departmental teams in evolving their practice with reference to the above	?	?	?
School 4: Primary			
1) Establish procedures to share and develop existing good practice identified in this report	?	?	?
2) Extend the learning opportunities for more able pupils	No	Yes	Yes
3) Clarify and define management roles to achieve a unified structure...	No	?	?
4) Make better use of existing procedures for assessment to inform curriculum planning	No	Yes	No
5) Develop formal strategies for evaluating standards of achievement across the curriculum	No	Yes	No
6) Produce a policy on sex education and ensure that religious education is included in the pupils' annual reports	Yes	Yes	No
7) Review communications with parents and arrangements for parent and teacher consultations	Yes	Yes	No
School 5: Secondary			
1) The achievements of pupils with high ability often less than satisfactory. The headteacher and staff should consider how this situation can be improved	No	Yes	Yes
2) Set a realistic timescale for the admission of all subjects into the SDP and how the role of co-ordinators can be developed to ensure the benefits of planning can be translated into classroom delivery...	Yes	Yes	No
3) Organisation of teaching groups should be reviewed by the headteacher and staff to establish curriculum access through greater differentiation of work Consideration should also be given to the desirability of in-class support for reception teachers	Yes	Yes	No
4) The headteacher should consider the benefits which an effective senior management team can bring to the school...	Yes	Yes	Yes
5) The governors should consider adopting a financial and planning strategy which also looks to the medium and longer term	Yes	Yes	Yes
6) The headteacher and governing body should seek to establish written policies and procedures in those areas where they do not exist	Yes	Yes	Yes
7) The governing body and headteacher have done much to develop parental involvement in the school: this is a strength and efforts should continue to develop further links with parents	Yes	Yes	No

Only four of the five schools agreed to participate in this second stage; the fifth school had a new headteacher from whom no response could be obtained. Seven people were interviewed on this occasion, one by telephone. Six had been interviewed in the original study. Data from this set of interviews supported an analysis which allocated comments to categories related to distance, purpose and morality; it offered a tentative test of the operation of the new public management in education. Table 10.2 presents abbreviated and categorised responses.

FINDINGS

The findings from the analysis of the first set of interviews are reported under headings which relate to the potential for a supportive process. These focus ultimately on the key issues in the inspection report and the action plan, how instrumental the inspection was in identifying them and how helpful the inspection team's involvement was. The intention was to analyse the follow-up interviews in a similar way but there were surprises in what people offered in the interview which were much less a considered reflection on the past inspection event and its products and more a judgement of the process and relationships in the previous and impending inspection. This actually facilitated an analysis related to distance, morality and purpose.

The empowering report

One school in particular felt that their OFSTED report, notably when inspectors had exceeded their remit, had been a useful tool in their dealings with the LEA. To quote from one OFSTED report: 'leadership and organisation at a senior level are good, financial planning has responded extremely effectively to the increasing constraints of the budget, there is little scope for further economy, the current level of resourcing is restricting the development of necessary learning opportunities.' The headteacher found this comment 'very supportive': 'The report put things into context and it helped us in dealing with the LEA afterwards.' Another member of staff reported that 'For the first time people who knew what they were talking about came in and said what a really good job we were doing, I felt valued'. There were examples of teachers unsure of their own performance, very concerned before OFSTED, feeling a major sense of reassurance afterwards in knowing they were doing the right thing in the right way.

Planning and management

Four of the schools visited felt that their planning process was more than adequate and had been unaffected by OFSTED. In one school, however, where there was not a tradition of planning, major improvements came about: 'we had little to show in terms of long term planning before, therefore it helped us to develop and

Table 10.2   Impact of OFSTED on the school three to four years later

Impact	Main comments
School 1: Secondary	
Distance/morality (waste)	'I feel more strongly than ever that this [OFSTED inspection] was a waste of money.'
Purpose/morality	'We did have a lack of teaching documentation, but did we really need all this? We certainly did not need OFSTED to tell us.'
Morality	'Head and deputy took early retirement, though latter returned in a different [part-time] role.
Morality (fear)	'Everyone is desperately worried about the next inspection.'
School 2: Infant	
Purpose (devolved surveillance)	'The school now has an LEA inspection every other year to look at particular aspects.'
Distance/purpose	'OFSTED changed the nature of the development plan, gave us different priorities, even if we didn't agree with them.'
Distance/morality	'OFSTED always wanted to have something wrong . . . they would look for criticisms.'
Morality (fear)	'Sometimes dreads the prospect of the next inspection because of personal pride and the recollection of the enormous stress on herself and her colleagues last time.'
Morality(damage)	'It was extremely difficult to get the staff up and running again, [after the inspection] so in fact the school lost a year's impetus.'
Morality (fear)	'So much work, so much tension. Personally it was traumatic.'
School 3: Secondary	

This school had a new head and wanted nothing to do with any review of inspection under a previous regime.

Impact	Main comments
School 4: Primary	
Primary	'In the short term it had an effect; in the long term it will have little effect.'
Distance/purpose	'We know the problems, we do not need anybody to highlight them.'
Purpose/morality	'It [OFSTED inspection] could be done much better – criticism with help would be useful.'
Morality (fear)	'We are all more apprehensive now. Now you know what to expect, it's going to be worse than it was before.'
School 5: Secondary	
Distance/morality (surprise, non-negotiable judgement)	'Just learnt that a statistical trawl by OFSTED had put the school onto the "at risk" register; two departments had fallen below the required percentage of "satisfactory-or-better" lessons. There had been no warning of this.'
Distance (powerlessness/predictability)	The head felt he could write the OFSTED action plan now and saw the new OFSTED inspection framework as more hostile.
Purpose(devolved surveillance)	LEA inspection making a more positive and constructive contribution to the school.
Purpose	All points on the action plan had been fulfilled.
Purpose (compliance)	'All it did was to highlight things we already knew, and give some impetus.'
Morality (fear)	Senior member of staff seeking to leave (early retirement): 'I will not go through another OFSTED.'

to prioritise'. Even when it did not lead to major changes in the way planning was carried out it did lead to a re-prioritisation: 'It made us emphasise and prioritise the qualities of teaching and learning. The staff probably saw no difference but they were sharper. It made us tie up loose ends and get things finalised'.

One school appreciated the help in instigating the planning process. In another, 'we have had a management plan for a very long time, the action plan has nothing that we were not already doing. They really had to look for things to say'. Other research has shown (Earley *et al.*, 1996b) that headteachers and governors tend to be more positive than staff. Almost all staff interviewed felt that the reports were too superficial and that many of the key issues in schools were missed: 'We expected it to pick up a lot of things that were not right but it didn't – it was just a paper exercise – OFSTED were blinded by paper.'

Most schools are already committed to the process of short and long-term planning and the question arises as to the effect of OFSTED inspections on a normal planning routine. If OFSTED enhances planning, which it can do in schools which are at the very beginning of the process, what is the effect on schools which already have a detailed planning cycle, who are clear about priorities, who are working to goals agreed in consultation with all the staff? A governor of a primary school, speaking of the action plan, felt 'it was a useful tool to have on the wall'. In this school no long-term planning had taken place before. In another primary school the inspection led to a change in priorities and this had had negative effects: 'We changed our priorities so that we had to put other things on the back burner.' Almost all headteachers felt there was some value in an objective process of inspection. In any organisation the small uncomfortable things are often left. As one headteacher said: 'It did force us to finish a number of tedious, non-crucial tasks.'

One of the common themes in many OFSTED reports has been the improvement of the management skills of heads of department. As one head said: 'it helped us move the heads of department to appreciate their wider role as management.'

The developmental power of informal feedback

The universal comment which was common across all schools and at all levels was the fact that by far the most useful parts of the inspection process were the informal exchanges. The depth and frequency of these comments differed widely from one inspection team to another and within the inspection team itself.

One governor said: 'the only useful parts were when the inspectors went beyond their brief, discussed issues with us and gave advice.' A headteacher said the only useful part was the informal feedback when they did suggest some improvements. A head of department reported that 'the off-the-record comments were far more valuable than the report itself'. All the schools felt that the inspection teams had worked hard, 'They gave the taxpayer value – questioning everything, looking into all the teachers' cupboards', even if they felt the resulting report was superficial.

Professional friends

Relationships are crucial in the inspection process and teachers' perceptions of inspectors were varied (Brimblecombe *et al.*, 1996). In one school the inspection team were described as 'one in a hundred, a model inspection team, collaborative, supportive of the school, they came in and treated us with trust and respect'. Other schools did not necessarily share these sentiments, but all felt their teams had been rigorous with one headteacher claiming, 'we couldn't pull the wool over their eyes'. Having to justify everything clearly sharpened people's minds, 'It compelled us to focus on making good practice comprehensible to other people' (head of department).

The stress and disruption of inspection

During the week of the inspection and in the run-up, OFSTED had the effect in all schools of uniting the staff, producing what was referred to effectively as a 'Dunkirk' mentality. The importance of the role of the headteacher and senior management has been stressed in preparing the staff and pupils for inspection (Brimblecombe *et al.*, 1996). In some cases the bonding seemed to work, in others it was counterproductive: 'The inspector and the LEA adviser came in to talk to us to prepare us. Instead it put fear of God into us. After they had these meetings there was a real panic.' One senior management team arranged a series of preparatory meetings to equip the staff for the inspection and to defuse the tension. The effect was the opposite: 'Preparing us with lots of meetings increased the pressure and the stress. The headteacher went round the school like Clive Dunn saying, "Don't panic! Don't panic!". He was in a terrible state.' More critical than staff morale and stress was the fact that the normal life of the school came to a stop during at least the previous term. In one primary to be inspected at the end of November all Christmas preparations were delayed so that the school appeared to be serious.

The OFSTED inspection week is bound to disrupt any school. Afterwards there was an almost universal sensation of anti-climax: 'There was a lot of long term illness, some never recovered, some have been off school ever since.' 'One teacher left shortly afterwards, it was not just this but OFSTED was the final straw.' 'Shortly after two staff went off with long term sickness and have not returned. Both are first class teachers and got A1 reports but just couldn't cope with the stress.'

Normal school life was disrupted for a period of at least three months: 'It took four to five months for the school to get back to normal, it became so obsessed with administration that teaching suffered.' 'The effect afterwards was a total anti-climax. I wanted to bring in some innovations into the Sixth Form but the staff were simply not interested – such a reaction is not normal in this school.' Not only was this due to the cumulative effect of the pressure of the build-up and the panic of inspection week but also to the report itself and the feedback. Feedback is given in all cases to the headteacher and the senior management team. This is appreciated and one of the most valuable parts of the process. However, at the time of the research, relatively little feedback was given to teachers, though all teachers value direct feedback (OFSTED, 1994a, p. 26). As one teacher said when interviewed: 'No one ever even told us it was a good report; you're the first person to actually say that.' In one school when the report came out, 'They all looked for the negative, they felt demoralised and devalued. Afterwards I was devastated and needed anti-depressants.' A point made by Field *et al.* (1998) is that 'the language of reports is stylised and restrictive, operating largely within the parameters of assessment and accountability'.

Action plans

The OFSTED key issues for action for the five schools are reproduced in Table 10.1 in a necessarily abbreviated form. Columns 2, 3 and 4 indicate the school's reaction to each issue. Table 10.3 below summarises each school's reactions to the inspection issues.

Table 10.3   Issues in the action plan and school responses

School	No. of key issues	No. identified prior to inspection	No. subsequently in the action plan	No. where OFSTED highlighting of the issue was felt to be helpful
1	7	5	4	1
2	7	7	7	3
3	5	2	3	3
4	7	5	5	1
5	7	7	7	4
Total	33	26	26	12

Three quarters of the issues were identified by the school before the inspection. In relation to a third of the issues it was judged helpful that OFSTED had highlighted them. The main reason seems to be the impetus to action the report may have given. This does not point to a high return from the inspection effort and expense in relation to improvement and the action plan. In one school the action plan was done by the headteacher alone: 'No progress has been made on the action plan. I wrote it myself to meet the needs of the exercise and have since given it no further thought.' In another school it was reported: 'Our action plan has been a non-event.' Not only are schools asked to draw up action plans at a time when many people are uninterested, 'there is no real motivation', 'the staff were not interested, they were exhausted', but also at a time when most successful schools should be celebrating – the action plan makes people concentrate on the negative: 'I could not motivate the staff, they saw absolutely no point in the action plan.' In four of the schools there were staff who felt that the key points in the inspection report were trivial and that the whole process was debased.

In one school (see Table 10.1, school 1) a key issue 'Maintain the present thrust of policies that are proving successful' was officially answered by 'The governing body was reassured to learn that the inspectors had given such a clear endorsement of the range of ongoing developments'. Another key issue, 'Articulate more clearly the key area for future development' elicited the response: 'The governing body takes the view that to articulate areas for future development is not at all meaningful until it moves into a time scale extending beyond the present year's budget cycle.' Another: 'To undertake a strategic review post 16 provision and other aspects of curricular organisation' received the response: 'This school carries out a review of post 16 provision each year.' Another 'Take steps to meet the requirements for collective worship' was dismissed as follows: 'The governing body is keeping this difficult and sensitive issue under regular review.' In the above instance, inquiring whether OFSTED had accepted the last comment, the headteacher had asked the OFSTED inspector what steps he would advise and was told: 'I am asking you to take steps, I am not telling you what steps or in which direction to take them!'

In most of these schools, governors seemed not to have played a particularly active role in this part of the inspection. Though O'Connor (1996, p. 151) reports in her research, 'With only one exception governors had been involved in the action planning', and Earley (this volume) discusses the potential for greater governor involvement, the initial findings of Ouston et al. (1996b, p. 115) mirror those reported here. The general feeling from the governors interviewed in this study was support for the school and great scepticism about OFSTED: 'In our action plan, in a polite way, we rejected their findings. So what – what are they going to do? – throw out all the governors?' 'My view afterwards was "what was all the fuss about?" We don't need another of these.' Others clearly felt that OFSTED was an inspection to find out what was wrong. Many accepted that there were some shortcomings within the school, but resented the idea that inspectors were coming in to tell them about these.

MATURE REFLECTIONS

The lapse of time did not lead schools to a more favourable view of OFSTED inspections. Heads felt removed from, and disempowered by, a process which was without negotiation in judgements and without dialogue for solutions. The morality of the process was questioned in terms of waste, personal and institutional damage and most particularly, fear. The purpose, in terms of improvement, was not evident. The main comments are presented in Table 10.2. The data can only illustrate the thesis that the policy architecture is such that the process of inspection by OFSTED teams is distancing, subjugating and amoral, an experience it is dangerous to impose on those we wish to exercise professionalism (commitment, internalised standards, self-policing etc.).

Distance is evidenced by the perceived imperviousness of the system to teachers' views. It was done *to* them. It was 'a waste' (school 1), 'changed the nature of the development plan' (school 2) and schools claim to know their problems (schools 4 and 5).

The schools view negatively the OFSTED inspection purpose of making them do things they know they need to do, and even more so when it requires action they see as unnecessary (school 1). LEA inspections have been stimulated and judged helpful (schools 2 and 5) but mostly schools want help and advice to be coupled with the criticism.

Morality is interpreted broadly here involving respect for fellow professionals. The mentions of negative personal impact, early retirement and damage to morale are striking in number. 'Desperately worried' (school 1), 'traumatic' (school 2), 'apprehensive' (school 4) are amongst phrases applied freely by heads in respect of the last inspection, or that to come in around a year.

The effects are built into, not accidental consequences of, the process.

ASSESSING THE ASSESSORS

The action plan is the key element of OFSTED's approach to improvement. To produce this crucial plan in 40 days at a time when staff morale is low and often staff illness is high, denigrates the whole idea of having staff working together in teams to plan for the future. To base this improvement on judgements made in a one-week visit to a school also seems naive. Many people interviewed said that continuous assessment rather than examination would provide a fairer image of what was happening: 'It would be better to have one person in for a longer time to get a more balanced picture.' It might also be better to concentrate on areas of weakness. There is a clear feeling that to separate the audit (the inspection) from any responsibility to rectify weaknesses is false and is something that industry turned its back on a long time ago: 'The inspection was no value at all; we either knew it already or it was beyond our resources. It is important that inspectors don't just say what is wrong and walk away, they must be responsible for putting things right' (a governor who had worked extensively in training and personnel in industry). Many people in education feel, with some justification, that they know what is wrong with their schools. The present system of development planning, highlighting areas of weakness and how to overcome those weaknesses leads staff to bring their self-critical faculties into a formal setting: 'If we had the money we could identify areas of weakness and concern and get consultants in to report on them and then put them right. That's the sort of thing we are already doing. We don't need a sledgehammer to crack every nut.'

At a time of declining resources it would appear that to concentrate all the resources on areas of weakness would be more in line with current thinking. Similarly in successful schools money for inspection, anywhere between £15,000 and £40,000, could be devolved to schools which could focus this on areas of weakness. It is sometimes hard for a school governing body in a 'successful school' to justify spending £17,000 on an external inspection when two of the classrooms are empty because there are holes in the roof. The split between the inspection and positive action is also an area of concern. In most industries inspectors also have a responsibility for the maintenance of standards. OFSTED now are clearly stating publicly what is wrong. The past failure of LEAs to address the issue of failing schools and to deal with them in an effective way has actually led to the birth of OFSTED itself.

CONCLUSIONS

The perceptions of the governors, teachers, headteachers and senior managers interviewed differed widely depending on the nature of the school, the nature of the inspection and the nature of their role. Reportedly, in schools with little systematic planning, poor evaluation and monitoring, OFSTED provided valuable impetus. In some 'failing' schools it has finally highlighted deficiencies and put huge pressure on LEAs to rectify the situation. In the vast majority of schools which are successful, OFSTED has caused considerable disruption to the normal life of the school. In the lead-up, during it and afterwards the effect of the inspection upon staff and pupils has been dramatic. In many cases it has disrupted the day-to-day routines of the school, the long-term planning process and the process of assessment and evaluation. The result has been to produce bland and superficial reports invariably making statements about collective worship, about differentiation and generalised issues that most teachers in the school could probably have highlighted.

Major deficiencies in schools were missed by the inspection team while they reported issues that were common to almost all schools. In a time of shortage of resources (or at any time), should money be spent on a process that causes as much disruption as benefit? Teachers and governors have stressed that schools are already on the road to self-evaluation and have a culture to carry out real changes through long-term processes owned by teachers, senior managers and governors. The action planning necessitated by the OFSTED inspection was of little consequence with over three quarters of the issues already identified by the school and only a little over a quarter helpfully highlighted by OFSTED. Finally, the future of OFSTED must be to concentrate on areas of known weakness, either across all schools or in specific schools, and to focus resources into the formative process of school development in partnership with schools and the LEAs. The present process is subjugating, demeaning and deprofessionalising.

11

School Improvement or School Control? Teachers' Views on the Long-Term Value of Inspection

NIGEL CROMEY-HAWKE

The claim that the public audit and benchmarking of educational quality upon a national throughput model can and should promote much needed school improvement has become central to political rhetoric and the very existence of OFSTED. 'Audit' and 'school improvement', 'league tables' and 'standards' have become commonplace and, some claim, commonsense notions within an educational arena widened by an information revolution and possibly market forces. Questions remain, however, of whether teachers themselves consider that OFSTED's much vaunted mission, 'improvement through inspection', is actually happening. Do teachers, as major players within this drama, think that improvement has been provoked or facilitated, particularly within schools not deemed to be obviously at risk?

This chapter reports on the first part of a research project tracking some 21 secondary schools (through postal surveying) and two out of four case-study investigations over the period since their original inspections in 1993/4. Ultimately there will be three stages to the project: baseline (1993/4), stage one (up to 1997) and stage two (up to the millennium). Teacher estimations of the extent to which practice has changed and professional values affected have so far been considered through the baseline stage and stage one of the project. Whether headteachers, senior management teams (SMTs), middle managers and classroom teachers with no other responsibilities have seen these forces as facilitating improvement has been probed. Apparent differences between these groups concerning the value and effect of inspection and its potential for conditioning definitions of schooling have been considered, as well as some group's willingness to attribute any real or potential change agency function to OFSTED.

PROBLEMS OF DEFINITION

First, there was the need to clarify some terms and establish some positions. What constitutes 'improvement' for the various stakeholders is central to such an investigation. Whilst every teacher in every school undoubtedly has his/her own view on this, some starting point for the investigation was thought necessary. Hillman and Stoll's (1994, p. 2) definition was thought sufficiently broad in declaring improvement to be 'the sustained and systematic quest for the enhancement of pupil learning, in which strategic planning, goal setting and the development of a learning culture for all enables the school to both absorb and react to the rapidity of change within the post-modern world'. Almost universal acceptance of this definition by all involved in the early states of the project resulted in its adoption as a working definition.

OFSTED's performance-oriented definitions of the quality to which that improvement aspires, however, have been acknowledged as often sitting uncomfortably with teachers. Many schools involved in process models of quality management such as Investors in People seem to have been looking to more qualitative indicators of local relevance. On the one hand, OFSTED's promotion of a cost-effective competitiveness in a cause-effect analysis of the process of schooling was, therefore, acknowledged as almost certainly insufficient to explain how schools themselves viewed improvement. On the other hand, the widespread acceptance by teachers of the OFSTED framework (1993/6b) itself as a comprehensive set of descriptors of effective teaching and learning was also important. The recognition by large sections of the teaching profession that the findings of their inspections were very largely valid also suggested a significant commonality such that both the framework and the inspection reports themselves could be used as a starting point for these teachers to begin talking about how they had worked towards school improvement. Therefore, whilst no inherent supremacy of the OFSTED model itself was being claimed, either in inspection or school improvement terms, having professed a general satisfaction with it as a catalogue of effective teaching and learning, how these schoolteachers and managers reacted to its application in their unique contexts, became the focus of the study.

THE EVIDENCE BASE

Baseline 1993/4 surveying of the 21 secondary schools revealed headteachers to be initially optimistic about the improvement potential of inspection. Stage one 1995/6 surveying then showed them claiming to have carried out some level of action on over 80 per cent of their inspection issues. This was not matched by their judgements on the impact these had had on practice. Claiming largely 'thorough' levels of implementation they had not, however, seen significant levels of whole-school change resulting by 1995/6. Believing that they and their SMTs had higher levels of awareness of OFSTED than other teacher groups, they also considered that their practice had been significantly affected by inspection rather than these other groups. They also claimed largely process and organisational changes to result from these actions, with individual teaching and learning activities remaining most unaffected. Representing 17 LEAs across the country and schools of most secondary types, it is likely that their responses evidenced the complexity of explaining change as much as the problems of relating inspection to improvement.

CASE-STUDY INVESTIGATIONS

The headteachers of the two case studies reported here exhibited opinions largely representative of the whole postal survey group. The views of these headteachers and those of their SMT, middle managers and classroom teachers with no other responsibility were then probed through extensive interviewing throughout stage one (1995/7). Each interviewee was asked how far OFSTED was still affecting his/her practice, to what extent it was still in his/her professional consciousness, and how far inspection had changed his/her school. Scales of 0 (low effects) to 5 (high effects), were utilised throughout.

Case study: school A

This was an 11–18 coeducational comprehensive with full community status in an inner-city location of considerable deprivation: 920 were on roll, making up a strong multicultural intake. Key issues identified in their 1993/4 inspection are presented in Table 11.1.

Table 11.1   Key issues identified in the inspection

Inspection issues	Headteacher's 1996 survey raw implementation score on 0–5 scale
Needs of the more able	3
Attendance	5
Post-16 efficiency	4
Teaching and learning strategies (TLS)	3
Information technology (IT)	3
Worship	0

Headteacher's views

Generally happy with the conduct and findings of the original inspection the headteacher, in post six months prior to OFSTED's 1993 visit, found the provision of its statutory change agenda very timely. In confirming his judgements about the school he felt initially enthusiastic that together his staff could work towards them. In five interviews with the head over the two years of stage-one fieldwork that enthusiasm had been tempered by the need to respond to other agendas (notably the gaining of full community status) and other demands. By nature very tenacious, he had pursued attendance monitoring through four successive short-term post-holders and expensive electronic recording of individual lesson registers. He felt the 3 per cent improvement over this time had been worth while, taking them up to OFSTED's 90 per cent figure (below which schools potentially trigger reinspection). As a strongly multicultural school he rejected the worship issue as unworkable and misdirected, but it had been debated at whole-school level. The needs of the more able had been addressed through further education liaisons, although little evidence could be given yet of improved outcomes. Post-16 efficiency had also been significantly improved *via* those networks. Although teaching and learning strategies (TLS) remained an area needing attention in his view, the more recent rapid turnover of staff had been instrumental in bringing new blood and ideas into the school. A new 'teaching code of practice' strong in pupil entitlement terms had resulted, but in the head's view had yet to impact upon practice.

This headteacher now considered inspection and the continuing existence of OFSTED to have real potential in school improvement terms, although he believed it was not perceived as such by either himself or his staff at the time of the original inspection (1993) or up to a year afterwards. The 'fashionable denigration' (his words) of OFSTED and his own belief in the need to seek validation for the issues in their own terms, not merely as OFSTED's requirements, led him consciously to eliminate 'inspection' and 'OFSTED' from all attempts to address these issues during the two years following inspection. Most recent 1997 interviewing, with reinspection looming and fears of falling into at least three of OFSTED's more recent criteria for the identification of failing schools (attendance, GCSE results and exclusions, – OFSTED, 1997d) revealed him to be regretful on the one hand that he had not more obviously used OFSTED earlier on as a direct tool in performance management terms, yet still convinced his more collegial approach was morally and professionally right. This was in a school perceived by its LEA, its community and through numerous national and international awards to be a beacon of comprehensive education within a very difficult inner city context.

The headteacher also considered that OFSTED's contribution to the wider performance management movement had been significant, but that earlier fears of its potential for conditioning definitions of schooling were now being addressed. He considered that SMT and governors now recognised its limited, not all-embracing, nature and as such valued it, perversely, more rather than less as they used it as just one of an increasing number of evaluative mechanisms. He was already adopting a less passive attitude to reinspection and endeavouring to reculture his staff into this view also. They had been encouraged to think of themselves as near as possible equally in charge of the process as the inspectors, where they would clearly present their views of what constituted effective schooling and how they went about achieving it. His responses to the 1996/7 survey reflected this deliberate and overt focusing upon OFSTED as one means towards improvement, with middle managers playing a vital role in putting ideas into classroom practice.

Senior management team

The deputy head (curriculum) and senior teacher (achievement) interviewed over 1996/7 had contrasting views over the actual effects of inspection, although both agreed upon its potential for facilitating improvement. The curriculum deputy was not impressed with its cost-effectiveness, considering the sums of money involved would have been more productively used in improving the staffing of the school and providing resources for learning. The inspection told him nothing new, he claimed, but did make it easier to persuade governors to use £35,000 of the school's own budget for the expensive electronic attendance monitoring hardware, and staffing to monitor it. While the headteacher considered this money well spent, he did not. He personally thought OFSTED to be seriously conditioning definitions of schooling, but he 'accepted that that is the game being played in town and if I'm going to play it I had better be playing by their rules'. He clearly saw part of his 'game playing' role as moderating and filtering the influences of such forces as OFSTED upon classroom teachers and, to a lesser extent middle managers, so that they could concentrate upon the core tasks of teaching and learning. School improvement was, for him, very much a senior management rather than a specifically teaching activity. His improvement agenda was directed, for example, at 'cracking the culture that does not make possible the commonplace, positive mutual observation by colleagues of each other so that they can learn and keep on learning from their own practice'. OFSTED's own early activities seriously set this back, he thought, but he was hopeful that its recent apparently less draconian and impersonal image of recent months indicated a change for the better. As teachers became more familiar with it and OFSTED itself appeared to moderate and learn from its own practices, then respect, trust and eventually 'improvement through inspection' may result, he thought.

The senior teacher (achievement), perhaps because of the nature of her role, made more direct use within her work of both inspection findings and wider OFSTED pronouncements. Considering the school generally very well led, she acknowledged the major tasks on hand to be the reculturing of classroom teachers in particular, as well as pupils, into a more performance-oriented attitude, but accepted that this was often difficult to distinguish from notions of raw accountability in teacher performance terms. To this end the school had developed an achievement plan. This took the form of a three-year vision for the school against which specific annual school development plan (SDP) targets for middle managers were directed. The result of a weekend off-site INSET session for all SMT and middle managers, it had set performance goals which mirrored OFSTED's own categories. Attendance, academic achievement and cost-effectiveness all featured strongly, defined in relation to the school's own understanding of how school improvement related to their context. The Director of Achievement saw this as prompted by the headteacher, 'inevitably' (her words) driven by OFSTED, but declared herself personally and professionally comfortable with its underlying principles. Whilst recognising that it would not get anywhere near national figures for these categories, she saw Hillman and Stoll's (1994) notions of being systematic and sustained in any quest for improvement as essential. Recognising that the actual inspection findings of 1993/4 were, in her words, in many ways 'empty figures' and 'not specific enough', she valued the part OFSTED has played, albeit painfully, in contributing towards a wider awareness of performance management in schools.

Middle managers

The long-serving Head of Science had expressed strong views in the baseline interviewing about the whole process of inspection. Whilst impressed with its rigour he also found that it led to superficiality. In agreement with his subject's findings and those of the school as a whole, he felt little would actually change as a result, though, as (at the time of the research) advice, INSET or any other forms of resourcing were not tied to the inspection package. As a school improvement force he doubted its value then, a view more entrenched by the second round of interviewing in 1996/7. He considered the attempts made to implement the key issues by the SMT and headteacher to be noble, but inevitably doomed unless the wider culture of the school actually did become more performance orientated and wider social forces helped raise expectations of pupils. He matched the headteacher's scores on the extent to which OFSTED was in the professional consciousness of middle managers, but added that this was only because it had been forced into their professional world over the last two years, not otherwise. He also matched the headteacher's score of its effect on practice in relation to whole-school issues such as attendance, and at middle manager level in terms of systems, but thought it had had a limited impact on individual classroom practice.

Some similarity in views were represented through a Head of Arts and Leisure, in post since 1996, two and a half years after inspection. Having inherited well documented policy and action towards the inspection areas since 1994, she considered the school had been optimistic to the point of unrealism in its target-setting. 'It's not that the will's not there, or the organisation is not there – I don't know what OFSTED would make of this – but if you have got a difficult class you've got to have your own set of priorities first.' As a middle manager she had had problems sometimes, she said, in reconciling the vision, targets, policies, etc., of the school (valuable though they be) with what actually went on in practice, a view shared by other middle managers and teachers within the school. The need to respond constantly to complex and unique situations within any classroom and their teams, set within a context of high teaching loads, she claimed made it very difficult actually to reflect on inspecting findings.

Teachers

Teachers' responses to questions about the type and extent of implementation of inspection issues fell very much into the category of, as one put it, 'Well, we struggled for it and we tried, but [I] don't know how much good it's done'.

When asked why they acted upon any particular issue, responses were always in terms of their own professional judgements, not as a result of OFSTED. Both interviewees scored the extent of whole-school change as 3 on the 0–5 scale, as did their head. One of these two teachers considered the early inspections to be crude and now meaningless; both had accepted the head's lead in wanting to get more from it next time. They also scored themselves at 4 on the 0–5 scale for OFSTED being in their professional consciousness, although also said that this was due to their inner-city status, the butt of inspection attention they felt. Initial claims not to have acted on their key issues as a result of their statutory nature, but because they considered them valid, were later moderated. They both considered the headteacher's more open management style as more significant in bringing about school improvement though, by building transparency and teamworking. The simple introduction of regular middle manager and whole-staff meetings for the first time when he arrived was still one respondent's abiding memory. The other voiced the view that he was not surprised no greater levels of change or extent of implementation had been claimed. Until OFSTED started to value schools and teachers like himself through the inspection process, rather than continually denigrating them, individual morale and motivation would be low. OFSTED's attempts to facilitate this through recognising teacher excellence *via* individual scoring or banding of teaching quality were thought to be divisive, however. This teacher wanted what he termed the 'torrent of vilification' issued centrally by OFSTED to be compensated for by an equal if not greater celebration and praise, especially important in their context where already low pupil expectations and authority tolerances could sink even lower if the teachers who tried to uphold these values were themselves being repeatedly publicly shamed for apparent poor practice.

Case study: school B

This was an 11–16 coeducational split-site comprehensive, which has since moved to one site with some new buildings. There are 780 on roll in a large town, but within a new, small unitary LEA. Key issues identified in the 1993/4 inspection are given in Table 11.2.

Table 11.2 Key issues identified in the inspection

Inspection issues	Headteacher's 1996 survey raw implementation scores on a 0–5 scale
Religious studies	2
Worship	0
Special educational needs	5
Timetabling and pupil grouping	3
Assessment and marking	2
SDP linked to funding	5
Information technology	2

Headteacher's views

At the time of inspection this school was operating as a split-site 11–16 comprehensive, years 7–8 in run-down Victorian buildings one mile across town from the 1960s year 9–11 site. Following the staff as they commuted between double lesson blocks of a six-period day exhausted the inspection team, it was said! Showing a rapid improvement in all levels of results since 1987 from a very low base, the school was then acknowledged to be consistently in the top three of the large LEA's value-added calculations, although still below national average GCSE scores in most subjects. A long-serving headteacher very much saw the inspection as his swan-song, retiring 18 months afterwards, just as fieldwork in stage one was initiated. Under this original headteacher the SEN area was tackled first. For long having imposed a policy and structure considered outmoded by most others, including the LEA and the SMT, he appeared to have been virtually forced by the governors' and the curriculum deputy head's use of the inspection report, and the release of long anticipated legislation (the Code of Practice), to concede change. The incoming headteacher solicited the help of another member of the extant SMT, a senior teacher, to complete the 1996 survey and when interviewed revealed that he had originally accepted this senior teacher's view that this SEN action was wholly school and legislation driven, not attributed to inspection. His own investigations with the governing body since led him later to believe firmly they had been OFSTED prompted.

Whatever the stimuli, both the head and the senior teacher agreed that dramatic change had resulted. Since taking up post in September 1995, one and a half SDP cycles after the original inspection, this new headteacher had increasingly used the OFSTED criteria for effective teaching and learning within INSET presentations, SDP documentation and discussion. He considered the inspection itself to have provided a timely audit of the school prior to his appointment, but had deliberately not treated the resulting key issues as a recipe for improvement since.

Suffering from its pre-1987 poor image the school had long been struggling to have its value-added worth recognised in the community, rather than by just educational professionals. The headteacher considered the generally encouraging inspection report did much to raise teacher morale in this respect by providing national validation of its teaching quality. Indeed, these issues had not been revisited since the original burst of activity towards them in 1994/5 (hence their low implementation scores). He had seen improvement very much in terms of school culture and environment, and had tried to direct the school's energies into the move on to one site, with some £2.8million of new buildings, and the seeking of dual-use community status.

Agreeing with the baseline project's assessment of the school as very fragmented, even Balkanised (Hargreaves, 1994) up to 1995, he had been endeavouring to build a more open style of management and more teamworking as the basis for future improvement. Whilst acknowledging the inspection's very real effect in prompting change in such an extreme situation as

SEN at the school, and upon a technical aspect of SDP/finance, he felt that otherwise it had had little effect upon practice. He did consider, though, that the continued existence of OFSTED as a wider force had and would continue to have real effects upon schools. He saw it as now firmly embedded within the performance management movement evidenced most obviously through the *Excellence in Schools* white paper (DfEE, 1997a), just one of the 27 initiatives the school had had to respond to between June and October 1997. His aim was to build greater knowledge and acceptance of this movement (not just of OFSTED) amongst his staff. He was conscious of his responsibilities in seeing that the school obtained as good a report as possible should they visit again, but the original inspection issues carried little weight for him as the school had in the mean time simply changed so much as to make them largely irrelevant. To this end he had already highlighted within staff INSET and the SDP key areas such as attendance, exclusions and behaviour in terms of OFSTED's criteria for identifying failing schools – none of which featured as concerns in the original inspection report.

Senior management team

Since inspection the very active deputy head (curriculum) responsible for much of the immediate implementation of the action plan had left for his own headship. His successor, appointed almost coincidentally with the new head taking up post in 1995 therefore had to take up a report of an inspection neither he nor the head had actually experienced. This deputy features in other discussions of this project, and for the purposes of this account the extant members of the original inspected SMT are dealt with. New headteacher and SMT effects were obviously difficult, though, to disentangle from any inspection effects. Once again, however, the complex reality of schools having to initiate and sustain improvement efforts under such circumstances was felt to justify rather than negate their inclusion in the evidence base.

The two colleagues interviewed (out of the extant three inspected SMT) agreed on scores of 2 (on a 0–5 scale) for the overall extent of implementation of their key issues by 1997, and 2 (on a 0–5 scale) for overall change to the school. Of these two, the senior teacher (staff development) was clearly of the view that the school had changed mostly in structural ways, rather than in terms of staff values. The new headteacher's rather optimistic views on changes in IT had been moderated at his insistence in their joint 1996 survey submissions. Both he and his SMT colleague, a deputy head (pastoral), felt that practice in assessment and religious studies (and the wider issue of differential teacher performance identified by the new headteacher) had not noticeably improved either. Investors in People accreditation had been sought since the original inspection, but initial enthusiasm had waned and the initiative had largely collapsed. A once strong appraisal system, acknowledged by staff and the LEA to have been working well, had also lapsed during the headteacher and deputy interregnums and move to one site. Clearly of the view that they had had 'to keep things afloat' (deputy head, pastoral) during this time they both acknowledged potential for improvement within the inspection system, yet its limited effect upon them. The latter felt that the principles of systematic and sustained planning and evaluation implicit within the view of school improvement here were the very ones that had moved the school forward under the new headteacher. She saw an anachronistic situation though, where the school's popularity, location, buildings and exam performance had dramatically improved unrelated (except for SEN), in her view, to a significant part of the original inspection's findings.

Middle managers
Generally considering the school to have responded poorly to the inspection findings since 1993/4, the two heads of faculty interviewed gave lower scores (3) than the headteacher for OFSTED's continuing effect on their practice. The head's assessment of 3 for the extent to which inspection was still within their professional consciousness they both mirrored, one even thinking it slightly low. Like other schools, however, they would have given generally lower scores all round for such factors two years ago. This perhaps tailing off then renewal of interest was not characteristic, one head of faculty claimed, of other changes over the last decade, other than the existence of the National Curriculum itself. Whilst other initiatives had come and gone

> this one is sticking with us, despite a radical change in government – inspection has already moved beyond its immediate context of teacher and LEA bashing – a lot of us viewed it like that at the time of inspection, it was fashionable to ridicule it – it is coming of age now, though, it is maturing. I think it is emerging as a significant force in education.

Whilst not having actually implemented many of their key issues, both these middle managers felt that they ought to have responded generally better as a school. They could explain why they had not done more in very real terms of staffing, site upheaval and resourcing (the school had lost a split-site bonus of £90,000 from their annual budget). They recognised that as a school they would be held accountable within any reinspection for this limited improvement in terms of the inspection areas, and were anxious that their SMT and the headteacher present as good a case as possible to OFSTED should they return. The school was, after all, going from strength to strength in the perceptions of local community and, they were told, by its LEA.

Teachers
One of the teachers interviewed here found it hard to identify areas of real change other than with SEN that could be attributed to inspection, as so much else seemed to have happened since. The two most significant factors in facilitating school improvement were claimed to have been the move on to one site and the new headteacher. They separately rated OFSTED at level 3 in their

consciousness, though not level 2 as did their head. Like their middle managers they felt disappointed on the one hand that, looking back, only limited effects could be perceived as a result of inspection; but on the other both were relieved that more had not been thrown at them in pursuit of those issues at the time. One now claimed to relish the prospect of reinspection as a potential validation of the recent change and a benchmarking to facilitate future growth. When asked why action had been taken on specific issues in the past though, like those in school A, she responded in each case that it had been the result of her own professional judgements, not OFSTED's requirements.

The second teacher, newly in post in 1993/4 and having the opportunity of length of service punctuated by a period of maternity leave to look afresh at the institution when she returned, commented that whilst structures and processes (such as SEN, timing of the day, etc.) had changed, significant aspects of some SMT and individual teacher thinking and practice had not. Like the middle managers, she thought that until such differential performance was tackled, conflicting messages about expectations would continue to be sent to the pupils and parents and whole-school improvement would not really move forward. The demise of the aforementioned appraisal system and the 'failure' in her terms of the inspection system to facilitate such 'culling' of staff, were sources of great professional frustration to her.

GENERALISED FINDINGS

A significant factor emerging from the fieldwork investigation has been what can be termed 'denial'. In the early stages of interviews large numbers of respondents, other than the headteachers, had expressed clear and outright denial of any effects of these inspections upon their professional judgements or those of their teams. Despite claiming that OFSTED continued to have a noticeable place in their professional consciousness, most respondents had initially denied actually acting upon many issues as a result of OFSTED's identification of them. Interviews throughout early 1996 showed this particularly strongly amongst teachers and middle managers, but also some members of SMTs. The headteachers were clearly of the view that they were acted upon because of their statutory nature. This may, of course, be symptomatic of a lack of confidence by other than headteachers when faced with a largely unknown researcher. Some respondents did temper or reassess this initial rejection of OFSTED as a potential change force later on in the same interview. Such instinctive rejection of OFSTED seemed to extend to recognition of its use by schools in their own literature as well, though. Almost universally denied by SMT, middle managers and teachers right up to 1997, the reality showed the continued use of inspection quotations and data within school handbooks, job descriptions and marketing literature. The 1996/7 survey also showed heads acknowledging this use (34 per cent of them declaring such use within their marketing literature, 30 per cent within appointment literature and processes and 20 per cent in appraisal). Gentle production of the relevant documentation resulted in almost universal recognition that instinctive rejection, rather than simple forgetfulness, was likely to have been at work here. When asked to comment generally on this issue, all headteachers in all the case-study schools identified in various ways the culture of 'blame and shame' as a probable cause. For the two case studies described here this was a cause for concern as they particularly strove to build cultures of reflective practice as routes to improvement. For the head of school A it provided further evidence that his strategy of eliminating all references to inspection and OFSTED in what became an almost covert drive to fulfil the inspection action plan was a double-edged strategy, where public recognition of OFSTED's role within school improvement had to be balanced with notions of professional ownership and self-actualisation. As reinspection looms, it will be interesting to see if there are increases in the willingness and frequency with which 'inspection' and 'OFSTED' enter into discussions of school improvement, as opposed to simply inspection preparation within these groups.

Schools would thus seem to be claiming that they have acted on a wide range of their original inspection findings after two years, but this activity tailed off during the 1995/6 period three years from these inspections. A renewal of interest is apparent now, prompted by actual or potential reinspection. In relation to the baseline findings of 1993/4, staffing changes have resulted directly from inspection reports as was anticipated and in the case studies continue to do so. These more often than not take the form of internally awarded incentives to cover a specific area of responsibility related to an inspection issue. The expectations that the role of governors in influencing future change was likely to be limited is born out, with the exception of action on obvious or serious weaknesses. The baseline view of headteachers that little or no money would be directed at fulfilling OFSTED's key issues now seems largely true, again with notable exceptions for such obvious areas of concern. Other than a spate of activity immediately post-inspection, INSET has only recently been used to return to considering the original 1993 issues, almost certainly due to the likelihood of reinspection.

Headteachers and SMTs clearly considered themselves to be more conscious of OFSTED and inspection, almost certainly due to their management roles, but their perception of the place of OFSTED within the minds of their middle managers and teachers was often not one shared by these groups themselves. Middle managers and teachers considered they thought about this more than their senior colleagues gave them credit for, yet when asked to ascribe reasons for carrying out many improvement initiatives they rejected OFSTED and inspection as stimuli.

The sense of empowerment heads identified in their middle managers immediately following inspection (baseline data) was now considered by both headteachers and those middle managers to have largely gone. General dissatisfaction and a disappointment amongst the latter with what they perceive to be limited amounts of change and/or improvement seemed to be commonplace.

There was still general agreement that inspection could and should lead to school improvement, but in terms of Hillman and Stoll's (1994) definition, which was widely found acceptable, it had been the 'systematic' and 'sustained' elements that had been most problematic. Whilst the underlying principles of 'planning for performance' seem to have become more widespread through an increasingly pervasive and creative SDP movement, the actual inspection issues had often had limited effects, except in more obvious or extreme cases of concern. This had not been because they were devalued as potential routes to improvement, rather that schools felt that for a variety of reasons they had not been able to deal specifically with them. Rapid and radical change, the very intensification of teaching itself, alternative initiatives such as Investors in People or the seeking of community school status as routes to improvement had otherwise taken up their energies. The principles of consistency and the evidencing of any such systematic quest for improvement against the 1993 issues which form the basis of the reinspection model were already giving cause for concern, it is suggested, as schools struggled to justify their practice in the increasingly public arena that is education.

The role of key change agents, especially at senior management level has, once again, been shown to be vital. Recent levels of such staff turnover, evidenced here but acknowledged as a national phenomenon, seem to have created problems of continuity of action and consistency of interpretation of inspection issues to the point that maintaining any momentum in implementation has been difficult. Gender differences in attitudes to or implementation of inspection requirements do not seem to have been relevant at this stage.

CONCLUSION

Whilst barely half completed, an evidence base is emerging, it is claimed, that shows schools beginning to change in their attitudes to inspection and to OFSTED as an organisation itself. Initial rejection, side-lining and resentment at perceived misdirected state intrusion would appear to be moderating. In many cases, OFSTED and inspection seem to be becoming institutionalised within the teaching profession and to be increasingly valued, albeit from a low starting base. The potential for 'improvement through inspection' is being increasingly recognised, it is suggested, by many groups within schools. Early arguments claiming the invalidity of snapshot judgements and their inevitable limitation to something like specialist fields of inspection knowledge, not wider and perceived to be more relevant fields of school improvement knowledge, also seem to be changing. Whilst the absence of any real input into the process that formulates these inspection judgements is still recognised as a source of concern, schools as stakeholders would seem to be engaging with the principles underlying inspection, if not the specific inspection findings themselves. This is not because they necessarily disagree with those findings, for this would logically negate their validity, and therefore reinforce their status as limited to inspection knowledge alone. Rather, that force of circumstances often means they are not specifically being implemented, although the principles underlying them are being absorbed into the culture of teaching. Whether this constitutes widespread and insidious corruption of definitions of good schooling is as yet uncertain. The 'denial' so far being expressed by some teacher groups is highly complex but an area, it is suggested, where school improvement and inspection may well stand or fall.

Will cultures of teamworking and reflective practice really emerge at all levels to promote systematic and sustained improvement if there is not widespread openness and recognition of the contribution all sides are making towards effective schooling? This is not to support blindly any OFSTED role in facilitating change, rather it is for schools to acknowledge it when it is present, to engage with it professionally and to temper it and make it their own. Will accountability on the one hand and professional autonomy (so important to teacher creativity) on the other, come to coexist in anything like a relationship of mutual pressure and support based upon respect and trust? It should be hoped both OFSTED's handling of reinspection and schools' responses to it will more clearly show whether what has so far been largely a one-way trade consolidates state control or, as is tentatively suggested here, schools reassert their autonomy to an increasing extent by their proactive participation in 'the game that is currently being played in town' as the deputy head so colourfully described it.

Acknowledgements

The research reported here has been supported by a studentship from the Economic and Social Research Council (R.00429544074). The author is particularly indebted to all those who have so willingly given of their time, often under very pressing conditions.

12

Inspection without Direction: Schools' Responses to OFSTED Requirements in Moral and Spiritual Education

MARGARET MATHIESON AND MEL VLAEMINKE

In the first year of this study we interviewed a deputy head of a community college highly rated by OFSTED inspectors in every area except spiritual education. Anxious to improve their college's rating in this area, staff asked, she said, for inspectors' guidance for the future. Not one felt sufficiently confident to provide definitions or practical help.

This anecdote, from a study drawing heavily on interviews with policy-makers, inspectors, senior managers of local schools and colleges, their teachers and pupils, illustrates several of the concerns we explore in this chapter, the aim of which is to report upon a sample of schools' responses to OFSTED's requirements in the areas of moral and spiritual education. First, we shall provide a brief background to our investigation; secondly, discuss OFSTED requirements and their implications; and finally report what we saw and heard about the impact upon teachers of the expectations currently held of them.

BACKGROUND

Our interest in this investigation originated in our earlier studies in curriculum history and our long and varied experiences of schools during our careers as teacher trainers. Aware that there was nothing new about schools in this country being held responsible for their pupils' characters, we were curious to discover the effect upon teachers of persistent accusations of failure to discharge this responsibility, and of their efforts being brought under inspectorial scrutiny.

With this in mind, we needed to ask what factors appeared to explain the high priority being given to goals which have long been held by educational institutions, and long been sought through assemblies, systems of rewards and punishments, and teachers' choice of material, topics and strategies as they undertake their professional responsibilities. Part of the answer was to be found in repeated official expressions of concern about the likely consequences of current educational reforms, that is, the prescriptive and specialist nature of the National Curriculum. On the one hand, reforms had been introduced which emphasised measurable targets in order to remedy this country's declining international competitiveness; on the other, these changes created anxieties in some quarters about the perceived loss of those morally improving experiences which have characterised schools in this country since Thomas Arnold's advice to his prefects: 'What we must look for here is, first religious or moral principles; secondly gentlemanly conduct; thirdly intellectual ability.' David Pascall, Chairman of the National Curriculum Council (NCC) in 1992, expressed his regret that it had taken three years since the introduction of the National Curriculum for the spiritual and moral dimensions of educational reform to receive their proper attention. Pascall indicated the way forward likely to be taken by the government when he said: 'From being almost totally overlooked...the spiritual and moral dimensions have, over the past months, assumed much greater significance...the time is now right, as we consolidate our work...for spiritual and moral issues to share the stage' (Anglican Heads' conference, September 1992).

Policy-makers who succeeded Pascall appeared to be gripped by two anxieties. Society was in a unique and dangerous state of moral dissolution; schools were failing to discharge their responsibilities for teaching pupils the difference between right and wrong. Hastily the conclusion was reached that the promotion of moral and spiritual education would be an official requirement and become part of OFSTED inspections.

Both assumptions demand further consideration. During the period between the murders of James Bulger and Philip Lawrence and the euphoria succeeding new Labour's victory, our society was depicted by politicians, church leaders, spokespeople in the media and the 'man in the street', judging by the talk shows and MPs' postbags, as deeply confused about moral issues and behaviour. At York Minster, Dr Hapgood said that the empty tomb that heralded knowledge of the Resurrection was 'an appropriate symbolism at a time when as a nation we have stared into the darkness of a violent society and something of our own moral emptiness' (*The Times*, 12 April 1993). At the same time as Dr Hapgood's Easter message, Melanie Phillips wrote of 'a real and deep rooted fear, not just of teenage hoodlums, but of a society which appears to have lost its moral bearing so emphatically that it seems to be in danger of careering into anarchy in personal and social behaviour' (*Guardian*, 2 April 1993).

Not everyone subscribed to these apocalyptic views. Historians pointed out that murders, rapes and fraud had been committed in earlier societies and that both rich and poor had recurrently been perceived as 'immoral' in their sexual behaviour and parenting. Sociologists reflected on the interconnected changes of globalisation, detraditionalisation and social reflexivity, that is, the replacement of past certainties by the need for people to take more decisions for themselves. At the same time, thoughtful politicians asked for attention to be given to the widening gap between rich and poor as this affected housing and health, and especially to the likely consequences of severe unemployment in parts of the UK for the moral welfare of society.

The media, instead, encouraged by leading figures in education and government, who raised their public profiles by scapegoating schools and teachers, repeatedly identified these softer and easier targets for hostile critical comment. Ignoring the complexities of social changes, especially as these had affected the traditional institutions of marriage and family and, even more wilfully, ignoring children's inescapable awareness of public figures' moral failings, which were making nonsense of John Major's 'back to basics' campaign, numerous prominent politicians and leading figures in education fastened upon the notion of 'relativism' as the central explanation for society's problems.

Their simple analyses and recommended remedy were anticipated by David Pascall, who, at the beginning of this decade, appeared to reason thus: many unpleasant events are taking place in our society; if teachers and churchmen were doing their jobs properly, these would not happen. Where control can be exercised, that is, in the schools, insist that traditional values are taught and inspected, since clearly these are being neglected. 'Education', he announced, 'cannot be value-free. It's vital that schools don't abandon their responsibility as they have tended to do. They have tended to think these things are too controversial. That's not good enough.' It is a criticism which has been taken up and strengthened throughout the decade, surfacing in such ill-considered comments as appeared in the *Sun* newspaper that 'We'll be letting kids choose whether they'll murder old ladies next' (20 October 1994). Among the ironies to which we shall point at the end of this chapter is that it is by precisely those who have criticised teachers most harshly for moral relativism that the mixed bag of definitions of spiritual education has been produced as aids to the re-establishment of moral absolutes in schools.

OFSTED REQUIREMENTS: PAST AND PRESENT UNCERTAINTIES

From the autumn of 1993, as part of the new OFSTED inspection framework, inspectors were required to report on schools' performance in the promotion of pupils' spiritual, moral, social and cultural development. SMSC, as it quickly became known, formed one of four discrete topics within each report, alongside educational standards achieved, quality of education provided and efficient management of financial resources. Although each of those three areas is susceptible to varying interpretations, it can be argued that the inspection of SMSC was distinguished by the absence of even a background of discussion or negotiation, let alone a broadly agreed consensus. There was little official guidance, for either inspectors or schools, about what constituted success; as one senior HMI told us (in 1996): 'If I am brutally honest, a large number of current HMIs have not much idea of how to implement this.'[1] Early inspection reports reveal a curious mixture of school features presented as evidence alongside fairly relentless criticism, especially at secondary-school level. We became particularly interested in what were to become the most persistently problematic aspects, moral and spiritual.

Several levels of difficulty can be identified. First, the concepts of morality and spirituality are highly complex ones which have exercised philosophers, theologians, psychologists and others throughout history. Little more can be said about that here, except to offer an underlying cautionary tone to any discussions which appear to simplify or underestimate the complexities involved. OFSTED's attempts to explain and refine its criteria have been harshly characterised by one professor of philosophy as 'platitudinous, pretentious, meretricious, shambolic, incoherent, nonsense, ambiguous, riddled with inconsistencies, perversely unbalanced, shot through with relativism, composed of compromise and fudge' (Flew and Naylor, 1996, p. 18).

Secondly, the role of formal education in promoting moral and spiritual development is a contentious matter which many countries have confronted at some point in their history. Here, the close association between the Church of England and schools of all kinds – from the top public schools to hundreds of denominational primary schools – has given religion an officially approved place in schools, without its purpose or practice ever having been clearly articulated. But this implicit association gave rise to an assumption that the religious element of school life took care of spiritual matters at the same time as it underpinned moral development. By the latter part of the twentieth century, with society becoming less evidently Christian in the face of growing secularisation on the one hand and an increasingly multifaith population on the other, maintained schools had tended to retreat from the overtly Christian standpoint of earlier times. As we have indicated, from the early 1990s a strengthening body of opinion was calling for a change of heart on this issue. Senior figures in education whom we interviewed in preparation for our study of schools produced a number of intriguing possible explanations. There had been, we were told, a long history of tensions within the Department of Education and within HMI over interpretations relating to religious education, so that, for example, the *Curriculum Matters* series of the 1980s omitted RE because agreement could not be reached. Our attention was drawn to the prominence of a number of committed Christians, especially Roman Catholics, in education policy-making. There was a viewpoint which suggested that in our media conscious age, more headlines could be grabbed by calling for the salvation of the nation's youth than by proposals to reform the geography curriculum. As one HMI told us: 'Taking the high moral ground is always going to sound good – you can't measure it or dispute it so it's an easy one to trumpet.'

Apparently aware of the special difficulties in this country of assuming an interdependence between religious experience and moral and spiritual values, policy-makers have been at pains to separate them in official documents. However, it is not surprising that teachers have tended to view them as part of the same ideological package. NCC thinking on moral and spiritual education was often delivered on a religious platform – to RE advisers or Anglican bodies – and the apocalyptic treatment favoured by the media contributed to a sense of revivalist fervour. At the same time, considerable energy was going into the development of a new framework for religious education through the SACREs (Standing Advisory Councils for Religious Education), as constituted by the 1988 Act, which also introduced the controversial requirement that schools must provide a daily act of collective worship of a broadly Christian character. It is significant that, at the time of writing, the issue of collective worship is again under review, with religious leaders sharing in a call for reform of the law because 'teachers have neither the time nor the inclination to oversee religious assemblies' and evidence points to a 'declining interest in Christianity among children' (*The Sunday Times*, 8 February 1998).

Further difficulties arose from the ideological stance taken by Dr Nicholas Tate who, as head of the School Curriculum and Assessment Authority (SCAA), attracted wide publicity in January 1996 on the occasion of the conference 'Education for Adult Life'. He said: 'the loss of the religious basis for morality has weakened its credibility... This is one reason why religious education must continue to be a vital part of every child's curriculum... Its role is crucial. This is why its well-documented neglect in schools is so highly regrettable' (Conference, 15 January, 1996); and 'in spite of the miseries we see around us every day, there are grounds for optimism. The comeback of RE is one of them' (*The Daily Mail*, 15 January 1996). He was highly critical of what he interpreted as teachers' moral relativism – 'if ever a dragon needed slaying, it is the dragon of relativism' – which he defined as 'the view that morality is largely a matter of taste or opinion'. This was in contrast to his own conviction which echoed Pascall in stating that 'there are some moral matters which should not be called into question. This is how it is, this is how it has been, this is how it must be'. In particular, Tate attacked teachers' attachment to self-esteem – 'it is possible to place too much emphasis on self-esteem (a peculiarly late twentieth century preoccupation) and too little on some of the traditional moral qualities' – and to personal and social education – 'We need to find ways of giving it greater rigour and coherence... How in particular can it contribute to society's efforts to maintain structures centred on the traditional two parent family?'

The solution, Tate recommended, lay in the creation of a forum of opinion with a brief to identify the shared values of our society. The Values Forum, a diverse body comprising 130 representatives of assorted interest groups, such as parents and governors, the world of work and researchers, met several times over a period of 18 months before producing a largely uncontroversial statement of values. Having tested these by a MORI poll of 1,544 adults and surveyed 3,200 schools and 700 organisations (how this survey was done is not clear), SCAA claimed to be giving teachers the assurance that they can all teach values in the expectation of receiving society's support and encouragement. The single 'difficult' issue – whether marriage should be recommended – on which five members of the forum dissented from their colleagues, remains unresolved. SCAA engaged the services of Oxford academic Marianne Talbot (who had also attacked teachers' moral relativism at the original conference) to develop these values and other aspects of SMSC into a teachable package. The extensive materials which have been assembled are being trialled in a limited number of schools from late 1997 and may, in time, generate some helpful advice to all teachers. The second cycle of school inspections has, however, already got under way.

A further layer of uncertainty in the official rhetoric and execution of inspection can be identified in the wide-ranging interpretations placed on SMSC by OFSTED team members. Variously described to us as 'the most important part of school life' and 'often dumped on the lay inspector', the judgements made on teachers' work include some bizarre pieces of evidence. From an analysis of approximately 100 OFSTED school inspection reports, there was praise for one primary school headteacher for 'setting high standards of conduct', and for a secondary school whose 'pupils are well dressed'. Opportunities 'for contemplation and reflection' were commonly applauded, as were a secondary school's 'weekly prayer group which is an excellent experience for the pupils concerned' and a primary school where 'children are encouraged to consider the awfulness of human suffering, and the awe and wonder of creation'. In contrast, one nursery and infants school was criticised for not 'bringing pupils to a point of worship'; in a primary school it was judged that 'assemblies emphasise friendship, tolerance, care and celebration of success, but do not always secure a daily act of collective worship'. It is difficult to imagine what criteria could have been used to determine that 'the strong Christian ethos is good' or to demand that acts of worship should be of 'a more consistently high quality'. The frequent use of the term 'quality' in relation to pupils' spiritual, moral, social and cultural development is odd, implying that it is possible to be bad at those things and for outsiders to measure the deficiency. This deficiency approach has been expanded upon in draft guidance from the Qualifications and Curriculum Authority (QCA) which suggests that people who are lacking in these areas of development are likely to 'feel powerless, lethargic and hopeless', to lack 'self-belief and generosity of spirit', to be 'governed by self-interest' and to have 'closed minds and/or fear of those who are different'. It remains to be seen if teachers find this kind of guidance helpful.

FINDINGS

The anecdote which opened this chapter highlights the experience of many schools which struggled to determine how to respond to the OFSTED judgements they received on their work in promoting pupils' spiritual, moral, social and cultural development. Their difficulties were exacerbated by widespread criticisms of weaknesses in the teaching of religious education, and of the 'failure to observe statutory requirements' in relation to collective worship (almost universal in secondary schools). Both of these are constrained by practical considerations: there is a national shortage of trained RE teachers, which is only recently (from 1997) being addressed; few secondary schools have a room which can accommodate all pupils for collective worship; and some school staffs have legitimate conscientious objections to active participation in either or both.

However, schools and their governing bodies have, of course, had to respond to judgements made by OFSTED inspectors and their action plans frequently specify targets and strategies. A common response has been to make a fresh staff appointment, often in RE, sometimes in PSE, to co-ordinate and revitalise work in these areas. Leicester, where the research was undertaken, with its rich multifaith traditions, is considered fortunate in the quality of RE teachers it can attract. This has helped to remedy the low status and poor teaching too often associated with RE – 'bringing RE out of the shadows and giving it a place in the sun' (Lofthouse, 1996) according to one local commentator. Compliance with the local agreed syllabus, which was already under way in most schools, has been effected relatively smoothly, supported by LEA documentation and in-service training. There are now coherent schemes of work, assessment procedures and new curriculum support materials. At opposite ends of the educational spectrum, a Church of England primary school whose RE provision was criticised has revised its whole curriculum with special consideration for the ages and abilities of the pupils; while a 14–18 upper school has introduced compulsory short-course RE examinations. At post-16 level, RE provision seems still to be problematic for schools and colleges; one college offered A-level but no student chose it.

The boost given to RE has, in a number of cases, been identified as the trigger for wider changes in school provision of moral and spiritual education, though the two do not necessarily go hand in hand. Another favoured approach has been to stimulate staff discussion of moral and spiritual issues during a training day or staff meeting, as a preliminary for an audit of provision across the curriculum. In one school, the twin aims were 'to re-examine and redefine our own values for the second millennium', and 'to conduct an audit to ascertain what and where SMSC education is happening in the curriculum and then propose ways in which it should be developed'. The rewriting of the school's mission statement and guiding principles was also envisaged. In some instances, PGCE students on placement have been asked to undertake surveys of this kind. One such group was disappointed by the muted response to its meticulous questionnaire; another generated a detailed document outlining possible slots in the curriculum for the promotion of moral and spiritual values.

Overall, we found that teachers respond positively to initiatives which help to define their school's values and validate their own work in promoting debate about moral issues, but are less comfortable in the spiritual or religious domain. Hence, opinion in one 11–14 high school had polarised, with some bitterness, around the contrasting views of the atheist headteacher and the Christian head of humanities, while the majority of the staff in a 14–18 upper school declined to assume greater responsibility in developing an improved programme of collective worship, as required in the OFSTED report. It is worth remembering, of course, that a conscience clause still permits both teachers and pupils to withdraw from collective worship, which rather undermines proposals to strengthen its central role in school life. An experienced primary education specialist recently suggested that, given the choice, even the parents of primary school children may well choose to reduce the time spent on assemblies, on the grounds that 'it seems strange that, in a country where most adults choose not to take part in corporate worship, we should require our children to do so' (Chamberlain, 1998).

Our investigation[2] proved unequivocally that teachers are neither casual nor irresponsible in their approach to moral and spiritual education. From our findings, five broad themes are offered here for consideration.

Teachers take their responsibility for moral education very seriously

Every teacher we met affirmed unreservedly his/her role and that of the school's in developing pupils' moral sense, including their sense of self, their responsibilities to others, their families and wider society. We observed many examples of good practice. Given the nature of school communities, teachers have an obvious vested interest in promoting orderly, considerate and honest attitudes. It is an ever-present feature of school life, encouraged through an ethos based on 'respect for persons', and through the curriculum.

In our experience few teachers were content with generalities and rhetoric in these matters. When asked to review progress in this area of school life, one of the secondary schools in our sample identified its assertive discipline programme as of special value. Wishing to reduce and, if possible, eliminate 'confrontation' between staff and certain pupils, teachers voluntarily attended a demanding INSET programme designed to provide a supportive common framework and, most importantly, to achieve consistency of approach based upon 'respect for persons' in the school community.

The primary schools we visited tended to approach SMSC education in a holistic way, with all parts of the curriculum, as well as assemblies, exploring a theme like 'Friendship' or 'Birthdays'. We observed moral themes skilfully integrated with a wide range of learning experiences, such as letter-writing, diary-keeping, music, artwork and ICT. In secondary schools we were impressed by the variety of opportunities taken to explore moral issues. For example:

- English departments consciously selected texts for the thought-provoking moral issues they raise, and were confident about exploring questions related to personal motivation and ethical dilemmas.
- Drama and the performing arts lessons provided striking opportunities for exploring individual differences and alternative viewpoints.
- History teachers exploited the ethical implications of memorable past events.
- Geography and science teachers seized opportunities to introduce consideration of dilemmas relating to resources, or the gains and losses of modernisation.

- Science students at more advanced levels were encouraged to discuss current theories about the origin of the universe, or the nature of being.
- A-level economics lessons included regular topical debates.
- A-level sociology students were encouraged to think about their academic achievements and impediments to learning in relation to gender differentiation.
- In PSE, all pupils in one school engaged in a weekly written dialogue with their tutor.
- RE, as well as exploring difficult concepts like miracles and prayer, drew forth discussion on pupils' varied cultural experiences of marriage and childbirth.

Teachers are conducting moral education on the basis of well considered professional principles

We have been repeatedly impressed by the thoughtful and sensitive approach shown by teachers when approaching moral issues in the classroom. This approach derives not from moral uncertainty on the part of the teachers, nor from any wish to inflict moral uncertainty on their pupils, but from a conviction that pupils are most likely to develop moral codes if engaged in a discourse about issues, and encouraged to express their own opinions, listen to alternatives and arrive at principles which are meaningful to them. This is an approach which respects the varied personal and family experiences of pupils.

The negative way in which 'moral relativism' has been portrayed confuses the process with the ultimate goal. It represents a misunderstanding of teachers' views, and could undermine their skilful work in this demanding area of pupil development. As Taylor (1998) has recently pointed out, 'there is a danger that inspections may have low and rather generalised expectations about school practice in values education, whereas in its working out, teachers and schools may be more sophisticated in their approaches and conscious of the complex interrelationship of issues'. The alternative, an 'absolutist' or 'fundamentalist' approach, would in some ways be easier for teachers – but many believed that it would not work. Referring nostalgically to past times when it did appear to work fails to take account of the massive and rapid changes in the world in which youngsters are growing up, which do pose challenges to teachers, and to meet which, thoughtful analysis and assistance would be welcome. But from the evidence of our contact with teachers, we concur wholly with the senior HMI who said: 'I find this whole notion of us being awash in a sea of moral relativism difficult to recognise.'

Teachers are held in high moral esteem

The success of teachers' commitment and skill in promoting pupils' moral development seems to meet with greater approval from the general public than from OFSTED and the curriculum and assessment agencies (NCC/SCAA/QCA). Public opinion polls (e.g. ICM/*Guardian*, 1996; MORI/SCAA, 1996) consistently show that of all occupational groups teachers are rated the most highly for the moral examples and moral lead they give. Doctors, police officers and athletes also do quite well; pop stars and politicians do not; religious leaders are somewhere in the middle of the ratings.

Polls also show high levels of agreement among respondents of all ages when asked about specific moral dilemmas, such as shoplifting or bad language, which suggests that the concerns over lack of moral training and declining moral standards are overstated.

The terminology associated with moral and spiritual development is intensely problematic

It seems to us that the language used in the current debate has often been unhelpful. For example, the contrasting interpretations of 'relativism', as indicated earlier, are confusing, as is the recent criticism of 'self-esteem', widely held by teachers and educational researchers to be a necessary precondition for positive attitudes and values. 'Spiritual' is perhaps the hardest term to define in a way which is universally acceptable. We encountered a wide range of views, all sincerely held, about the desirability and the nature of spiritual development in a school context. In denominational schools, where a consensus between school, governors, parents and pupils exists, 'spiritual' is closely aligned with 'religious' – 'they are synonymous' was the opinion of one Roman Catholic headteacher. In other institutions, there was a recognition that school life may provide moments when insights of the kind some people would call 'spiritual' are possible, but that the personal, private, unpredictable nature of such insights do not lend themselves to institutional organisation and, even less, to the scrutiny of inspectors whose own understandings of 'spiritual' are also likely to be personal and intuitive. Amongst the examples we encountered of schools' pre- and post-OFSTED efforts to acquit their spiritual responsibilities were

- the multifaith secondary school where it was felt that respect for parental wishes was best observed by avoiding spiritual matters;
- the primary school where parents had indicated they did not wish the teachers to promote spiritual development;
- the school where a calculated emphasis was placed on 'awe and wonder' during inspection week;
- a number of schools where religious symbolism – especially the lighting of candles and periods of silence – was invoked in the attempt to promote spiritual development;
- the importing of outside religious enthusiasts to enhance the school's efforts. (This last solution, although adopted with the best of intentions and normally with careful vetting, seems to us to be particularly ill-advised, especially in the light of the evangelical fervour and organisational acumen possessed by certain charismatic and fundamentalist religious groups.)

It is difficult not to conclude that a believer and a non-believer have fundamentally different understandings of 'spiritual' and that it is unfair to expect teachers to unravel these highly complex theoretical positions and turn them into teachable concepts. The efforts of QCA to do this for teachers, by means of a broad definition which locates spiritual development in every area of the curriculum – a sort of spiritual relativism? – are misplaced. As Carr (1995, pp. 84–5) suggests, such efforts represent a 'general scattergun strategy' by which 'the spiritual comes to be characterised in terms of various vague feelings of awe and wonder in relation to everything under the curricular sun'. He concludes that 'it becomes less and less easy to see how education might begin to engage with it in any meaningful way'.

Teachers are demoralised by the statements which suggest they lack moral commitment

The aggregate effect of the themes outlined so far has been to create a situation in schools which is profoundly unsatisfactory. In an educational climate in which teachers are under great pressure from their own policy-makers, orchestrated by sections of the media, the persistent criticism which implies that they are irresponsible, timid or amoral produces frustration and anger at all levels of the profession. It has been suggested to us that such criticism actually makes their job more difficult by conveying to parents and pupils that teachers are neglecting their responsibilities.

Two statements in recent publications point to issues of grave concern:

> Everywhere we went we were told that teachers often felt oppressed by excessive and ill-informed media criticism.
>
> (School Teachers' Review Body, 1997)

> The new ethos of schooling is not only alien to the arts but very possibly detrimental to the personal, spiritual, cultural and social development of children, and to the personal and professional well-being of teachers'.
>
> (Ross and Kamba, 1997).

The teachers whom we met during our investigation would, we believe, add to the last comment the detrimental effect of ten years of ill-judged comment relating to spiritual, moral, social and cultural education. Current initiatives are not working on a blank sheet and will not succeed if that is assumed to be the case. Some of the desirable qualities identified in official documents – respect, trust, understanding, humility, confidence – need to be shown *towards* teachers as well as *by* them. For there is a cruel irony in vilifying teachers for their perceived responsibility for society's moral dissolution while expecting them to draw upon their dwindling professional confidence and lead the nation back to the path of righteousness.

Notes

1. All our interviewees were guaranteed confidentiality, so it is not possible to attribute remarks. We were repeatedly impressed by the openness with which they spoke, and represent their views faithfully here.

2. We interviewed 20 headteachers and around 40 teachers, and observed teachers and other school staff in six case-study schools – three primary schools and the three secondary schools (age ranges 11–18, 11–14 and 11–16) to which most of their pupils progressed at 11; two denominational (Roman Catholic) and two multifaith (with predominantly Hindu but also Sikh and Moslem pupils); four in city locations and two in a county town.

Section 4
Reinspection and Beyond

13

The Inspector Calls Again: The Reinspection of Schools

BRIAN FIDLER AND JACQUELINE DAVIES

INTRODUCTION

When OFSTED inspections first began in 1993 there was a substantial body of opinion that thought that schools, once inspected, would never have a second inspection. The first inspection was treated as an ordeal to be endured and although each school formulated an action plan and began implementation, progress soon ran out of steam. This view was reinforced by the difficulties there appeared to be in appointing sufficient inspectors particularly for primary schools and there was the substantial volume of criticism of some of the first inspections. Others dwelt on the cost of inspections and thought that the money would be better spent by schools themselves rather than on inspection.

However, inspections continued and some schools were highlighted where conditions were very bad. These schools had often existed in this state for some time and only inspection had brought the situation into a sharp focus and led to the initiation of some concerted and resourced action to try to improve the situation. Research by ourselves and others has revealed that schools found some development potential in the inspection process (e.g. Earley *et al.*, 1996a; Ouston *et al.*, 1996a). Not all teachers described the process as developmental but the general view was that aspects of the inspection process contributed to the development of the school. All these factors contributed to the political decision to continue with a second cycle of inspection, a decision ratified by the incoming Labour government in May 1997.

Our research indicates that the way in which a school approaches the inspection process is a major determinant of how it will subsequently view the developmental potential of inspection. The first round of secondary school inspections is complete and that of primary and special schools (at the time of writing) due for completion by the summer of 1998. We have considerable research evidence on the development of secondary schools following their first inspection. We are following ten of these schools through their reinspection and five have now completed the main stages of reinspection. The following advice and examples are based on this accumulated research evidence.

In the ensuing discussion the 'school' may be used as shorthand for the corporate voice of the staff of the school. Inevitably the influence of senior staff is likely to be stronger than that of other teachers in this corporate approach and governors also play some part. Except where it seems important to distinguish between different groups of staff in schools, the term 'school' will be used in this reified way.

THE OFSTED REGULATIONS

The original intention when OFSTED was established was that schools should be inspected once every four years. In May 1996, confirmed in December 1996, the then Secretary of State announced that schools would no longer be inspected on a four-yearly cycle. They would be inspected 'at least once within a six-year period'. Most schools interpreted this to mean that they would not be inspected for six years. The reasons for this change in policy have not been given, but it may reflect the expense of inspection. There were to be some schools which would be inspected more frequently than once in six years. These would mainly be schools giving cause for concern.

In March 1997 OFSTED announced that 650 secondary schools would be reinspected in the academic year 1997/8. The criteria for selection were that the schools chosen would 'provide a secure and representative basis for reporting on the education system as a whole', or schools that 'provide models of good practice' and those 'whose performance is weak, or show significant decline since their previous inspection', (OFSTED, 1997d). It will not necessarily be six years after their original inspection even if the school gives no cause for concern. Therefore, some schools are being visited again by OFSTED inspectors three or four years after their first inspection.

If predicting the timing of reinspection is problematic, what about the inspection process? Here again there are some difficulties. Experience from one inspection is not necessarily a good guide to reinspection. One source of change has been that the inspection process itself has been a moving target. There have been no less that three changes to the inspection framework. In 1994 there were some minor changes, in 1996 there were more radical changes and there have been further changes for reinspection, which are discussed below. These changes have been in addition to the myriad of small and procedural changes, which have been made or provided as guidance to inspectors, based upon the experience of inspection in practice.

The framework on which reinspections will be carried out has a number of changes compared with the latest previous revision in 1996 and is considerably different from the original framework that operated for the first two years of inspection. Particular features of the 1997/8 inspections are

- grading of the performance of each teacher and the offer of feedback;
- assessment of the extent of progress on the key issues for action since the previous inspection
- more indication in the inspection report of what the key issues for action involve.

In *Inspection and Re-inspection of Schools from September 1997* (OFSTED, 1997d) distributed to schools in August 1997, it was made explicit that progress on the first inspection's key issues would be the starting point for the reinspection.

It can be expected that inspectors will wish to see documentary evidence of progress since the last inspection. Following the last inspection each school was required to produce an action plan (our research found no schools which did not do so). Progress on fulfilling the various measures contained in the plan should have been reported to the governors' annual meeting for parents (this was less consistently done). Thus there should be some documentation on progress since the last inspection. Of course this is the minimum, there may have been regular reports to governors and the school's development plan may have progressed measures in the action plan each year.

Our research has shown that most schools reported rapid progress on some items on their action plan while other items were recognised as being more long term. In a well run school it could be expected that the school would have prioritised its development and also paced itself on longer-term issues. Thus schools should be able to demonstrate appropriate progress on their action plan over the intervening years between inspections. School documentation should help with this; otherwise for new senior staff it may require some detective work to piece together the picture. (Our results showed that over three quarters of the key issues were well progressed three years after the school's first inspection.)

THE IMPORTANCE OF THE REGISTERED INSPECTOR

In addition to changes in the framework for inspection a further source of variation between inspections has shown up. Our research has drawn attention to the critical importance of the leader of the inspection team – the registered inspector – and to a lesser extent the other inspectors in a particular team. The OFSTED inspection framework was intended to ensure that inspections around the country were similar. Inspectors carrying out inspections under the OFSTED framework received a week's familarisation with the framework and were examined on some aspects of their ability to work within the framework.

Lead inspectors were given a little more training and they were to have a pivotal role in the new-style inspections. They were to plan and organise the inspection, and were responsible for submitting the inspection report. The registered inspector in charge of an inspection is the first one to visit the school before the inspection (and so provides continuity throughout the inspection) and presents the findings to senior school staff and governors afterwards.

The extent of variation in the way inspections are carried out has become apparent as schools have compared notes after inspection by different teams, as the reports on different schools have appeared, as school staff have trained as inspectors and as research results have been published. It is clear that a registered inspector has a great deal of influence on the way inspection is carried out in an individual school. There are a large number of contractors who bid for inspections and even more registered inspectors who lead inspections. Thus the experience of inspection by a team led by one registered inspector is only a partial guide as to how another inspection with a different lead inspector will be carried out. This finding is borne out by the research evidence from the first round of inspections and the emerging evidence from reinspections. The reinspection research is showing that the majority of schools do not get the same inspector the second time round (only one of the ten will be seen by the same inspector). In interviews before and after reinspection, senior teachers have expressed concern about the importance of the registered inspector's personal interests and attitudes. The respondents felt that the approaches of these different registered inspectors varied.

This means that while the experience of a previous inspection is of some value in preparing for the next, it also may be a very inexact guide. In addition to the changes to inspection and the differences due to variations by individual inspectors, there are also differences in how inspection affects individual schools. It is the contention of this chapter that individual headteachers and senior staff need to work out an approach to reinspection which is appropriate for their own school. This represents a contingent view of the world. Rather than there being one best way to prepare for inspection, the approach needs to be tailored to be the best for an individual school. The next section sets out some of the factors that need to be considered in choosing and planning an approach.

It is worth paying attention to preparing for inspection because in addition to the public cost of inspection a great deal of school resources will be consumed by inspection. Anyone trying to estimate the amount of staff-time and other resources consumed by inspection is likely to come to the conclusion that the cost to a school is at least as great as the contracted cost of inspectors. It therefore makes sense for any school to try to look upon this resource as an investment and to aim to generate a return that benefits the school. Inspection can also be conceived as an opportunity. The impetus of an OFSTED inspection may make changes possible, which were regarded as inconceivable in the ordinary course of events. Properly used, an inspection represents an opportunity to carry out some developments which are worthwhile but which would be unlikely to happen without the threat of

OFSTED. If this opportunity is missed it may be a number of years before a similar opportunity presents itself.

APPROACHING REINSPECTION: SOME CONSIDERATIONS

The following criteria are intended to provide a series of issues that need consideration in order to formulate a personal and institutional approach to reinspection. Some of the considerations involve the way inspection is perceived by the leaders of the school, some depend on the state of the school and some depend on an assessment of the members of the inspection team when they are known.

Reason for inspection

When systematic school inspection was first mooted there was a strong emphasis from politicians for it to be seen as a means of holding the school to account. However, as inspection has evolved, a further aim of contributing to the improvement of schools has received greater emphasis.

Accountability
The accountability of schools has been of increasing importance since the 1970s. During the 1980s there was a redirection of emphasis away from public accountability to government and those employing teachers towards accountability to consumers and clients (Kogan, 1988). This new strand of accountability expected market mechanisms to achieve its impact since the income of schools was made dependent on the numbers of children who were recruited and retained. However, such market mechanisms had an uneven impact on schools and, in any case, this was a direct accountability to lay people. OFSTED inspections introduced an external professional dimension into the accountability process. On the one hand, professional judgements on schools were to be reported to OFSTED and summarised for government and the general public through the Chief Inspector's annual report, whilst on the other hand individual reports were made public at a local and national level. The reports provided a professional judgement on a school, which were intended to inform the choices of lay consumers operating through the market mechanism. Since this would influence the income of the school through the number of pupil units of finance there would be an obvious incentive for schools to receive what was perceived as a 'good' OFSTED report.

Our evidence from the first round of inspections is that those schools which aimed to get a 'good' inspection report and hoped to escape any criticisms were the ones which appeared to be more disappointed with the inspection process and have obtained least out of the process. For whatever reasons, their schools did not escape some criticisms from the inspectors and so this aim was not fulfilled. Also as the opportunity had not been seized to make improvements there were no compensating advantages for the school. Thus it does seem important to keep in mind the possibility of helpful outcomes for the school rather than just obtaining a 'good' inspection report and escaping criticism. In the case of reinspection this may be even more important for schools which obtained a 'good' report in their first inspection, especially if the school regarded this as flattering, since there is a possibility, and perhaps even the likelihood, of a less good report after reinspection.

The reinspection research suggests that there is a problem with overgenerous first reports. If a school was said to be functioning well in 1993 then a more rigorous inspection in 1997/8 might find little, or even negative, improvement.

Improvement

Once set up OFSTED quickly took up the maxim 'improvement through inspection' and there are obvious features of the inspection process that may lead to improvement, but it seems rather unlikely that these will happen unless the school plans to use inspection in this way. Inspection offers two contributions to improvement – the period before inspection and the period after inspection. Those who advocate that inspection should take place with very little advance notice or schools themselves which adopt the stance of 'take us as you find us' (and who wait for the inspectors to identify key issues for action) take a rather administrative and summative view of inspection. This is likely to limit the possibilities for improvement because the period before inspection is not used positively. Schools can use the period before inspection more formatively to prepare for inspection by auditing their documentation and policies and by evaluating their practice. The pressure of inspection can be used to make improvements to practice prior to inspection. In this approach, inspection then offers 'free consultancy' on how the improvements are working. It is the school's basic approach to the purpose of inspection that may limit opportunities. An approach that seeks to manage the inspection process so as to maximise the possibilities and opportunities for improvement also relies upon appropriate attitudes to inspection.

Attitude to inspection

In addition to views about the purpose of inspection, school staff will inevitably have views about how the forthcoming inspection should be approached. We may categorise responses to inspection as varying from the defensive to the proactive. There may be a middle position in which the school takes a *laissez-faire* approach, either believing that as a good school there is no need to change either before or after an inspection or alternatively treats the whole inspection process as charade. This is a game that must be won but should not be taken too seriously.

Although each individual member of staff will have his/her own response to inspection this is likely to be mediated by the view which the headteacher and senior staff take. The actions of senior management can make teachers feel even more pressurised and beleaguered. Alternatively some of the fears can be allayed such that staff are able to approach inspection in a more positive frame of mind.

Defensive stance

Schools of all kinds, from those with a good performance to those that are near failing, may be so fearful of inspection that their basic stance is a defensive one. The threat of inspection produces a great deal of stress amongst staff because inspection is seen as an attack – an attempt to find weaknesses and criticise the school and its staff and not to look for strengths. While such an attitude may be inevitable to some degree, unless it is redressed it leads to a 'victim' mentality, which not only does not help the individual, it also is unlikely to yield positive benefits for the school and its pupils.

Proactive stance

Benefits for the school and a more positive frame of mind for staff are more likely to result from trying to seize the initiative and attempting to steer the inspection process. This requires that the school thinks seriously about the opportunity which inspection offers as well as the possible threats and tries to manage the process. The basic stance is to ask what the school wants from inspection and to seek to achieve this. The headteacher's report offers the first opportunity to influence inspectors. This may be by identifying problems that are being tackled or by pointing out areas of the school's work which are thought to need particular scrutiny. The school's basic approach to its work and the philosophy of the headteacher are clearly indicated by the content of the headteacher's report. This can be supplemented when the registered inspector visits the school and is briefed by the headteacher. During the course of the inspection the visits of inspectors can be monitored and the progress of the inspection can be checked with the lead inspector every day. After the inspection some of the threats posed by a poor inspection report can be minimised by checking the factual basis for any judgements in the report. Finally, the way the inspection report is picked up by the school, by the parents and by the press should be managed. In addition to a press release for the media, a school can produce its own commentary on the inspection findings. This may accept some points but seek to refute or downplay others.

Previous experience of inspection

Whilst the previous two factors depend on personal philosophy and style of leadership, this factor is informed by previous experience of inspection. As has been pointed out, changes can be expected in a reinspection compared to the first inspection; nevertheless experience of a previous inspection will be influential. Partly this will be an emotional response – previous experience will either leave a positive or a negative feeling about inspection and this will condition feelings about reinspection. In addition to such general feelings, previous experience will have indicated possibilities that could be exploited to improve inspection from the school's point of view. In addition, hearing about the experience of inspection from other schools and research projects will raise possibilities that are strengthened by a knowledge of precedents.

For a headteacher or member of a senior management team who is new to the school there may be two sets of experience to draw on – the personal and the institutional. Sharing personal experiences in a systematic way and analysing similarities and differences will begin to indicate the extent of the variation in the first round of inspections to which we have alluded earlier. Teachers who have experienced inspection elsewhere are also a valuable source of evidence.

Good previous experience

If previous experience of an inspection was a positive one this is likely to be influential in planning for reinspection and lead to expectations of another positive experience. This is likely to be the best frame of mind for tackling reinspection provided it does not lead to complacency.

Positive experiences may be of a number of kinds. They may not necessarily mean that the report was highly complimentary, but that the report was much better than feared, or that it was the spur to development that was worthwhile. It often means that the inspectors' report presented a view of the school which staff could recognise. Our research has discovered the existence of all three reactions.

Individual teachers will have had a range of reactions to the OFSTED experience; unfortunately it seems to be the case that bad news is more newsworthy than good experiences and so it is the horror stories that are broadcast and retold. Thus it is quite possible for a whole series of individuals to think that their positive experiences are unusual because they only ever hear about the negative experiences of others. A systematic sharing of experiences which tries to give equal weight to the positive as well as the negative will lead to a much more balanced picture.

Poor previous experience

Whatever the prevalence of positive compared to negative experiences of OFSTED there certainly have been some bad experiences. Schools and individual teachers appear to have had negative experiences, the causes of which, in some cases, lie with the school and its personnel and, in others, do not.

Where individuals approach reinspection with negative feelings based on their personal philosophy of inspection, the experience of inspection is likely to make little change to this point of view. As earlier noted, some schools went into their first inspection seeking to escape with a clean sheet and were disillusioned when the result was different. It appears that such anticipation of the outcomes of inspection is unrealistic and reduces its positive impact. Rethinking inspection may be necessary to begin to change such preconceptions before they begin to influence the next inspection in an unhelpful way.

Some negative experiences, however, result from either the way in which the inspection was conducted or the repercussions for a school following inspection. The reasons for negative experiences seem to lie in three main areas:

- inadequacies in the framework;
- unfamiliarity with or misunderstanding of the framework and how it should be operated
- rogue inspectors.

There appears to have been more progress on the first two causes than the last. Some points have been improved – the framework revised (simplified and greater emphasis on development); some misunderstandings and their clarifications have appeared in briefing from OFSTED; and the paperwork and proformas are better. However, too little appears to have been done about individual poor inspectors or the training and development of inspectors in general.

Poor inspectors may be inadequate in a number of ways. They may have poor knowledge of that which they are inspecting (and we have come across a number of examples of that). Poor inspectors may organise their work inadequately. Staff may be observed on an uneven pattern or too late in the inspection to make a valid contribution to the report. Some inspectors who carry out few inspections may not be very familiar with the framework or, more likely, changes to the framework. In a different vein, inspectors may have poor interpersonal skills. They may appear negative and critical because of the unbalanced nature of their feedback or actions. Finally, they may show poor judgement based on the evidence. In many ways under current procedures, this is the least tractable area for the school to pursue although an appeals system was introduced in spring 1998 (OFSTED, 1998a).

Our research found evidence of most of the failings listed above. Fortunately, most of these have been individual inspector failings and it has been the registered inspector who has been able to alleviate the situation to some extent. However, it has still badly influenced the way inspection is perceived. Where the problems lie with the registered inspector the situation is extremely difficult. OFSTED, until very recently, had no well-known procedures for dealing with situations of this kind. Schools have reported their irritation at finding no clear way in which they could present their complaints and have them investigated. A complaints procedure with an ombudsman has been set up but it remains for further research to investigate how well known this is and how credibly it operates.

Any analysis of the validity of inspection findings identifies the basis on which inspectors make their judgements as crucial. The framework does not consist of a series of criteria-referenced statements, even though it has been drawn up to give this impression. The procedure requires the collection of evidence, which then forms the basis for judgements. However, the evidence, particularly on classroom observation, is norm referenced. It does not consist of a systematic series of highly objective observations of what teachers actually did and the responses of children. (Indeed, this approach in the USA has also been found to be problematic.) Instead it identifies a number of areas to be studied but this observation and data gathering require some judgement rather than being entirely objective since they are inevitably selective. Thus any bias or poor selection will affect the evidence gathering stage and not only the judgement based upon the evidence. This makes clear the unparalleled importance of a sound basis for judgement by inspectors. One crucial factor in this is that they need a wide range of experience on which to norm reference their judgement based on the collected evidence. Another crucial factor is the need for a systematic procedure for collecting and weighing the evidence to form judgements. There appears to be no systematic development and testing of inspectors on these two criteria. This is a huge weakness in the quality assurance of inspections. The belated weeding out of a small number of rogue inspectors after four years appears to be a huge failure of quality control.

Thus a school may have to take the initiative in cases of suspected poor inspection. The inspection framework offers some protection and this needs to be exploited. There should be a systematically collected evidence base (examples of key issues for action depending on only one piece of evidence abound). Thus there not only needs to be evidence to support judgements but also that evidence needs to be representative. For research evidence this involves not only representative sampling but also triangulation – using different sources of evidence to crosscheck the findings. In a less rigorous way this still should be a test applied by inspectors – is there sound evidence to support an important judgement? Finally, when the evidence is agreed, the framework gives the independence of judgement to the inspector. However, there is no reason why there should not be discussion of how the judgement has been made. Indeed the extent to which heads reported that they negotiated with inspectors is very clear. In our 1996 survey just over three quarters of secondary heads reported that they 'negotiated' with inspectors over more than factual aspects of the report.

There are also negative experiences of what happened after inspection. Particularly in the first inspections the press – local and national – picked up findings and sometimes chose to emphasise the critical aspects of the reports. This was quite unfair where a school was no worse than other local schools but it was one of the first to be reported on. The sheer number of inspections has caused them to be less newsworthy and so this is less likely to be an effect unless a school is found to be failing on reinspection.

The largest effects of inspection have been felt in those schools deemed to be 'failing' or in need of special measures, and the larger group deemed to have serious weaknesses. The 'naming and shaming' of such schools was traumatic particularly for the first few schools. The process of gradually coming to terms with the effects of a very bad inspection report and its consequences have been documented (Earley, 1997). Whilst for those staff in the schools and particularly those deemed responsible for failure such consequences were very hard to bear, looked at from the perspective of children in the school, in the longer term, judgements might be more balanced as the next section indicates.

State of the school

The state of the school can be expected to be an important factor influencing how the reinspection is viewed. Our research evidence indicates that most schools made considerable efforts to be seen in a good light during the inspection week. In our 1996 survey only 13 per cent of secondary heads said that inspectors would see 'a typical week' during inspection. Further small-scale research examining inspection from the perspective of school children indicated that they did not consider that inspectors were seeing normal teaching (Gillies, 1996). More worryingly, in this research pupils reported that they wished that school and teaching were always like they were in the inspection week. Thus it is not so much the fact that inspectors will see a prepared performance which needs discussion but the extent of the preparation.

At opposite ends of the performance spectrum decisions on how to approach reinspection can be expected to be different.

Schools likely to be 'failing' or having serious weaknesses
The designation that a school is deemed to be failing its pupils or as having serious weaknesses depends upon a range of factors, so it is not easy to predict with certainty that a school will be placed in either of these categories. The ground rules have been clarified and there is case history as a guide but there is some evidence that schools are not very good at predicting how they would be judged (Watling *et al.*, 1997). Outside observers such as LEA advisers appear to have been better placed to judge the weaknesses of schools. Thus for schools which are uncertain of the inspectors' likely findings and/or categorisation, or who have a very weak department or section, some pre-inspection check-up would probably be worth while so that the likely results of inspection can be predicted and hence planned for.

How far a school should seek to prevent itself being so categorised is less easy to say. To some extent this must depend upon an assessment of how far the school, post-inspection, considers that it can improve relatively unaided compared to such possibilities when resources, attention and help are triggered by being designated in the 'at risk' categories. Although the stigma of being in one of the 'failing' or 'serious weaknesses' categories is undesirable it may be the only way in which a school has a good chance of remediating the situation. This is likely to be the case where a school has been in a poor state, for whatever reason, for a long time. The school may simply have lost the capacity to improve without a great deal of outside assistance. If this is accepted the school can still plan and attempt to influence how this should happen. In this way senior staff can help prepare others for the likely verdict which may make it a little easier to accept than when it is quite unexpected. Although being designated in one of these categories is very traumatic, the increasing evidence from schools which have been designated as failing is that, with the extra assistance which is provided, most are able to improve sufficiently to leave the failing category within two years (OFSTED, 1997a).

Where the view is taken that more damage in both the long and short term will be done to the school through being classified in one of these two categories then the plan should be to 'put on a show' which will prevent this. Although OFSTED inspections are often accused of being snapshots it is when a 'show' is being planned that the picture looks rather more complex. Inspectors should examine evidence of children's work and documentation over a period. This means that either the plan to avoid categorisation has to be long term or else the evidence from the inspection week has to be sufficiently compelling that the evidence showing the past situation is viewed as out of date in an improving school. Whatever the tactics during inspection, the long-term and credible strategy should be of improvement in the interests of both children and staff.

Schools likely to be satisfactory or better

Schools without the pressure of possible failure can afford to take a more relaxed view of the extent to which a 'show' needs to be put on. However, it should be surmised that OFSTED inspectors expect that special efforts will be made, and so they will make appropriate allowances for this when they make their judgements. This may disadvantage schools that show only their typical work.

The more major decisions required are likely to be how far schools indicate areas of weakness, areas where improvement in the past has proved intractable and areas where more objective and impartial evidence would be welcomed by the school. The research evidence here is somewhat mixed. Some schools, which indicated weaknesses in the headteacher's form, have reported that the inspection seemed to be dominated by this issue in a way that was quite undesirable. However, evidence from our 1996 survey of secondary heads showed that 61 per cent of schools did indicate some areas of weakness before or during the inspection. This decision will be particularly acute where the school knows or suspects that it has one or more very poor teachers (Fidler *et al.*, 1998).

Often good schools reported that they gained little from inspection in terms of new insights into how they should improve or areas in need of improvement. There are two contrary thoughts here. First, research by OFSTED refutes the initial assertion. It is claimed that evidence gained from talking to schools before inspection and comparing this with inspection findings indicates that schools were better at recognising their strengths than their weaknesses and that weaknesses were thrown up by inspection which schools were unaware of (OFSTED, 1998b). Secondly, if nothing new was discovered during inspection this should act as confirmation that the internal school monitoring procedures are working. The value of such confirmation should not be underestimated. It gives confidence that the school is not complacently unable to see its own weaknesses.

State of staff

A managerial consideration affecting how to approach reinspection is a judgement about the staff of the school. An OFSTED inspection gives an opportunity both before and afterwards to prioritise and focus on particular developments. The most should be made of this opportunity.

A forward-looking and innovative staff

Where the staff and the school as a whole are already making improvements, inspection can legitimate and reinforce such actions. Advantage might be taken of inspection to ensure that developments in the school are co-ordinated and focused on children's learning or some particularly difficult issue (which would not ordinarily be tackled) could be attempted. This is particularly likely to be the case where there is a necessary development or one required in the longer term which is currently unacceptable or unpalatable to staff. The effect of a forthcoming inspection can be used to mobilise the political will to overcome these objections.

Staff are coasting or in need of improvement

Where staff as a whole, or sections of it, are coasting and resist improvement or where areas of work are weak and not improving, inspection offers a potent motivator. It may be that contrary to the advice given earlier about reducing the stress induced by inspection, lethargy might be shaken off if a greater sense of anticipation and heightened concern were generated by a forthcoming inspection.

Inspection team

Much of the earlier considerations offered in this chapter might have, finally, to be conditional on an assessment of the inspection team. Some information on the team will be provided before reinspection. This may be particularly useful if the team or members of it are not already known to the school. Further information can be requested. Important criteria here are: specialist qualifications in the subject areas being inspected (Millett and Johnson, 1998); teaching experience including phase, length and recency; and inspection experience. However, it is likely to be the registered inspector who is of critical importance since he/she sets the tone and plans the inspection, deals with problems during inspection, gives feedback after inspection and is responsible for the production of the inspection report. Although some information on paper may be of some value, such considerations as interpersonal skills may also be important and only possible to assess in person. Asking for the names (or looking up on inspection reports if they are not forthcoming) of previously inspected schools would provide the names and phone numbers of heads who could give some experience of the person as a registered inspector.

The majority of secondary schools inspected in 1996 said they had confidence that the inspection team would carry out a professional inspection and most schools reported afterwards that this had happened. However, a small proportion (just over a quarter) reported otherwise and so any school needs to be prepared to change its plans if at the stage of meeting the registered inspector or later, confidence in a professional inspection is lacking.

Confidence in inspectors

Most secondary schools questioned said that they had confidence in the inspection team at the start of the inspection. Most retained this or increased their confidence over the course of the inspection and reported that they could speak freely to the lead inspector. This would appear to be a precondition for an inspection that is to yield value for a school.

Lack of confidence in inspectors

The situation is very different where confidence is lacking at the start of the inspection or events reduce confidence as the inspection proceeds. In this case the activity becomes one of damage limitation. Every action needs to be logged and as much confirmation as possible obtained about practices so that any dispute can be seen to depend on evidence rather than personal dislike. The attempt should be to limit the damage at every stage including the circulation of a summary of the report to parents afterwards. Some schools have accompanied this with a commentary by the school. As earlier noted, new procedures are being implemented by OFSTED (from spring 1998) to deal with complaints and appeals against the inspection report (OFSTED, 1998a). These should be used and reported so that other schools are aware of the number of complaints about inspectors.

PLANNING FOR ACTION

The whole emphasis of this chapter has been to suggest that schools should try to see what opportunities an OFSTED inspection offers and try to treat it as such. Our research has suggested that those who approach inspection in this way are more likely to value its developmental potential than those who don't. Inspection may present a way to accomplish a difficult change because staff are more receptive to school improvement in their preparation for inspection. It may offer an opportunity to unite the staff by working together against an external threat. It certainly offers an opportunity to carry out 'spring cleaning' – bring documentation up to date, review procedures and try to envisage how the school will look to outsiders.

Such a proactive approach requires preparation. This chapter has suggested a number of criteria to consider in order to decide how to approach inspection and as a summary to this chapter we offer this checklist of advice on preparing for reinspection:

- Decide on an approach subject to meeting the inspectors.
- Ask – what do we want out of inspection?
- Seize the impetus which inspection can provide.

- Prepare using self-evaluation and external help.
- Progress and chart action since the last inspection.
- Review documentation.
- Prepare staff, children, parents and governors.
- Use the headteacher's form to indicate areas for special attention.
- Check on inspectors beforehand.
- Be prepared to cover up and limit the damage if the inspection appears to be being conducted unprofessionally.
- Reassess the original approach if circumstances change.
- Hold daily meetings with the lead inspector to discuss progress.
- Ensure that evidence is seen of noteworthy features of the school's work.
- Ask for evidence which substantiates judgements.
- Evaluate and negotiate the wording of the report and summary.
- Prepare press release and commentary on the report (if necessary).

14

Conclusion: Towards Self-Assessment?

PETER EARLEY

THE PUSH TO IMPROVE – INTERNAL AND EXTERNAL MECHANISMS

Demands are increasingly being made on schools to demonstrate that they are effective and that they are improving. Pressure has been exerted on them to find ways of enhancing achievement, to raise standards and, for their own survival if nothing else, to attract pupils. Local management, open enrolment, the publication of (raw) attainment data and regular OFSTED inspections have all played a part in this sharper focus on school performance. The new reality facing schools is that they must improve but the key question is how? In simple terms, the school improvement debate can be seen as being polarised between those who advocate either internal or external factors as the most significant mechanism for change. The former stress the importance of school review, self-evaluation and school self-improvement, all predominantly internal mechanisms in which the school itself is seen as the main change agent. The latter point to the significance of external forces, such as school inspection or audit, conducted by bodies such as OFSTED or the LEA, and see them as the main driving force for school improvement.

Mortimore, a leading writer in the field, has described the school improvement debate in terms of two opposing groups: the doves and the hawks (Preface to MacGilchrist *et al.*, 1997). The doves argue that unless schools are able to do things for themselves then any change is likely to remain superficial. For change to be successful and improvement to be embedded, there is a clear need for 'ownership' on the part of those responsible for 'delivering the innovation' or raising standards. The hawks, on the other hand, tend to perceive self-review or school evaluation as an easy option and soft-centred, and argue that without the hard edge that external probing (supposedly) brings to a school, difficult questions and judgements will invariably be shirked.

Of course, the reality is likely to be that a combination of the two is required for successful change to occur and that both internal and external pressure (or challenge) and support are needed. Whether more of one than the other is needed is likely to depend on a number of factors and according to the institution in question. Fullan (1991), for example, has argued for the need for a judicious mix of both. Pressure and support are both required for change to take place but, he suggests, support without pressure is likely to lead to waste and pressure without support to stress. The 'pressure–support' notion has also been taken up by Barber (1996) and has become a central plank of government policy in conjunction with target-setting and the five-stage cycle of school self-improvement (DfEE, 1997b).

It is important, however, to be reminded of the tensions and contradictions – explored in several chapters in this volume – between external inspection or audit whose main purpose is *accountability*, as opposed to external inspection for school development or *improvement*. Accountability or inspectorial evaluation – judging in order to justify performance to others – has usually been contrasted with developmental or professional evaluation – judging in order to improve. The key question is whether the main concern of the activity in question is *improving* or *proving*; is it about being able to 'improve' an institution such as a school, or is it more about being able to 'prove' something to others (e.g. that the institution offers value for money)? It could be argued that one of the difficulties with the OFSTED inspection process is that it claims to be able to do both; to act as an accountability mechanism whilst also bringing about 'improvement through inspection'.

Research has shown that effective or 'confident' schools – what in the recent literature have variously been called 'intelligent schools' (MacGilchrist *et al.*, 1997), 'learning organisations' (Senge, 1990) or 'thinking' schools (Bradley, 1989) – have particular strengths in self-review and evaluation. Such schools are said to thrive on critical review and reflection on practice, and have the capacity to manage change well. How such schools achieve this position is less clear. It has long been known, for example, that 'good teachers make for good schools' but the converse is also true and in a kind of symbiotic or reciprocal way, teachers and their schools feed off and develop each other. In this sense school culture is crucial (Rosenholtz, 1989; Stoll and Fink, 1996). Promoting a culture of 'restless self-evaluation' has been described by Barber (1996) and others as a central feature of improving schools but how such a culture is achieved is clearly the key question.

In those schools where there is a need to develop a culture of self-evaluation and continuous improvement, external inspection may play an important role in its promotion. The Nuffield research into secondary school inspection, for example, found that nearly seven out of ten heads, whose schools were inspected in 1996, reported having undertaken a 'thorough review' prior to their inspection. In addition, many schools were using or had made use of the inspection handbook as a staff development tool, to audit the school's strengths and weaknesses and to review the school's priorities. Indeed, OFSTED, in a recent publication entitled *School Evaluation Matters*, encourages schools to use the inspection framework as a basis against which to evaluate their own practices (OFSTED, 1998b). Yet it is generally agreed there is a clear need for *both* internal and external approaches to evaluation and review, perhaps if for no other reason than to confirm an institution's quality assurance and review procedures. Barber (1996) notes that 'though the current system of externally imposed inspections is often contrasted, usually deprecatingly, with a self evaluation model, the reality is that both are essential'. In a similar vein Hargreaves (1995) remarked that: 'the most effective audit of a school comes about by neither internal self-evaluation nor external inspection. Some combination of both probably does the job better than either alone'. Each on its own is of limited value and neither is sufficient to bring about real improvement in schools.

Various contributions to this volume have shown how a growing number of schools and LEAs are emphasising the importance of self-evaluation and attempting to embed such practice so that it becomes an integral part of the school's culture. In Chapter 5, for example, an LEA initiative was described which was designed to support all schools in setting up rigorous programmes of self-review, linked to the school development plan. Schools were making use of benchmarking information or performance data, available both nationally (from QCA and OFSTED) and locally (from 'value added' analyses and from school profiles produced by the LEA). The case studies in Section 2 have clearly demonstrated that external perspectives, both from OFSTED and the LEA, are an important part of school improvement and can help promote self-scrutiny and evaluation. They show that OFSTED inspection *can* contribute to school improvement, particularly in validating agendas for change, but that inspection was merely a snapshot evaluation, likely to compare unfavourably with, where it existed, a school's more rigorous and ongoing system of self-review.

It is worth noting, however, that there is some evidence to suggest that schools are better at diagnosing their strengths than their weaknesses, and even schools which claimed to have effective review and evaluation processes in place were not always able to predict accurately the inspectors' main findings. OFSTED recently conducted a study of 100 primary and secondary schools which showed two thirds of the 'key issues' identified in secondary school reports were not anticipated as weaknesses by the schools themselves, whilst in the primary sector only just over a quarter of the key issues had been previously identified as priorities (OFSTED, 1998b). (Almost all schools involved in this study felt that their inspection report was fair and accurate.) Similarly, there is evidence from the accelerated inspection programme of a London borough that some schools were not very good at predicting how they would be judged by the inspectors (Watling *et al.*, 1997).

In addition, evidence from the further education (FE) sector, where self-assessment is perhaps more established than in schools, suggests that assessments by the colleges themselves tend, on average, to be one grade higher (on a five-point scale) than the assessment by FE inspectors (Dixon, 1996). Also, interestingly, the area of quality assurance (one of the five areas graded under the FE inspection framework) was found, on average, to be awarded the lowest grade by the inspectors. Self-assessment is not therefore easy and outside observers such as OFSTED inspectors and LEA advisers may be better placed to judge the weaknesses of schools. But the credibility of any self-evaluation process demands that it is moderated and checked. This can be undertaken by outsiders (acting as critical friends?) who endeavour to ensure that the process is rigorous and thorough and does not become too cosy or complacent or simply self-affirming rather than self-evaluative.

External inspection undertaken by the LEA or OFSTED can therefore have considerable value and it is likely to be trusted by parents and governors and seen as offering a wider perspective. Schools with experience of both approaches generally acknowledge the valid contribution of each but it is the external perspective that is likely to be seen by the outside world as more important, particularly with its perceived harder edge and measurable performance indicators.

However, a further tension can be created if schools put on a front for the inspectors and attempt to disguise their weaknesses and limitations. If this is the case, and there is evidence of this occurring in some schools, then internal review or self-evaluation may appear to be the less rigorous approach but it is, at least, likely be more honest and to see the 'real' school. Also, of course, as Hargreaves (1995) and MacBeath et al. (1996) note, teachers will be less likely to reject the findings from a process that they have helped to design and which is conducted by people who know the school and its context and whom they can trust. The ownership of the findings will be crucial for their successful implementation.

In Section 3, Lonsdale and Parsons note the paradox that, despite the efforts devoted to the notion that schools should produce development and improvement plans based on a diagnosis of their *own* needs, this voluntaristic approach to school improvement has been superseded, and in their view devalued, by the imposition of the OFSTED process. They, like other commentators, make a distinction between quality assurance and quality control, and see inspection as more akin to the latter and as occurring too late in the process to be of any great value. Inspection appears to achieve its accountability function but they are less convinced of its value as an improvement tool, seeing inspection as unlikely to motivate teachers to achieve higher standards. For this to be achieved there is a need for a supportive, developmental and threat-free approach to quality improvement. They conclude that the OFSTED inspection process is subjugating, demeaning and deprofessionalising. If inspection is seen as something done to teachers by someone else, then teachers are less likely to see themselves as stakeholders in the school improvement process. The inspectors' key issues for action may not necessarily be those that the school would have identified or seen as areas of priority.

For many commentators, self-evaluation is the crucial mechanism for achieving any kind of school improvement. Underpinning everything is said to be questions of ownership and empowerment. School improvement has to be in the hands of teachers and other stakeholders and this, it is claimed, is unlikely to be promoted by top-down directives or an inspectorial approach to development.

INSPECTION: COST AND CONTROL?

Two additional concerns are expressed by several contributors to this volume and elsewhere. First, that inspection, like other auditing devices, is itself conditioning the shape of what is being audited and exerting a controlling influence. Secondly, the ever-growing cost of inspection, part of what Power (1997) has recently termed 'the audit society' or the 'audit explosion', is also a concern. These both warrant brief consideration.

The power of audit

As argued elsewhere (Ouston *et al.*, 1998a), there is an increasing awareness of how patterns of accountability, such as OFSTED inspections, are changing the values and practices of teachers. Harland (1996) has argued that educational evaluation can lead to compliance, patterning and surveillance. These may also apply to educational accountability and inspection: 'Compliance is the most straightforward: is the school performing as it should? OFSTED inspectors focus explicitly on compliance. Patterning is more subtle and has been referred to...as league-table thinking and OFSTED speak. Teachers take on the values and language of the accountability mechanisms' (Ouston *et al.*, 1998a, p. 120). Drawing on Foucault's (1979) ideas about surveillance, Harland (1996) argues that teachers may begin to regulate their own behaviour in line with what they perceive the government expects. The latter point is supported by the Nuffield secondary inspection research finding that as schools gained more knowledge of inspection, they were more likely to make changes *before* inspection rather than afterwards (Ouston *et al.*, 1997). The nature of the audit influences performance and schools change their practices to conform to what they think the inspectors expect (a variant of teaching to the test?). The inspectors or auditors 'have become part of a surveillance system that professionals incorporate into their thinking' (Ouston *et al.*, 1998a). The recent publication by OFSTED of guidance and advice for schools on how to use the inspection framework for the purposes of school evaluation (OFSTED, 1998b) is a further example of regulation and the encouragement of conformity to an imposed model.

The greater emphasis on the 'audit society' (described below) is, as Power (1997) suggests, a reflection of the lack of trust of the professionals who provide the service. But it is this lack of trust that can be compounded by the inspection process itself: 'The purpose of audit and accountability is to raise standards of service; however the process of audit may lead to declining standards of performance through the lack of trust and autonomy of professional staff' (Ouston *et al.*, 1998a, p. 121).

The cost of audit

A second concern raised about inspection, which must be seen in the context of a wider social phenomenon, centres on its cost. A feature of contemporary society, affecting not only the education sector, has been the growth of the regulatory state, or what Power (1997) has called the 'Audit Society' or the 'audit explosion'. It is suggested that the costs of this ever-growing army of 'waste-watchers, regulators and inspectors' is phenomenal, particularly when the time spent in preparing and providing information for the audit or inspection is taken into account. Power estimates, for example, that the overall cost of complying with the regulatory requirements of the audit at least doubles the direct running costs. Fidler and Davies in this volume also point to the additional costs of OFSTED inspections and agree that the real cost of an inspection is probably at least double the public cost. An analysis of the real cost, however, in terms of a full cost-benefit analysis would also have to include the effects of inspection on the activities of staff, both in the period leading up to the inspection week and afterwards. It has been suggested, for example, that inspection-related activities have taken school managers and teachers away from other more important activities and that pupils may have been affected in various ways, not all positive (Duffy, 1997). Similarly, the after-effects of an inspection may lead to a period (sometimes quite lengthy) of 'post-inspection blues', or to unusually high rates of absenteeism (Fitz-Gibbon, 1998). A proper analysis of the cost (and value) of inspection or audit would need to consider all these factors (Earley, 1996b).

Clearly, monitoring the management of public resources is necessary; as noted earlier, internal evaluation or self-regulation on its own may lead to complacency or worse. With a total schools' budget of approximately £14 billion it may not seem unreasonable to spend just over £100 million each year to monitor how it is managed. Similarly, on a smaller scale, £17,800 (the average cost), spent on the inspection of a secondary school, once every four to six years, could be seen as offering value for money when considered against that school's annual expenditure budget of £2–3 million. Research into inspection suggests that there is general agreement that some form of accountability mechanism is desirable; it is more a matter of ensuring that the process is cost-effective. If the main aim of inspection is accountability this may be the case. If it is to effect school improvement then there may be better uses of this resource, particularly for those schools not deemed to be in difficulty.

What is apparent however is that the audited or the inspected soon learn to play the game and regulatory audit can become a ritual. But, as suggested above, far from just measuring behaviour, audit has the very real potential to alter it. The performance of auditors and inspectors themselves has also become subject to audit. An extreme example of this is given by Power (1997) who describes the abattoir industry as currently having more than two regulators for every 'doer'. According to Power the lesson is not the Kafkaesque vision of more and more bureaucracy but to shift regulation and auditing from a largely box-checking external exercise to an organic internal one, perhaps through stakeholding mechanisms. He makes a distinction, as does Kogan (1988), between professional audit, undertaken to improve the quality of service, and external audit, which attempts to control the service. Can OFSTED inspection be expected to do both effectively or is the alternative, more cost-effective, approach, to encourage institutions to assess themselves, and for the inspectors to inspect and accredit the processes of self-assessment? The framework for the reinspection of schools, with its emphasis on progress made since the initial inspection and the school's capacity to secure further improvement, shows evidence of the first steps towards such a development.

TOWARDS SELF-ASSESSMENT

As the inspection cycle has grown so has the annual cost of school inspections; from about £60 million in 1993 when the first inspections took place, to about £160 million in 1997/8 at the completion of the four-year cycle for primary and special schools. As argued above, the cost-effectiveness of the system, particularly in terms of school improvement, has been raised and the trend away from quality control (by OFSTED) towards quality assurance and self-evaluation (by the schools themselves) can perhaps best be seen in these terms.

In the FE and higher education (HE) sectors there have already been distinct moves from inspection or audit to various forms of self-assessment (e.g. Dixon, 1996; Kelly, 1996; FEFC, 1997a; 1997b). The statutory sector appears to be following this trend as witnessed by the framework for the reinspection of schools (with its greater emphasis on a school's capacity to manage change and quality-assurance mechanisms) and the publication of OFSTED's guidance document *School Evaluation Matters* (OFSTED, 1998b). Evaluation is most effective when people internalise quality standards and apply them to themselves. The move towards self-assessing institutions is a recognition that, for the vast majority of schools, a rigorous form of evaluation, underpinned by comparative performance, is likely to be an effective mechanism for achieving improvement and raising standards. Both internal and external perspectives are needed but after the first round of school inspections (and as institutions mature) the focus of inspection is likely to centre on the assessment of a school's capacity to self-assess or evaluate.

MacBeath and his colleagues (1996), building on the approach to school self-evaluation adopted in Scotland, argue that school evaluation should be honest, valid and reliable; comprehensive, reflecting the things that matter to people; and developmental and empowering, helping the school to set and monitor its own progress in a climate of mutual accountability. It should be part of the ongoing activity of a school rather than an extra imposed by some external agency, providing as it does, an opportunity for a school to recognise and celebrate its achievements (*ibid.*). It is suggested there is a need for dedicated 'evaluation time' and on the basis of research, undertaken for one of the teacher unions, MacBeath and his team advocate 'a model in which external evaluation focuses primarily on the school's own approach to evaluation rather than a spit and polish inspection' (MacBeath et al., 1996).

Similarly, both Hargreaves (1995) and Moon (1995) see inspection as important but mainly for validating the effectiveness of the process of internal review, as in the HE and FE sectors. There is no research evidence to support the notion of improvement by mandate nor it should be said of the autonomous self-improving school. Schools need the challenge of an external perspective but as MacBeath (1996) suggests there is a need for a rigorous and realistic national framework of internal and external evaluation in which all stakeholders have a place in the process.

Wragg (1997) has also pointed to the importance of school self-evaluation which he believes ought to be part of an external inspection and be accredited. LEAs, he suggests, should identify schools which are not effectively evaluating what they do. If a school is unable to evaluate itself then it would not be licensed or accredited because self-evaluation would be a precondition for being awarded a licence. If a school was found by the inspectors to be doing well it would be awarded a five-year licence allowing it to continue with its self-monitoring procedures. At the end of the five years the school would have a scaled-down or 'light touch' inspection and the licence would be extended for a further five years. After ten years the school would expect to receive a full inspection. Wragg (ibid.) sees such a scheme as involving schools in their own inspection and in combining the best of local and national traditions of inspection and advice. It should challenge schools to improve what they do and then license them to do it (ibid.).

In many ways much of what Wragg is suggesting is already occurring in the non-statutory sector. From September 1998, FE colleges are able to apply for 'accredited status'. Self-assessment schemes have been introduced whereby colleges regulate their own activities and are judged or assessed by a panel of peers from other high-performing colleges. It is intended that this will provide an incentive for underachieving colleges to improve but currently 'quality assurance' is the weakest aspect of college practice (Dixon, 1996) and 'management and governance' tend to be the areas where the colleges' opinion tends to be more favourable than the inspectors (Crequer, 1998). Early experiences of the new FE system in which the inspectors scrutinise the evidence the colleges provide rather than create evidence from scratch has been very positive and the process has been seen as rigorous and developmental (ibid.). The revised FE model of college inspection gives due recognition to internal evaluation and quality-assurance processes. Inspection is leading to the development of self-assessment skills within the institutions and whilst the latter on their own cannot provide a valid measure of accountability they are very important in quality improvement. If the process is rigorous then inspection becomes one of sampling the evidence to test the validity of the self-assessment rather than being a repetition of the self-assessment (Kelly, 1996). Quality marks – which are found in colleges and schools – such as Investors in People, the Chartermark, ISO 9000 and the British Quality Foundation award provide further evidence of an institution's ability to assess and act upon that assessment.

Clearly, there is no magic wand for school improvement. Many schools are likely to need assistance in assessing their own effectiveness and in acquiring the necessary skills to become self-evaluating institutions and to ensure the existence of a culture of continuous improvement. Self-review and self-assessment can raise professionalism and help to develop a culture of evaluation, the driving force of a successful improvement strategy (Barber, 1996). Most recently, self-evaluation has become incorporated into notions of good management and as part of the core activity of development and improvement planning. Yet effective self-assessment is far from simple; a certain level of institutional maturity is needed in order to have the confidence to be able to identify and address the issues raised.

External inspection may be more effective at 'proving' as opposed to 'improving' and there is a consensus that the most likely way to achieve improvement is through developing a culture of self-evaluation at all levels in the school. However, if an organisation, like a school, is to improve, external professional commentary has to combine constructive criticism with a recognition of that organisation's achievements. If this does not happen even justified criticism is likely to be ignored. Achievement needs to be recognised and a climate of success created. The role of external inspection in the creation of both a culture of evaluation and a climate of success will, no doubt, continue to be discussed with great fervour.

References

Audit Commission (1998) *Changing Partners: A Discussion Paper on the Role of the LEA*, London: Audit Commission.

Baginsky, M., Baker, L. and Cleave, S. (1991) *Towards Effective Partnerships in School Governance*, Slough: NFER.

Ball, S.J. (1996) *Who Controls Schools Now – and How Well?* Stoke: Trentham Books.

Ball, S.J. (1997) Good school/bad school: paradox and fabrication, *British Journal of Sociology of Education*, Vol. 18, no. 3, pp. 317–36.

Ball, S.J. (1997) Policy sociology and critical policy research: a personal review of recent education policy and policy research, *British Educational Research Journal*, Vol. 23, no. 3, pp. 257–74.

Barber, M. (1996) *The Learning Game*, London: Gollancz.

Bottery, M. (1996) The challenge to professionals of the new public management: implications for the teaching profession, *Oxford Review of Education*, Vol. 22, no. 2, pp. 179–97.

Bradley, H. and colleagues (1989) *Thinking Schools: Support for Innovation Project*, Cambridge: Cambridge Institute of Education.

Brimblecombe, N., Ormston, M. and Shaw, M. (1996a) Teachers' perceptions of inspections, in Ouston, J. *et al.* (eds) *OFSTED Inspections: The Early Experience*, London: David Fulton.

Brimblecombe N., Shaw M. and Ormston, M. (1996b). Teachers' intentions to change practice as a result of OFSTED school inspections, *Educational Management and Administration*, Vol. 24, no. 4, pp. 339–54.

Broadbent, J., Laughlin, R. and Read, S. (1991) Recent financial and administrative changes in the NHS: a critical theory analysis, *Critical Perspectives on Accounting*, Vol. 2, pp. 1–29.

Brodie, D. (1995) *Planning Planning*, London: EBS Trust/BBC.

Carr, D. (1995) Towards a distinctive conception of spiritual education, *Oxford Review of Education*, Vol. 21, no. 1, pp. 84–5.

Cerny, P. (1990) *The Changing Architecture of Politics: Structure, Agency and the Future of the State*, London: Sage.

Chamberlain, R. (1998) We are gathered here for what?, *The Times Educational Supplement*, 13 March.

Clarke, J. and Newman, J. (1997) *The Managerial State*, London: Sage.

Close, D. (1994) *Inspection Report: Uxbridge High School*, London: Close Associates for OFSTED.

Corrick, M. (1996) Effective schools, effective governing bodies? in Earley, P. *et al.* (eds) *Improvement through Inspection? Complementary Approaches to School Development*, London: David Fulton.

Creese, M. (1995) *Effective Governors, Effective Schools: Developing the Partnership*, London: David Fulton.

Creese, M. (1997) *Effective Governance: The Evidence from OFSTED*, Ipswich: School Management and Governance Development.

Creese, M. (1998) The strategic role of governors in school improvement, in Middlewood, D. and Lumby, J. (eds) *Managing Strategy in Schools and Colleges*,

London: Paul Chapman.

Creese, M. and Bradley, H. (1997) School improvement and the role of governors: findings from a pilot project, *School Leadership and Management*, Vol. 17, no. 1, pp. 105–15.

Crequer, N. (1998) Lighter touch finds favour, *The Times Educational Supplement*, 6 February.

Department of Education and Science (1989) *Planning for School Development*, London: HMSO.

Department of Education and Science (1991) *Development Planning: A Practical Guide*. London: HMSO.

Department for Education (1992) *Choice and Diversity: A New Framework for Schools*, London: HMSO.

Department for Education and Employment (1996a) *Self-Government for Schools*, London: HMSO.

Department for Education and Employment (1996b) *Looking at National Curriculum Assessment Results: What LEAs are Doing?* London: DfEE.

Department for Education and Employment (1997a) *Excellence in Schools*, London: HMSO.

Department for Education and Employment (1997b) *From Targets to Action: Guidance to Support Effective Target-Setting in Schools*, London: DfEE.

Department for Education and Employment (1997c) *The Road to Success: Four Case Studies of Schools which no Longer Require Special Measures*, London: DfEE.

Department for Education and Employment (1997d) *On Target for School Improvement: A Report of the DfEE/OFSTED Governors' Conference*, London: DfEE.

Department for Education and Employment (1997e) *Setting Targets for Pupil Achievement: Guidance for Governors*, London: DfEE.

Department for Education and Employment/Office for Standards in Education (1996) *Setting Targets to Raise Standards: A Survey of Good Practice*, London: DfEE.

Dixon, S. (1996) Towards self-assessing colleges, *FE Matters* (Further Education Development Agency (FEDA) paper), Vol. 1, no. 1, pp. 1–30.

Duffy, M. (ed) (1997) *A Better System of Inspection?* Hexham: Office for Standards in Inspection (OFSTIN).

Earley, P. (1994) *School Governing Bodies: Making Progress?* Slough: NFER.

Earley, P. (1996a) Governing bodies and school improvement: a research agenda, in *Teamwork for School Improvement: A Report of the DfEE/OFSTED Governors' Conference*, London: DfEE.

Earley, P. (1996b) School improvement and OFSTED inspection: the research evidence, in Earley, P. *et al.* (1996) (eds) *Improvement through Inspection? Complementary Approaches to School Development*, London: David Fulton.

Earley, P. (1997) External inspections, 'failing schools' and the role of governing bodies, *School Leadership and Management*, Vol. 17, no. 3, pp. 387–400.

Earley, P., Fidler, B. and Ouston, J. (1996a) Introduction: OFSTED inspections and school development, in Earley, P. *et al.* (eds) *Improvement through Inspection? Complementary Approaches to School Development*, London: David Fulton.

Earley, P., Fidler, B. and Ouston, J. (eds) (1996b) *Improvement through Inspection? Complementary Approaches to School Development*, London: David Fulton.

Esp, D. and Saran, R. (1995) *Effective Governors for Effective Schools*, London: Pitman.

Fidler, B. Earley, P., Ouston, J. and Davies, J. (1998) Teacher gradings and OFSTED inspections: help or hindrance as a management tool? *School Leadership and Management*, Vol. 18, no. 2, pp. 257–70.

Field, C., Greenstreet, D., Kusel, P. and Parsons, C. (1998) OFSTED inspection reports and the language of educational improvement, *Evaluation and Research in Education* (in press).

Fitz-Gibbon, C. (1998) Ofsted: time to go? *Managing Schools Today*, March, pp. 22–5.

Flew, A. and Naylor, F. (1996) *Spiritual Development and all that Jazz*, Campaign for Real Education.

Foucault, M. (1979) *Discipline and Punish: The Birth of the Prison*, London: Penguin.

Frost, R. (1995) *Improvement through Inspection*, London: National Commission on Education.

Fullan, M. (1991) *The New Meaning of Educational Change*, London: Cassell.

Further Education Funding Council (1997a) *Validating Self-Assessment* (Circular 97/12), Coventry: FEFC.

Further Education Funding Council (1997b) *Self-Assessment and Inspection* (Circular 97/13), Coventry: FEFC.

Gann, N. (1997) *Improving School Governance: How Better Governors Make Better Schools*, London: Falmer Press.

Gillies, C. (1996) Pupils' perceptions of OFSTED inspections: survey findings of questionnaire responses, paper given at British Educational Research Association (BERA) conference, University of Lancaster, September.

Gilroy, P. and Wilcox, B. (1997) OFSTED, criteria and the nature of understanding: a Wittgensteinian critique of the practice of educational judgement, *British Journal of Educational Studies*, Vol. 45, no. 1, pp. 22–38.

Gray, J. and Wilcox, B. (1995a) *Good School, Bad School*, Buckingham: Open University Press.

Gray, J. and Wilcox, B. (1995b) In the aftermath of inspection: the nature and fate of inspection report recommendations, *Research Papers in Education*, Vol. 10, no. 1, pp. 1–18.

Habermas, J. (1984) *The Theory of Communicative Action: Reason and Rationalisation of Society*, Cambridge: Polity Press.

Habermas, J. (1987) *Theory of Communicative Action: The Critique of Functionalist Reason*, Cambridge: Polity Press.

Handy, C. (1995) *The Empty Raincoat*, London: Arrow.

Hargreaves, A. (1994) *Changing Teachers, Changing Times: Teachers' Work and Culture in the Post-Modern Age*, London, Cassell.

Hargreaves, D. (1995) Inspection and school improvement, *Cambridge Journal of Education*, Vol. 25, no. 1, pp. 117–25.

Harland, J. (1996) *Evaluation as realpolitik*, in Scott, D. and Usher, R. (eds) *Understanding Educational Research*, London: Routledge.

Harris, A., Jamieson, I. and Russ, J. (1996) *School Effectiveness and School Improvement*, London: Pitman.

Hillman, I. and Stoll, L. (1994). Understanding school improvement, *School Improvement News (SIN) Research Matters*, No. 1.

Hoggett, P. (1994) The modernisation of the UK welfare state, in Burrows, R. and Loader, B. (eds) *Towards a Post-Fordist Welfare State?* London: Routledge.

Institution for School and College Governors (1996) *Inspection – A Weapon or a Tool, a Post-Mortem or a Health Check? The Governors' Analysis, Occasional Papers, 4*, London: ISCG.

Kelly, F. (1996) Higher and further education colleges: approaches to institutional self-review, in Earley, P. *et al.* (eds) *Improvement through Inspection? Complementary Approaches to School Development*, London: David Fulton.

Kogan, M. (1988) *Education Accountability: An Analytical Overview* (2nd edn), London: Hutchinson.

Laar, B. (1996) Ready for inspection, *The Times Educational Supplement*, 18 October.

Laing, R. D. (1970) Knots, in Ainscow, M. and Conner, C. (eds) (1990) *School–Based Inquiry*, Cambridge: Cambridge Institute of Education.

Layder, D. (1994) *Understanding Social Theory*, London: Sage.

Lofthouse, M. (1996) Religious education, in Kitson, N. and O'Neill, J. (eds) *Effective*

Curriculum Management, London: Routledge.

MacBeath, J. (1996) A stake in quality, *The Times Educational Supplement*, 2 February.

MacBeath, J., Boyd, B. and Rand, J. (1996) *Schools Speak for Themselves*, London: National Union of Teachers.

MacGilchrist, B., Myers, K. and Reed, J. (1997) *The Intelligent School*, London: Paul Chapman.

Maw, J. (1996) The handbook for the inspection of schools; models, outcomes and effects, in Ouston, J. *et al.* (eds) *OFSTED Inspection: The Early Experience*, London: David Fulton.

Maychell, K. and Pathak, S. (1997) *Planning for Action. Part 1. A Survey of Schools' Post-Inspection Action Planning*, Slough: NFER.

Mclaughlin, R. (1991) Can information systems for the internal NHS market work? *Public Money and Management*, Autumn, pp. 37–41.

Millett, A. and Johnson, D. (1998) OFSTED inspection and primary mathematics: are there new insights to be gained? *School Leadership and Management*, Vol. 18, no. 2, pp. 239–55.

Moon, B. (1995) Judgement and evidence: redefining professionality in a new era of school accountability, in Brighouse, T. and Moon, B. (eds) *School Inspection*, London: Pitman.

O'Connor, M. (1996) The OFSTED experience: a governors' eye view, in Ouston, J. *et al.* (eds) *OFSTED Inspections: The Early Experience*, London: David Fulton.

Office for Standards in Education (1993/6a) *The OFSTED Handbook: Guidance on the Inspection of Schools* (first published in 1993 and revised annually), London: HMSO.

Office for Standards in Education (1993/6b) *Framework for the Inspection of Schools* (first published in 1993 and revised annually), London: HMSO.

Office for Standards in Education (1994a) *A Focus on Quality*, London: OFSTED.

Office for Standards in Education (1994b) *Good Practice in Inspection. Guidance for Registered Inspectors and their Teams on Inspection Practice Valued by Secondary Schools*, London: OFSTED.

Office for Standards in Education (1994c) *Corporate Plan 1994, 1994–95 to 1996–97*, London: OFSTED.

Office for Standards in Education (1994d) *Improving Schools*, London: HMSO.

Office for Standards in Education (1994e) *Guidance on the Inspection Schedule*, London: HMSO.

Office for Standards in Education (1995) *Inspection Quality 1994/1995*, London: OFSTED.

Office for Standards in Education (1996) *Planning Improvement. Schools' Post-Inspection Action Plans*, London: HMSO.

Office for Standards in Education (1997a) *From Failure to Success. How Special Measures are Helping Schools Improve*, London: OFSTED.

Office for Standards in Education (1997b) *LEA Support for School Improvement, a Framework for the Inspection of Local Education Authorities*, London: OFSTED.

Office for Standards in Education (1997c) *The Annual Report of Her Majesty's Chief Inspector of Schools. Standards and Quality in Education, 1995/96*, London: HMSO.

Office for Standards in Education (1997d) *Inspection and Re-inspection of Schools from September 1997*, London: OFSTED.

Office for Standards in Education (1998a) External adjudicator to strengthen OFSTED's complaints procedure (Press Notice 98/07), London: OFSTED.

Office for Standards in Education (1998b) *School Evaluation Matters*, London: OFSTED.

Ormston, M. and Shaw, M. (1994) *Inspection: A Preparation Guide for Schools* (2nd edn), Harlow: Longman.

Ouston, J., Fidler, B. and Earley, P. (1996a) Secondary schools' responses to OFSTED inspection, in Ouston, J. *et al.* (eds) *OFSTED Inspections: The Early Experience*, London: David Fulton.

Ouston, J., Fidler, B. and Earley, P. (1997a) What do schools do after OFSTED school inspections – or before? *School Leadership and Management*, Vol. 17, no.1, pp. 95–104.

Ouston, J., Fidler, B. and Earley, P. (1998a) The educational accountability of schools in England and Wales, *Educational Policy*, Vol. 12, no. 1. pp. 111–23.

Ouston, J., Fidler, B., Earley, P. and Davies, J. (1997b) The impact of OFSTED inspection on secondary schools, paper presented at the BERA conference, University of York, September.

Ouston, J., Fidler, B., Earley, P. and Davies, J. (1998b) *Making the Most of Inspection? The Impact of OFSTED Inspection on Secondary Schools*. Final report to The Nuffield Foundation.

Parsons, C. (1994) The politics and practice of quality, in Parsons, C. (ed) *Quality Improvement in Schools, Colleges and Universities*, London: David Fulton.

Pathak, S. and Maychell, K. (1997) *Planning for Action. Part 2. A Guide to Post-Inspection Action Planning*, Slough: NFER.

Power, M. (1997) *The Audit Society*, Oxford: Oxford University Press.

Richards, C. (1997) The high price of inspection, *Guardian*, 3 June.

Riley, K., Johnson, H. and Rowles, D. (1995) *Managing for Quality in an Uncertain Climate: Report 2*, Luton: Local Government Management Board.

Riley, K. and Rowles, D. (1997) *Learning from Failure*, London: Haringey Council and the Roehampton Institute.

Rosenholtz, S. (1989) *Teachers' Workplace: The Social Organisation of Schools*, New York: Longman.

Ross, M. and Kamba, M. (1997) *The State of the Arts in Five English Secondary Schools*, Exeter: University of Exeter Press.

Russell, S. (1996) *Collaborative School Self Review*, London: Lemos & Crane.

Sallis, E. (1993) *Total Quality Management in Education*, London: Kogan Page.

School Curriculum and Assessment Authority (1997) *Target Setting and Benchmarking in Schools*, London: SCAA.

Senge, P. (1990) *The Fifth Discipline: The Art and Practice of the Learning Organisation*, London: Century Business.

Stiles, C. (1996) *School Governors and Inspection* (2nd edn), Coventry: AGIT.

Stoll, L. and Fink, D. (1996) *Changing our Schools*, Buckingham: Open University Press.

Stoll, L. and Myers, K. (ed) (1997) *Schools in Difficulties: No Quick Fixes*, London: Falmer Press.

Taylor, M. (1998) *Values Education and Values in Education*, London: ATL/NFER.

Thomas, G. (1997) School inspection and school improvement, paper delivered at British Educational Research Association Conference, York, September.

Thompson, M. (1996) The oral evidence, in Boothroyd, C. *et al.* (eds) *A Better System of Inspection?* Hexham: OFSTIN.

Walters, J. and Richardson, C. (1997) *Governing Schools through Policy*, London: Lemos & Crane.

Watling, R., Hopkins, D., Beresford, J. and Harris, A. (1997) *An Evaluation of the Accelerated Inspection Programme (AIP) in the London Borough of Waltham Forest*, Nottingham: Centre for Teacher and School Development.

West-Burnham, J. (1992) *Managing Quality in Schools*, London: Longman.

Wilcox, B. and Gray, J. (1996) *Inspecting Schools: Holding Schools to Account and Helping Schools to Improve*, Buckingham: Open University Press.

Wragg, T. (1997) Inspection and school self-evaluation, in Duffy, M. (ed) *A Better System of Inspection?* Hexham: OFSTIN.

Index